John Grindrod

John Grindrod grew up on 'the last road in London' on Croydon's New Addington housing estate, surrounded by the Green Belt. He is the author of *Concretopia: A Journey Around the Rebuilding of Postwar Britain*, described by the *Independent on Sunday* as 'a new way of looking at modern Britain'. He has written for the *Guardian, Financial Times, Big Issue* and *Modernist* and has worked as a bookseller and publisher for over twenty-five years. He runs the popular website dirtymodernscoundrel.com and can be contacted on Twitter @Grindrod.

D1534824

'*Outskirts* is the product of someone who has already written extensively and illuminatingly about the setting of twentieth-century lives, and the experience of Grindrod's very ordinary yet unique family upbringing forms a logical sequence underpinning much of what he says about the green belt.'
Gillian Tindall, *TLS*

'He takes us surefootedly through the protracted and often controversial story of the green belt's origins and evolution . . . one of the great virtues of his account is that, tolerantly and unsentimentally, he gets us close up to the green belt as it actually is today . . . All this would be enough to make *Outskirts* thoroughly worthwhile . . . I for one found some of his passages revelatory.'
David Kynaston, *Spectator*

'At a time when political parties seem to be eyeing up the green belt as a potential site for housing, John Grindrod's salutary memoir-cum-meditation is a reminder that not everything can be viewed in simple black and white – or green and brown – terms . . . [a] well-researched and engaging book . . . It allows the reader to reconsider parts of the country that they might have taken for granted, and offers its own modest encomium to a part of England that seems under threat.'
Alexander Larman, *Observer*

'*Outskirts* is dotted with funny anecdotes and familiar cultural references from a 1970s childhood. Grindrod segues elegantly between memoir and fascinating social history'
Countryfile

'One of the great strengths of Grindrod's book is his moving portrait of his late parents . . . His memories of his wheelchair-using mother are especially touching . . . Her enthusiasm clearly inspires Grindrod's own vivid descriptions of the green belt . . . [*Outskirts*] provides an excellent point of departure for an essential debate about its future, one that is likely to be contentious but is long overdue.'
P.D. Smith, *Guardian*

'A satisfying ramble through the Green Belt of past and future with a backpack full of research . . . the personalisation of plotted land facing competing political and conservational pressures makes for both a thought-provoking read and a compelling argument for quality of life remaining central to balancing the UK's developed land and open spaces.'
List

'Very topical . . . Although he declares early on that he can only "just about recognise a dock leaf and a field mouse", there is no lack of sophistication in his writing about the natural world. However, this self-deprecatory note is one of the pleasures in his understated account of "the dotted line" between town and country. Another is the humour, the Londoner's gift for irony . . . although the passages of memoir are interesting and moving, it is the historical sections that compel . . . Grindrod has the knack of putting an issue into precisely the right perspective'
John Greening, *Country Life*

'What better lens through which to view the current friction between nature and our engorged cities than the Green Belt? A brilliant idea, brilliantly executed.'
Tristan Gooley

OUTSKIRTS

Living life on the edge
of the green belt

JOHN GRINDROD

SCEPTRE

First published in Great Britain in 2017 by Sceptre
An Imprint of Hodder & Stoughton
An Hachette UK company

This paperback edition published in 2018

3

Copyright © John Grindrod 2017
Illustrations © Eleanor Crow 2017

The right of John Grindrod to be identified as the Author
of the Work has been asserted by him in accordance with
the Copyright, Designs and Patents Act 1988.

All rights reserved. No part of this publication may be reproduced, stored
in a retrieval system, or transmitted, in any form or by any means without
the prior written permission of the publisher, nor be otherwise circulated
in any form of binding or cover other than that in which it is published and
without a similar condition being imposed on the subsequent purchaser.

A CIP catalogue record for this title is available from the British Library

Paperback ISBN 978 1 473 62504 4

Typeset in Sabon by Hewer Text UK Ltd, Edinburgh
Printed and bound in Great Britain by Clays Ltd, Elcograf S.p.A.

Hodder & Stoughton policy is to use papers that are natural, renewable
and recyclable products and made from wood grown in sustainable
forests. The logging and manufacturing processes are expected to
conform to the environmental regulations of the country of origin.

Hodder & Stoughton Ltd
Carmelite House
50 Victoria Embankment
London EC4Y 0DZ

www.sceptrebooks.co.uk

To the Grindrods –
Marjorie and John, Ian and Paul

Contents

INTRODUCTION
The Last Road in London

I grew up on the last road in London. At the end of our front garden there was a privet hedge, and beyond the rickety pavement there lay a narrow grass verge, street-lights that glowed a dim orange from dusk, and the road. A tarmac outline to our estate: that was all there was to mark it from the little wilderness beyond. And that wilderness was the woods. It wasn't like all the other streets on the estate, where a row of identical council houses would stare back. Here we lived oppo-site a wall of old trees, the gentle slope of a valley and a cantankerous family of crows. In ten steps I could run from our front door and be in the countryside. On Sundays folk emerged from *somewhere* riding horses along the strip of land opposite, and if the council was feeling flush it would send big tractors to mow the first few feet of it. In their oak tree facing us the crows hopped and cawed and stretched their inky black wings. Owls that we never saw hooted at night. Every year the cow parsley and nettles, elm and ash were furi-ously growing up and dying back. They were constant reminders that, even without human intervention, the woods were quite busy enough thank you. There was life here that didn't need us. And yet here we were, so close, watching it all from across the road.

Behind our maisonette the housing estate stretched back in the direction of the town for a couple of miles, but from our front garden there was little evidence of any of that. We called it the woods, but in reality it was a valley of farmers' fields surrounded by trees, with dense woodland in patches round and about. Our lives were dominated by the wildlife in this valley, green in spring and summer, red and yellow in autumn, brown and black in winter. While little of it seemed to venture to our side of the street, I made sure I headed across there as often as I could. If it was a dry summer, the long school holidays meant I could play over the road until late in the evenings. There were crab apples, tree stumps and barbed wire, and as the year progressed, conkers and acorns. Not that I saw any of that. In my imagination I was in space, on another planet, or fighting off invading forces. The woods were whatever I wanted them to be.

We take for granted whatever we grow up with outside our homes. This is just how it is. I lived on this road for most of my first thirty years. Since then I've never lived anywhere less than entirely urban, and I miss it. Not the housing estate. Nor, if I'm honest, the countryside. What I miss is that strange sensation of the collision of both: living on the edge of somewhere, where the town stops and the country begins, on the brink of something that feels unknowable, whether that's the country or the town. 'I live in the last road in London,' I used to tell people. It wasn't strictly true, even though it felt like it might be. The last road in London. And opposite us, where the crows lived, the woods. The wild. The peculiar outer limits.

Despite our best efforts, on the small island of Great Britain there are still ancient wilds, woodlands and moors where few people venture, remote and apart from the towns and cities where most of us spend our lives. Places where nature still flourishes, red in tooth and claw, green in stem and shoot, pale in frond and fin. But much of the open space in Britain is not found in rugged highlands or spectacular National Parks. It is nearer the towns and cities where most of us live. A tame vision of the country, with little of that edgy glamour that people seek out for rambling treks, wild swimming or getaway weekends. It even has a name that suggests mere practicality; vanity, even, as opposed to mystery and grandeur. The green belt.

If mountains and lochs are the cinemascope version of our countryside, the green belts are the sitcom. Cosy, familiar, cyclical. To be seen in regular short bursts. They are the small, pretty flowers of Laura Ashley wallpaper rather than the awe-inspiring atmospheric excesses of Romantic painting. A frilly green doily around the edge of our cities. Here the wildlife is the grey squirrel, fox and wood pigeon rather than the beaver, otter or wildcat. City folk might go here for a

3

weekend cycle, but for a proper break seek adventure in the real wilds beyond. Highland or North Welsh folk might find this tame landscape almost funny. It is the place where cross people meet to try to put a stop to the modern world, whether it be wind farms, fracking or road-widening schemes. Yet it's also full of commuters building extra bedrooms and adding value, and farms with hillsides of yellow oilseed rape or golden barley. Where developers win some and lose some. And, of course, there's much that's more surprising than any of this too: strange small towns, landfill sites, abandoned military facilities, motorway service stations, follies.

In England alone, the green belt accounts for 13 per cent of our total land, in Scotland 2 per cent, in Northern Ireland 16 per cent. Yet most of us would be hard pressed to explain a few fundamentals about this strange phenomenon. What exactly is it? Is there more than one? If so, where can you find them? And why and how did they come about? Was it an ancient idea we inherited from the baronial landowners of yore? Or something more recent and practical, like health and safety laws or immunisation? Are there people we can thank for it? And why don't we know who they are? What do these green belts say about our temperament, our hopes and ambitions? Are they, indeed, an attempt to give us a national character? When it comes to answering these questions, have the solutions been hidden in plain sight? Have we not been able to see the wood for the trees?

New Addington, the housing estate I grew up in, isn't just on the edge of the green belt, it's encircled by it. Because of that the estate can never expand, and must remain content holding to the boundaries in its lofty hilltop position. This atoll of concrete and red brick sits surrounded by a sea of green, from the Kent woodland, valleys and hills to the south and east to the Surrey farmers' fields, golf courses and parkland to the north and west, leading all the way back to Croydon. Despite such greenness being the defining quality of the estate, it's only since I left that I realised that this was part of London's green belt. The term had always conjured up images of something far more posh than the fag-end of a council estate. Yet I could open the door at number 100 Fairchildes Avenue and see it, and in a few strides be in it.

I never ventured too far, though. At school we were made to do cross-country runs down the steep path into the valley at the end of the road, and then, inevitably, back up again, caked in mud. In spring there was the dense carpet of bluebells of Jewels Wood to the east and Hutchinson's Bank to the west. My dad and brother loved wandering round down there taking photos of the flowers and plants, the overgrown fallen giants brought down by the wind, or the burned-out cars that frequently found their way into the valley. Sometimes we went blackberry picking, prising the stubborn little berries from the snaggle-stemmed brambles. And every June we would make our pilgrimage across the fields to Biggin Hill, the Kent airfield made famous during the Battle of Britain, where a spectacular weekend of airshows would brighten up our lives. The displays would often take place above the valleys, skimming the treetops till the normally twittering, rustling woodland would shake with the roar of jet engines or ghosts of the Battle of Britain. As we munched our sandwiches, Spitfires and Hurricanes rolled overhead in the Kent sky as they had in earnest decades before.

Building began on this exposed Surrey hilltop in the mid-1930s. It was part of an explosion in private construction of suburban semis, maisonettes and flats that had taken place all across Britain, usually following the path of major arterial roads. With no such thing as an official green belt around London to stop it, building in the Surrey countryside was a doddle. The big name in the new science of town planning was Patrick Abercrombie. His profession intended to curb the excesses of this kind of private construction, and he didn't much like what he saw going on in Croydon. At the close of the Second World War, before the birth of our modern planning laws, he thundered:

Further development southwards from the built-up boundary of Croydon at Shirley must be stopped. Addington hamlet itself with its church, the burial place of five Archbishops of Canterbury, is as yet unspoiled, although threatened by pre-war development near Featherbed and Lodge Lanes. The siting of a new estate here is a regrettable example of what could happen under planning powers; a considerable distance from any work or railway station, with only bus transport to serve it, this project was approved and begun. It is now too late to call a halt to it completely, even though it is in a charming piece of green belt country.[1]

The 'green belt' he's referring to was at this stage almost a fantasy: small pockets of land had been bought up in the 1930s for safekeeping, but the broad acres we associate with it were little more than a gleam in the eyes of planners like Abercrombie. It was obvious that although 'charming', this piece of country had no protection from the speculative builders and developers. Writing wartime plans for the rebuilding of London, Abercrombie felt he had to come up with a solution for estates like New Addington, half-baked, half-built and heavily frowned upon. Not to help them gain the amenities they so desperately needed, but instead to cut them off neatly from the surrounding world.

We have reluctantly felt compelled to allow a certain measure of rounding off, but such growth that we do recommend – up to a maximum of a neighbourhood unit of 10,000 persons – must be used solely for meeting part of Croydon's decentralization needs, and not for further speculative development for persons coming in from outside. No industrial development should be contemplated.

A final coda to his rant had particular personal interest for me. 'The recent purchase by the Corporation of the Fairchildes Estate', he wrote, 'should prove a useful contribution to the open space needs of the Borough,'[2] I'd grown up in a maisonette at number 100 Fairchildes Avenue, and when my two older brothers and I had outgrown sharing a bedroom we moved up the road, to a three-bedroomed council house at number 46. Our new neighbours, Jean and Sid Brown, had been the only occupiers of their house, having moved in after the war. They would have seen all the changes the post-war world would bring to New Addington. But one thing would remain the same: the land adjacent to the estate. Residents of Fairchildes Avenue could look out onto an area that had once been owned by farmers who bore its name, and whose land had been bought not to expand the estate, but rather to stop it: to help form an early piece of what would become London's green belt.

By 1951, when Sid and Jean were moving into number 48 Fairchildes Avenue, work on the housing estate behind them was beginning again. But change was in the air. The council, rather than a speculative developer, now owned the estate. And thanks to the likes of

Abercrombie, planning laws became much tighter. By the mid-fifties the nascent estate at New Addington was constrained by its own footprint. There would be no further expansion outwards, and any pressure to build more houses would have to happen within its existing boundaries. Over decades New Addington would grow more urban and tightly knit, while the edges remained sharply defined, or as Abercrombie would have it, 'rounded off', like the solution to a particularly prickly maths problem. And there we would live, on the rounded-off edge of this strange unloved new estate, looking out at something equally strange and new: the green belt, a band of tame outdoors held in stasis.

When I think of the place where I grew up, I tend to focus on the built-up areas, to look behind at the houses and flats that contained the kids I never understood and the tight-knit groups of adults staring out at the world, filled with suspicion. It is easy to fixate on that, because if people know New Addington, that is what they know. But when I recall happier moments from my childhood, they were mostly tied up with the woods beyond rather than the estate behind. This makes me sound like nature boy. I was not.

How I'd love to be one of those people who can identify trees at a glance, or tell a bird from its song. I've tried, and it never works. I can just about recognise a dock leaf and a field mouse. My mum, Marjorie, who had grown up in urban Battersea, took to it all much more readily. She could tell a greenfinch or a jay just from a glimpsed movement in the treetops. The flora and fauna remained a constant source of fascination for her, a new world she spied through our Crittal windows. Because she was a wheelchair user for much of her adult life, having the countryside right outside our door was an incredible bonus. She could experience it without having to get her wheels stuck in the mud or being bumped about on the flinty soil until she was sick and dizzy. And she could always get in her Mini and take off round the lanes, with their evocative names: Featherbed; Sheepbarn; North Pole; Skid Hill. Many times she'd take a drive out there to relieve the monotony of being trapped at home, a housewife with three kids, no money and a wheelchair. I loved going out driving with her. She'd stop where the sheep were grazing in a valley, and those lairy South London parakeets were whirling about overhead. We'd sit in the little blue Mini and enjoy it, the countryside, where things were going on that didn't need 50p for the meter or cooking on a hob. I loved those tree-lined lanes, the leaves arching overhead to form a tunnel, a holloway, over the road. Throughout my childhood I had one recurring dream: of cycling down those lanes forever, the trees knitted together above, and sunlight through the leaves sparkling up the road ahead. The happiest dream.

We weren't an intrepid family. Not one of those who went abroad on holiday or tried fancy foods. In many ways I'd put our timidity down to a few simple things. We tended to stick together, so Marj's disability meant there were things that weren't for us – no public transport, steep steps or rugged terrain. Accessibility for wheelchair users in the 1970s and 80s was a pretty hopeless affair, and quite often even if we could get in somewhere she would be told she was a fire hazard. Despite that, Marj, with her long dark hippyish hair and a flair for bleak irony, was actually far more intrepid in spirit than my short, scruffy, cuddly dad, John, whose anxiety at changes in routine was if anything even more inhibiting. For example, even for postwar Britain my dad's tastes were narrow when it came to food: because of that, not for us the wonders of pasta, pizza, chilli, curry or chow mein. Even chicken was out (*dirty* he'd say, recalling some childhood trauma none of us ever went near). And so, through a combination of a lack of accessibility and a dearth of adventurous spirit, much of Marjorie's birdwatching skills were honed from the kitchen window while boiling spuds or frying chips. Finally, there was where we lived, built on a hill miles from Croydon, as isolated as Patrick Abercrombie had predicted in the 1940s. Living between the two worlds of the estate and the country might have emboldened some families. Not ours. Instead, we never really felt part of New Addington, and the countryside remained a mystery. Mum's romantic spirit aside, we remained timid, nowhere people.

This was illustrated most obviously when it came to Marjorie's eldest brother, Bert. He and Joan, his wife, lived upstairs from us. I only vaguely remember them: Bert tall and gaunt in a sombre suit, like an emaciated Gregory Peck, and Joan, all tight fifties waists and red lipstick. They had tipped off Marj and John back in the late sixties that the maisonette beneath theirs was empty. At that time my mum and dad and my two older brothers were living in a block of flats in Battersea, a couple of streets away from where they had grown up. Marj had seven brothers and sisters, and many of them had lived in the same block with their new families. It wasn't clear to me how or why they had made the leap from the Battersea flats to the maisonette on the edge of the countryside, but they did. Perhaps I would find out in the course of researching this book, I thought. Although the move would be a wrench, it was also an eminently practical solution. It was even in London – just: Croydon became part of Greater London in 1965. As part of the decentralisation strategy of the time, they were part of a generation of working-class people being encouraged to move out of the city, and gradually Marj's parents and all of her brothers and sisters followed suit, landing everywhere from the posh suburbs of Cheshire to the urban new builds of Slough. But we were insulated from this shock by the proximity of Bert and Joan, who would be living upstairs. Although, it turned out that when we moved in they didn't really want anything to do with us. Perhaps we were overly rowdy or too obviously working class for this aspirant couple. Apart from the odd reference to Lord Snooty there was no mention of them at home, they never popped down from upstairs and we barely saw them in their garden. Christmas cards would be posted through letterboxes, and little chat would be had. And so my uncle and aunt upstairs remained to me, like Mrs Columbo, quite invisible. We never did anything to change that. It wasn't for us to rock the boat, to integrate, even with relatives living in the same building. I learned early on that being self-contained was important. After all, who needs social skills?

I've always had a sense of having lived a life at the outskirts of both town and country, on the dotted line between both, and belonging to neither. And it is those dotted lines that make the green belt what it is. After all, it is the countryside designated in relation to the town, not a place that would exist in its own right. It is not an equal marriage. Cities can exist quite happily without a green belt – just look at Norwich, say, or Swansea. But the green belt can only exist where there is a town or city. It is a benign parasite, owing its continued existence to urban rules.

Now, all these years since I moved away, I want to try to go back in time and understand the green belt I used to see from my front door. The ideas behind it, the history of how it came to pass. I have a peculiar feeling that it might even tell me something about my own life. Because the more I think about it, the more I realise that so much of my head has been formed by it, from the outskirts, looking both ways.

Part 1

Sowing

I
An Origin Story: Enclosures
and the Sickly City

That day in late July the Hertfordshire green belt was going all out for best in show. Two cricket matches were in progress in Berkhamsted, and in the tall grass nearby the game's namesakes were buzzing lustily. I headed uphill beside acres of alternating crops, perfectly ripe golden wheat in this one, nodding green heads of barley in the next. Barley had played a big part in my childhood, growing in the fields facing our maisonette, and seeding itself in the verges. It was the perfect weapon for throwing as sticky darts, and hard to disentangle from heavy bowl haircuts. Butterflies made their chaotic way around me, often pairs in amorous pursuit. I'd come here with my partner, Adam, in search of the remains of the Battle of Berkhamsted Common. It sounds like it might have been a skirmish in the English Civil War, but it was nothing quite so grand. Although this quaint corner of Hertfordshire has seen its share of action over the years. The Anglo-Saxons surrendered to the Normans here in 1066, and it's where Oliver Cromwell's colonel Daniel Axtell came to a grisly end too, hanged, drawn and quartered in 1660. But our battle took place 800 years after Harold had fallen at Hastings, on 6 March 1866, which should have been a rather more peaceable period of domestic history.

These days, with its half-timbered Tudor houses, picturesque thatched cottages and ruined castle, the main struggle in Berkhamsted appears to involve parking. But back in 1866 the battle was triggered by an audacious land grab by the local aristocrat, the second Earl Brownlow. The common had long been a place where local people collected wood and grazed their animals. Brownlow sought to enclose it to make it part of his estate at Ashridge. This didn't seem a particularly exceptional move at the time. Enclosure had been creeping across the land in a systematic fashion for over a hundred years, following a succession of parliamentary Acts encouraging the practice. Around the country aggrieved villagers and peasant farmers were ever more resigned to the disappearance of their communal farmland, as government commissioners and rich landowners systematically robbed them of their ancient pasture. Yet Brownlow was an unlikely antagonist. Just twenty-four at the time, he was a weak, consumptive Christian socialist. A contemporary portrait of him by Francis Grant shows a slender, pale, straggly-bearded young man of despondent aspect accompanied by an even more miserable-looking large grey dog. His mother, Lady Marian Compton, was rather more vigorous. An accomplished artist and a generous patron, it was she who drove John to enclose the town's common land for their own private use. And, as if to prove his masculinity, he went about it in a particularly aggressive manner, having two rows of five-foot-high steel fencing erected around the perimeter to keep out the locals.

Much of the countryside around Berkhamsted is now within London's green belt, and I was determined to uncover an overlap between it and Brownlow's enclosure. It all seemed so easy when I first sketched out the route. The problem was, to do it I'd had to use a number of different maps, none of which quite seemed to correlate with the others. There was the interactive map of England's green belts produced by Dan Palmer and Mark Oliver for the *Daily Telegraph* website in 2012. Its boundaries around Berkhamsted looked pretty complicated to me, with only the southern part of Berkhamsted Common included in the protected land. There was a walk suggested by the National Trust to commemorate the battle, with Brownlow's enclosed area a dotted outline on the map. It was clear from this he hadn't enclosed the entire common, just the middle section, and the red dots on one map didn't seem to overlap the green area on the other. An alternate walk around the common contained few overlapping features with the other maps, apart from a place called Brickkiln Cottage. I knew this sat at the northern limit of the green belt. Staring at all three maps I began to feel sick. Pretty soon Adam and I resorted to GPS maps on our phones, and so now with five to consult we headed out to the National Trust shop at the Ashridge Estate, Brownlow's old pile, where I picked up another, just to be on the safe side. Six maps – what could possibly go wrong?

I suspect the Earl and his mother assumed the story of the common would end at the enclosure, but the people of Berkhamsted were outraged. Reports soon reached a new organisation that was looking for just such an opportunity to stick it to the man. The Commons, Open Spaces and Footpaths Preservation Society had been formed the year before by young London barrister and failed Liberal candidate, George Shaw-Lefevre. He soon attracted notable humanitarians to his cause, including philosopher John Stuart

Mill, textile designer William Morris and social reformer Octavia Hill. Suddenly, in Berkhamsted Common, they had a test case for a good, clean fight.

They had an inspired ally in a prominent MP, Augustus Smith, who had grown up in the area and was rather more willing to play dirty. Forget the courts, thought Smith, what they needed was some direct action. He chartered a train from the East End of London and imported a gang of 120 navvies to nearby Tring station. They arrived like a band of mercenaries in a 1970s action film. Under cover of darkness these tough guys worked alongside a group of plucky locals, first breaching the two lines of steel fencing and then destroying them altogether. The Society, with its whizzy legal brains, took it from there, bringing the case to court and winning, ensuring that the land remained in common use. It was an ignominious end for the sickly young Earl, who died the following year at the age of twenty-five.

We reached as high as we would climb on our walk and, as far as I could make out, we'd left the green belt. This was one of the strange mysteries of it. Why were some of these fields conserved and others not? Finding where the belt stopped and started on the ground was no easy task. After all, it is a thought experiment. No signs announce its location. Hedges and fences do not necessarily demarcate its edges. It doesn't discriminate between beautiful forest, fallow farmland or industrial neglect. And its origins lie in many sources, ones that oppose in ambition and purpose what we have now, as much as confirm it. As I shuffled between maps, a cockchafer beetle, or doodlebug, rose into the air before us. Once abundant on these hills, they had been driven to the edge of extinction by pesticides. Now it was part of a pattern of abundant life returning to these farmers' fields. The flora too was spectacular. Acres of crops and meek fallow pasture had given way to a meadow in giddy bloom. On the undulating chalky earth, golden grasses were surrendering to the flowers of tiny orchids, white flax and fronds of yarrow, and the intense yellow of mouse-ear hawkweed. Any moment I expected a Nazi-dodging nun to come sprinting down the hill in full song. Later, on our return leg we saw a sign: alpine meadow. Suddenly my Julie Andrews fantasy didn't seem so absurd. It was in this meadow I realised that, despite our six maps, we were entirely lost.

Into the woods we marched, and back into the green belt. We spied the plain Georgian outline of Brickkiln Cottage, the only real landmark we'd noted. Up to our armpits in fronds and thorns we stumbled across a post in the ground. It was branded with the National Trust logo and carried the legend 'Battle of Berkhamsted Common Anniversary Walk'. I gave a startled Adam a massive bear hug. This was what I had come to see, the boundary of the enclosure, a 150-year-old historical link beneath my feet. And what's more, it *was* in the green belt, after all. The countryside contained, one form of enclosure overlapping another. These events felt hard to relate to London, a city almost forty miles away.

Every few months Marj and John would round us up, sit us down in the living room and tell us about the old days. She would hold court in her battleship-grey NHS wheelchair, punctuating sentences with her long fingers and gleeful giggle. He, in a garishly patterned jumper, would be perched on the edge of his seat, nodding or tutting as necessary. My rebellious eldest brother, Ian, would be fiddling with his rebelliously flicky hair. Beside him would sit my middle brother Paul, the anxious sports casual. And me, the quiet youngest one, I'd be sat on the floor with my bowl haircut and plim- solls, wondering what on earth was going on and when I could get back to playing with my toy cars. On those wet Sunday afternoons we'd hear the lot. Battersea during the war. Bathing once a week in a tin bath. Sharing beds with brothers and sisters. Grabbing cakes from a smashed-in bakery window after one of the tram's frequent derailments. The tiny terraced houses, bare yards and nasty outside privies. The bombsites John played on, where he knocked out his front teeth. The coal-hole Marjorie dreaded, where she'd seen a skeletal phantom gloating in the shadows. There were all of the characters from their large working-class families too, summoned up before us like the chorus of a big show. The misbehaving brothers, the sisters thinking they were all that, the cousins that thought they were siblings. Uncles and aunts getting drunk and acting up, parents and grandparents constantly fighting, often violently. The good old days spread before us like the waiting room of Accident and Emergency on a Saturday night. By the time we were being told these stories in the 1970s those houses and streets were long gone, and many of the people with them. The mouthy bunch left were dispersed across the country, from Chester to the Isle of Wight. Those days living in the old Victorian slums were a lost world.

We should record these reminiscences, John and Marj used to say. They must have been aware that most of these stories were lost on us, three boys who were living a very different kind of life in a housing estate on the edge of the country. Out here surrounded by woods and green it was hard to relate to these tales of inner-city deprivation and wartime adventure. Yet no tape recorders were ever deployed, and now no record of their much-rehearsed exploits exists. It feels like a monstrous act of idiocy, that none of us dug out an orange BASF cassette and clunked down the piano keys on our tape recorder. We all knew we were making a mistake. It's almost possible that we did nothing just so we could really enjoy feeling guilty later.

Outside of these extraordinary Sundays they didn't much talk about the past. You might have almost thought they hadn't had one. It was kept apart, like an old scrapbook or box of slides, to be dusted off in specific quiet moments. I wonder if it was upsetting for them to dwell on it now that their circumstances were so different. I used to think they were doing all of these re-enactments for our benefit, to educate us about a world we had missed. Passing down stories through generations, like a shoestring Viking saga or a penny dreadful *Beowulf*. Tales of minor transgressions sitting in for major battles, uncles and aunts for dragons and gods. But now I think it was more to keep reminding themselves they had actually lived that life. Out on the edge of the countryside it was easy to forget their world hadn't always been like this. Atomised from their families. Green places to roam. Knowing the name of plants, flowers and birds, in Marj's case. She was a keen observer, her pale blue eyes taking in everything. She was used to sitting still in her chair for long periods without fidgeting, some kind of Zen master powered by tea and jam sandwiches. John just nodded and smiled. That was often his function, to nod and smile at one of Marj's remarks, to offer occasional support with a muttered *Cor yeah!*, *Weren't it!* or a long exhalation through his teeth, a form of approval that seemed common then but now seems to have fallen from favour. Here they were, attempting to fix a vanished world in their heads. Even their retelling of these tales was as if they were getting them straight, in case they were ever caught and questioned about the dodgy things their relatives had got up to in the war.

The past is a slippery thing. Even the bits I think I remember can be turned around by some new insight or moment of empathy. And those are just the events I witnessed first-hand. For anything pre-1970 I am reliant on the memories of other people, old newspaper stories with their long-forgotten agendas, or books where the very thing I want explained occurs in the gap between sentences. Attempting to extract information from the lazy grey of my unreliable memory has proven tough. It's like trying to retrieve coins dropped in the street, all rolling in different directions, one under a car and others down drains. So I have been talking to Ian and Paul about the old days, just like Marj and John used to. Only this time I've recorded them. These conversations help in some ways, and make them more complicated in others. They're surprising and often contradictory. I wonder if that was how it was for our parents, telling each other things about their lives back in the forties and fifties, fixing a new truth from half-remembered bits of the old.

I've always felt that the green belt sounds like a superhero. You can see it lined up with the rest. Green Lantern. Silver Surfer. Black Widow. The Green Belt has the purity of Wonder Woman, visiting the righteousness of a life spent in the Amazon jungle on the corrupt in our urban world. It has the serenity of Superman, a visitor from another planet, seeing bigger problems than the everyday worries of puny humans.

It is invoked as indiscriminately in political debates as Commissioner Gordon grabbing for the Batphone or J. Jonah Jameson rushing out a biased story in the *Daily Bugle*. It can make conservationists and housing campaigners angry like Hulk. Like all good superheroes and villains it has a complex origin story, taking in tragedy, science and mystical transformation. There are mysterious mentors, powerful opponents, seemingly insurmountable struggles, cities to keep safe. The Green Belt is a modern superhero brought in to right ancient wrongs.

What must the British landscape have been like before we came along to spoil it? No buildings. No roads, tracks, bridges or dams. The parks or gardens undreamt of, the fields, hedgerows, crops and livestock unneeded. The coast left undefended, the ground unmined. Before any of those human changes to the landscape, wildlife would have been quite different. The house mouse, a Neolithic interloper. Goats too, introduced some 5,000 years ago. Rats: a Roman invader. The first British skeleton of a rabbit dates back a thousand years. And then there are many of the trees that we are so familiar with: the horse chestnut, the cedar, larch, sycamore and, ironically, London plane. These and many hundreds of other plants and animals owe their existence on these islands to human intervention. It's enough to give Nigel Farage palpitations.

There are absences too. Lost species, great and small, vanished because of us. Sea eagles. Lynx. Wolves.

Great auk. From the speckled beauty moth, lost for a century, to the titans of the ice ages, 10,000 years ago. Would woolly mammoths and rhinos still be mooching about on meadows where branches of Next and H&M now stand if *Homo sapiens* hadn't made it onto the scene? Or would the changing climate have done for them anyway? Without all of this human activity would the Andred in the Weald, Arden in the Midlands or Caledonian Forest in Scotland still dominate our landscape? Would those teeming woodlands stand where the regulated fields of our ancestors now stretch? Farming in its most rudimentary form reached Britain around 4,000 BC. Humans forcing six millennia of continual large-scale change on the landscape.

The first town planner appears to have been God, if the Book of Numbers is anything to go by. Here the great deity advised Moses to found new cities and surround them with an agricultural belt. Pretty progressive for 14,000 BC. The idea of a settlement surrounded by countryside is as old as human civilisation. After all, for thousands of years that would have been the only option. Farms, hamlets and villages were surrounded by countryside simply because countryside was all there was to be surrounded by. Unless you were by the sea. If God wasn't available to plan your town then Thomas More might suffice. His book, *Utopia*, written in 1516, described a fictional island, a kind of Tudor *Sim City* in which he experimented with ideas of how society might best be organised. People should live in small towns separated by country, he thought, where the townsfolk could 'walk abroad in the fields, or into the country that belongeth to the city'.[1]

The ebb and flow of the forest in the five centuries up to the Tudor period had been dramatic. William the Conqueror created the first royal forest, or game reserve, in Dorset: the New Forest. Protected land covered a third of England by the time of Henry II a century later. Historian W.G. Hoskins describes how, by the thirteenth century, 'a great belt of forest extended from the Thames by Windsor through Berkshire and Hampshire to the south coast'.[2] Peasants were often fined for attempting to clear them for farming. Yet in the following few centuries the growing demands of the construction industry, shipbuilding and charcoaling led to a dramatic decline in woodland across Britain. The Scottish Parliament even declared in 1505 that the nation's once dominant forests had been quite destroyed.

Traces of historic man-made country before the enclosures can still be found, peculiarly preserved on the edges of our green belts. Looking at satellite images of the edge of Birmingham, where the urban sprawl abruptly stops, you can see an older pattern emerging through the sharp modern field boundaries. The narrow strips of medieval fields are still visible, scored into the lightly farmed landscape on the edge of the conurbation, ghosts which are untraceable in the more heavily worked fields further out. Protected by its proximity to the city this threadbare patchwork of an older, harder way of life still marks the land.

Many of the belt's origin stories come about through threat and adversity, bolstering its credentials as a superpowered force field, the planning equivalent of Wonder Woman's bullet-deflecting bracelets. In 1580 plague began one of its periodic assaults on London. There was panic among the 75,000 people who lived in overcrowded conditions within the old city walls, not to mention the additional 115,000 housed in an area beyond, known as 'the liberties'. On 6 July Elizabeth I issued a decree, introducing a country zone around the city for its protection. Any new building within the liberties was prohibited, and the zone extended three miles out from the city walls. But this *cordon sanitaire*, which started at what is now Drury Lane, proved impossible to police. Before you could say 'notice of proposed development,' rich folk were simply bypassing the system altogether and buying dispensations to build on this protected land, and so the city continued to spread. Rather than discouraging further growth, the Elizabethan 'green belt' increased population density within the old city walls to intolerable levels. I'm sure we can't imagine what that might be like.

Less than a century had passed before a victorious Oliver Cromwell suggested that there should be no building within ten miles of the edges of London. As an idea it had more in common with Elizabeth's than he'd have liked to have acknowledged. Behind both concepts wasn't a desire to protect country or city, but rather to keep out the poor, who were being drawn to urban areas from impoverished villages in search of work. It was a migration crisis dealt with as cruelly as in any other age. Shortly after the Restoration, another emergency engulfed the city. The Great Fire of London of 1666 destroyed 13,500 homes, leaving just 10 per cent standing. It also presented the people with a profound problem of rebuilding, much as would the Blitz on the same spot three centuries later. Proposals included introducing limits to the edge of the creeping city. Christopher Wren imagined an agricultural belt of twelve miles around London, and John Evelyn's rival scheme suggested encircling the metropolis with fashionable landscaped gardens and plantations. Neither were taken up.

Could London's growth problems be solved with maths? Sir William Petty, a scientist and economist in the age of extravagant powdered wigs, certainly thought so. In 1682 Petty published his *Essay on the Growth of London*. He estimated that the population of Restoration London stood at 670,000, and that it would reach over four-and-a-half million within two centuries, a prediction that would turn out to be pretty near accurate. He may have been Petty by name, but his ambition was anything but. To prevent the emergence of this megalopolis he imagined limiting the city to a maximum of four miles in diameter, and encircling it with a mighty agricultural belt. 'A circle of ground of thirty-five miles semidiameter', he wrote, 'will bear corn, garden-stuff, fruits, hay, and timber for the 4,690,000 inhabitants of the said city.'[3] Londoners still dealing with the devastation of the Great Fire rejected his notions just as they had Wren's and Evelyn's.

The Inclosure Act of 1773 did as much as anything to create the landscape we see today in the English countryside, and to disempower the majority of people who lived within it. This was the privatisation of public land on a grand scale, taking away the shared fields from peasant farmers and signing them over to powerful landowners instead. Over the next hundred years an astonishing four million acres of common fields were affected by the Act, as government commissioners travelled the land to deliver these tracts into the hands of the wealthy, alongside a further million and a half acres of previously uncultivated woodland and heath. This was a brutal redrawing of the map. A popular epigram summed up the view of the thousands suddenly pushed from the land:

> 'Tis bad enough in man or woman
> To steal a goose from off a common;
> But surely he's without excuse
> Who steals a common from the goose.

Some of those villages and fields nearest the cities found themselves slowly swallowed up as the suburbs began to grow. In Scotland the traditional run-rig system, where small strips of land around settlements were offered to individuals to cultivate, was slowly replaced by enclosed crofts, to much the same effect. The enclosure of commons had been one of two major factors in the desertion of the land by the British working poor. The other was the arrival of new industries in the mill towns, encouraging the great resettlement of once rural families to rapidly expanding cities like Manchester, Glasgow, Birmingham and Leeds. City life was soon characterised in art and literature as a world of vice, temptation and sickness. The novels of Charles Dickens and the cartoons of William Hogarth catalogue the ills of this new urban age: the work-house, the poorhouse, drink, disease, destitution.

Scottish botanist John Claudius Loudon revived the green belt concept in 1829. Here the adversity was internal: Loudon suffered from acute rheumatism and arthritis, and when an operation to correct a broken arm in his mid-forties left him in intolerable pain, he had to endure amputation of it from the shoulder. Yet, throughout, Loudon continued working. When, three years later, he considered the infirmity of Georgian London, a city brought low by disease, addiction and poverty, he saw surgery might again be the only solution. His essay *Hints on Breathing Places for the Metropolis* called for 'zones of country' around the city of London. 'Our plan is very simple', he wrote, by which he meant fiendishly complex. He talked of surrounding the centre of London with a zone of open country a mile and a half out from St Paul's Cathedral. The problem was, this proposed half-mile-wide belt of outdoors contained areas inconveniently built up, like Islington, Bethnal Green, Lambeth and Pimlico. No problem, said Loudon: the government would simply buy up this land and the buildings on it, and slowly depopulate them, returning them to country. Outside that ring of enforced green, urban life could again continue in a mile-wide band containing Paddington, Deptford, Clapham and Chelsea. Beyond that would be another forced zone of country and more need for demolition. In fact, these zones would continue alternately until they reached the sea. Loudon thought it might take 200 years to realise his plans, or until 2029. I've just checked and it seems that Islington is safe.

It seemed impossible to impose Loudon's ideas on an existing city, even one as sick as London. But what about building it into new ones from the start? Enter the pioneers of an age of empire, to whom no task was too intimidating. Take swashbuckling Colonel William Light. Born in Malaysia, he'd fought Napoleon's army in the Peninsular War and was declared Captain of the Nile for his work founding the Egyptian Navy. In 1835 he set off with his mistress, Maria Gandy, to a new life as Surveyor-General of the Colony of South Australia. Within two years he'd created the blueprints for a new city – Adelaide – with a carefully structured grid layout and a town belt surrounding it. For that he became known as 'the best gardener in Australia'. Then there was Captain William Mein Smith, who in 1839 was in the employ of the New Zealand Company, a commercial outfit set up to colonise the country. Smith was among the team proposing Wellington as a new settlement at the south-western tip of the north island. 'It is, indeed, desirable that the whole outside of the town inland, should be separated from the county sections by a broad belt of land', went instructions from the company.[4] No building would be allowed in this area. Smith set to work, creating a belt which today includes the city's spectacular botanical gardens, reached by funicular railway from the centre of town.

The fashionable town belt idea made its way to Britain in 1849, thanks to the rebellious but elegantly named James Silk Buckingham. His book *National Evils and Practical Remedies* included the plan of a model town. In an attempt to make it sound more conservative, he named it Victoria. It was a place of regular grid roads, free medical treatment, communal kitchens, no pubs and an agricultural belt. Buckingham's ideas echoed those of a new generation of moralising industrialists, who were erecting model villages at New Lanark, Saltaire, Bourneville and Port Sunlight. They were a reaction to the overcrowded, insanitary and run-down homes of the Industrial Revolution, like the terraced houses in Battersea where Marj and John had grown up. Decent council homes would be a long time coming, bringing the kind of goodness that philanthropists managed in miniature to millions. But it was a start, a sign that improvement could happen, and that life could afford to be a little more generous.

Crusading Methodists, Quakers and humanists helped propel this change in British society, be they businessmen or campaigning groups. But their help was not bestowed without caveat. Concern about the living conditions of the poor was tempered by disapproval that the working classes had the gall to take their pleasures in bawdy pubs and music halls. In the topsy-turvy moralism of the day, thoughts of the deserving and undeserving poor weighed heavily on their minds. There was only one thing for it: improving walks in the country. Thanks to the work of poets and painters during the Enlightenment, the natural world had increasingly come to be portrayed as a place of innocence and virtue. Let your spirit soar on hills, fields, parks and gardens, away from city depravity. Every window box an observance, every vase of flowers an epiphany. The walking groups set up were the first examples of a new phenomenon: townsfolk encouraged to experience the healthful properties of the country. One such organisation giving it a go was the Ladies' Sanitary Association of Manchester. They published pamphlets on everything from 'What Can the Window Gardens Do for Our Health?' to 'Every-Day Wonders of Bodily Life: With Numerous Engravings'. Their crusade against the sin of insanitariness involved taking slum children to parks for parties, away from the corrupting grime of the city. Our modern green girdles find their roots in such extraordinary organisations.

'Bring Beauty Home to the Poor' was the curious motto of another, a philanthropic organisation called the Kyrle Society. Consisting almost entirely of women, it had been founded in 1875 by social reformer Miranda Hill with a belief in the spiritual uplift brought about through contact with art and nature. Under their banner, schools and hospitals received aesthetic makeovers, members sought to provide the deprived with books, music and murals, and they campaigned for the protection of open spaces. Pretty soon Miranda's more energetic sister Octavia had taken the lead in the society, to spearhead a hugely successful crusade to turn abandoned London graveyards into parks.

Octavia Hill's overriding obsession was housing the poor, to which her campaigns for open spaces were intimately connected. A prolific essayist, in 1888 she produced one of her most far-reaching, *More Air for London*, which combined the two interests. It is as much a sharply written assault on privilege and complacency as it is a plea for nature. She produced statistics, the details of which were shocking. In prosperous West London there was one acre of open space for every 682 people. However, in the working-class east there was one acre of open space for every 7,481 people. West Londoners had access to more than eight times the open space of those in the east. Surely that needed correcting?

It wasn't cold statistics that drove Octavia, but a vision of children brought up never having seen a garden, park or open space. 'This is different from reason and science', she wrote. 'This is life, and this is pain.' She saw Hoxton mothers carrying children, toddlers by their side, long distances to the nearest park, Spitalfields clerks walking ever further to the country through a rapidly spreading suburban landscape. 'The need for quiet, the need for air, the need of exercise, and, I believe, the sight of sky and of things growing, seem human needs, common to all men, and not be dispensed with without grave loss.' She envisaged the creation of an extensive network of paths linking parks, commons, greens and woods throughout the city. She talked about how working men on the outskirts loved a country walk, as did their children, and how 'year by year these field ways are being turned into forty-foot roads, and houses come and the walk is gone'. Reading her essay it's hard not to get swept up in her passionate arguments and righteous anger. And in it she coined a name that would live on far beyond her crusade. 'Might it not also be possible to secure sometimes a green belt to a road newly cut across the country, plant it with trees, and make of it a walking and riding way?' Her phrase lives on today, transformed from the leafy boulevards she imagined to great tracts of British landscape.

Hill's fervour brought the idea back into circulation. Following a trip to the US, Conservative peer, ardent eugenicist and cheerleading Victorian imperialist Reginald Brabazon was an unlikely convert. This grizzled veteran of London County Council's Open Spaces Committee had been much taken with Chicago's linked park system. Why not the same for London? Strips of land meeting up within the city and surrounding it in a 'green girdle', connecting open spaces throughout London with 'broad sylvan avenues and approaches'. Fellow Conservative, ambitious William Bull, MP for Hammersmith, was similarly infatuated. This stout fellow stole Brabazon's 'green girdle' and was happy to parade about with it. Their ideas generated a lot of interest. In a 1908 edition of *Quiver* magazine, writer Frederic Morrell Holmes's article *Green Girdles Round Great Cities* expanded on a proposal put forward by Bull. Hampstead Heath, Crystal Palace Park, Richmond Park, Kew Gardens, Syon Park, Ealing Common and Wembley Park would all be connected in a continuous ring of green running between four and eight miles from Charing Cross. And proposals began to spread beyond London too. Holmes explained how Glasgow, Sheffield, Liverpool and Birmingham could benefit. 'Town after town could be viewed in a similar manner,' he wrote, 'and the beginnings of a green girdle would be found already in existence.' After centuries of good intentions, eccentric proposals and idealistic visions the green belt was suddenly beginning to sound rather more achievable.

Octavia Hill's final immense contribution would be co-founding the National Trust. Here was an organisation that would take on the ideals of Hill's earlier work, while also adding some of its own: to preserve landscape and building of historic interest around England, with a slogan: 'Common Land for Common People'. There was also the added impetus that in the late Victorian era substantial areas of land were coming onto the market, land that was likely to be built on unless saved. Unlike the acres being preserved by the other societies, these weren't commons with rights of way, these were vast private estates, entire landscapes even, including the Lake District, Derwentwater and Ullswater. All of these green spaces had their champions. As a new century dawned, the outskirts of cities awaited their turn.

Gresley House, a modern four-storey block just off the Wandsworth Road, was a transitional place for my family, before the green belt quiet of my childhood and after the cramped Victorian terraces of my parents'. It was part of an estate erected to replace the old slums, houses finished off by a combination of latent jerry-building, bomb damage and the fashions of town planners. Marj and John moved into their flat in 1961 when they got married. She hadn't moved far at all, having already been living in a flat with her parents on the same floor of the block. Ian came along the following year; Paul, during the World Cup of 1966.

'I remember it *distinctly*,' said Ian, which immediately made me as unsure as I was about my own memories. 'The whole block was *dominated* by our family.' He has a knack for dramatic sweep. Ian used to tap dance and once appeared in an advert with Ronnie Corbett. That kind of showmanship doesn't just vanish. 'All our uncles upstairs, cousins . . . Everything was done on the open balconies. You could look out and you could see Battersea Power Station. That was my idea of a view. It was chaos all the time.' Our family lived on the third floor of the block, right in the middle. Marj's mum and dad were a few doors down. Two of her brothers lived in flats above them. Her aunt lived underneath. Housing conditions might have improved – inside toilets, hot running water, all mod cons – but it was still intensely built up. This attempt to tame the teeming life of the city was just one of the things that inspired – or frightened – the green belt into existence.

Many small, square, black-and-white photos exist of my family grinning, pouting and playing up on the concrete balconies of Gresley House. Marjorie with a beehive and thick black eyeshadow with her equally dramatic-looking Siamese cat, Simon. John with his skinny mod ties and thick Michael Caine specs. Ian grinning, looking like a right handful. Toddler Paul dreaming of somewhere to kick a ball. I've lived in

South London my whole life, but couldn't quite picture exactly where these flats were. So, one sunny October afternoon in 2015, I set off to find them, to see just where my family had left to come to New Addington. For sentimental reasons I decided to navigate using their old 1960s edition of the *A–Z of London*. 'New' it screamed on the front, in a way that very much wasn't. Here the map helpfully obscured itself with fluffy yellowing paper and porous lines of black ink. Still, it had lived in that flat, back in the sixties, and I never had. It would lead me there like a lost dog to its grieving owners.

The Patmore Estate in London is bounded by Battersea Power Station, New Covent Garden Market and the brick viaducts holding busy railway lines leading to Victoria and London Bridge. The map led me from Stockwell tube station and past the famous scallop-roofed bus station. Here were rows of small Victorian terraced houses, and there a succession of sculptural tower blocks surrounded by low railings and mown lawns. Quite suddenly, and before I was ready, these side streets opened out onto the noise and rush of Wandsworth Road. Hang on, I thought, was that *it*? I felt like I'd been robbed of an intrepid trek. Above a row of gaudy new supermarkets and offices rose the corner of a low-rise council block, hidden in plain sight by its own unremarkable decency.

Four storeys in brown brick and white concrete. An unmistakably postwar design, stripped of decoration and as regular as a bottle rack, with just a hint of those modest thirties council blocks in the scale and positioning. I'd investigated blocks just like this for my previous book, *Concretopia*, which told the story of the postwar rebuilding of Britain, and I admired the mild modernism, even down to the curved roof on the service tower – a nod to the Festival Hall perhaps. And back in the sixties it would have all been here for Marj and John: the busy shops, the noisy road, the rowdy pubs. This was a world they'd known all their lives, a place turned upside down, first by the Blitz and then by the planners, those socially concerned people out to sweep away the slums as eagerly as any Victorian moralist. It had been goodbye to the nasty, poky houses they had grown up in, and hello to all mod cons. While the city gentrifies around it, the estate remains what it had been when it was built: affordable housing for working-class tenants. Gresley House had been built in the late 1950s, designed by architects Bridgwater, Shepheard & Epstein. Later I would discover something remarkable, a connection that would both baffle and delight. The second of those designers, Peter Shepheard, had also been one of the architects of London's green belt. More on him later, a man for whom my parents could count themselves doubly thankful.

I'd like to say that tracking down my family's old home was a revelation. On Gresley House steps I sat down and wept. Here my strange, unknowable family finally made so much sense. But it wasn't like that at all. There was no ghost of Marj and John in the street furniture, or on the balconies and walkways. Rather, the overwhelming feeling was one of embarrassment. Gresley House, it turned out, was just a very short dawdle from a flat I'd shared in Stockwell in my thirties. All those years I promised myself I'd check out their old haunts. Instead I had been, what? Too busy? Self-obsessed? Bone idle? Too lazy to open an *A–Z* that was for sure. The big thing, of course, was how different it was from New Addington. So tightly packed, no sky, no green. One block of flats among thousands of other homes in an unbroken pattern for miles.

An elderly man looked down at me from the third floor as I snapped pictures of the block on my phone. I ambled down and through a gate at the side, and suddenly I was in a secret garden – there was green here after all. But of course there was: these flats were the result of efforts to open out the centre of London, to provide breathing spaces. They were the green belt in miniature. On this side of the block each flat had a small private balcony which overlooked a quiet municipal garden. Ash and cherry trees were beginning to drop their leaves onto the cropped lawn. Four 'no ball games' signs punctuated the façade. As I sat on a bench and looked around I could hear children playing in the distance, and the odd car trundling down a side road. Considering where I was it was surprisingly peaceful. Not the woods I had grown up with but still, a secret bit of green to escape to. It was relatively easy to imagine John tapping his foot along to The Shadows in the front room while fiddling with some wireless equipment, or Marj laughing along to the saucy exploits of Julian and Sandy in *Round the Horne*, a family favourite. [Sample joke: Kenneth Williams: 'I warn you, Mr Horne, this young lady's an expert in Judo.' Betty Marsden: 'Yes, I am a green belt. You know what that means?' Kenneth Horne: 'Yes. I mustn't build a factory on you without permission of the local authority.'] With their family ties and old friends, the familiar paths, shops and pubs, in a way it was hard to see why they wanted out. But maybe that was why. Here it all was, crowding in on them. Brick and tarmac as far as the eye could see, everyone popping by to see how you were at all hours, the pattern of life laid out before them with no choices to be made at all, and in the background the old familiar haunts being flattened under the bulldozer.

I am writing this on what would have been Marjorie's seventy-ninth birthday. Not that she would have thanked me for revealing her age, which she kept a secret as if national security relied upon it. I might not have recordings of those family reminiscences from the 1970s, but I do have something of hers. A diary from 1960, the year before she married John. It's not a big journal. In fact it's a tiny week-to-page pocket job, with a thin blue leatherette cover. Each entry is a brief dashed-off sentence at most, often just a word. Pages are covered with her lean italic scrawl, chaotically applied in either blue ballpoint or very faint pencil. It starts off chirpily enough, with numerous visits to the ITA Club in Camberwell, a place I can find no record of, although she did have a penchant for trad jazz at the time. She was accompanied by a number of different men, punctuated by repeated proposals by John. *He's so nice. He asked me to marry him again.* They were, in many ways, an odd couple. John with his love of slapstick and grubby bits of machinery; Marj and her air of mystery and quick wit; John the dyslexic, Marj with her love of words; chaotic, shambolic John and image-conscious, glamorous Marj. When I reached the summer in her diary it was clear that something had gone very wrong. She was in and out of work with illness, from bad feet to terrible headaches. From June onwards every page recorded stiff necks and thumping headaches, doctors' appointments and hospital visits. She had been very ill before. This was worrying.

Little was understood about her illness. It was believed that a cyst had grown inside her spinal cord, one that could have potentially destroyed it over time. This was syringomyelia, and the name for this type of cyst was a syrinx. Frightening, alien words, and no help when explaining to friends or relatives what was up. Syringomyelia is caused when cerebrospinal fluid, a liquid which flows between the brain and spine, begins to collect within the spinal cord. Typically it leads to loss of sensation, especially of extremes of temperature, and sometimes to chronic pain and paralysis. Back in the 1950s when Marjorie was first diagnosed little was known about the disease or how to treat it. It was mistakenly expected that she would develop many more cysts, and so preventative measures were taken. She had several invasive procedures on her spine and underwent many years of radiography, both to pinpoint and track the progress of the syrinx and to attempt to kill it and any future cysts. Legend went that Marj received so many x-rays that by the time she'd reached her thirties she'd had the maximum dose of radiation recommended for a lifetime. *You glow in the dark*, John used to say, proud of her singularity, her strangeness. It was as if she had undergone the kind of trial faced by a superhero in an origin story. Marked out with exceptional powers by a trace element and a dark personal fight.

During all of those years of sickness and treatment she was a big reader. It was her chief escape. But reading wasn't always a steadfast friend. One novel contained a character with syringomyelia. After reading it she fell into despair. The character was confined to an iron lung – one of those terrifying, room-filling diving-bell-type tubes – in which he was cut off from the world. Not only could he not move or speak, all he could do was look about him in mute horror. This nightmarish vision refused to leave her. She told me about it decades later, still angry with the writer for depicting her illness so shockingly, as a gruesome plot twist, and angry too with the doctors for not alleviating her fears. As it turns out, as with so much representation of illness in fiction, it was nonsense. But at the time, as a young working-class woman with a little-known disease, there was no way for her to know this. In fact, given the lack of information coming from her doctors, that depiction was one of the few things she had to go on. The numerous operations on her spine and the experimental nature of it all left her worse off than before. By the time she was married in 1961 the cyst was long gone, but all of that tampering with her discs had left her hunched and with limited movement, occasionally dependent on a wheelchair to get about.

Whether living in the city had any effect on her developing the disease I do not know. Victorian campaigners would have said so, for to them cities were sick. After all, even in the early century if you were a poor woman in an industrial town, just giving birth safely was a miracle. Beyond that, the child would have to dodge an epidemic of health problems, such as rickets or tuberculosis, diseases that thrived in the terrible conditions in which people lived. By the time Marj and John were born in the 1930s, conditions in many of those areas hadn't improved markedly since those days. Correspondingly, the story of my parents is also one of sickness. A constant companion in their marriage and their lives. Not that it stopped them. She went from date to date, job to job, a mysterious, self-contained figure in a world where everyone knew everything about everyone else.

What drove her on? Hope? Frustration? Bloody-mindedness? Fury? Absolutely. As a superhero she didn't lack for motivation. But this makes her sound like some kind of remote figure, and she wasn't. She could be silly – finding new ways to trick John into checking to see if double cream was fresh so she could dab his nose in it. Often when faced with a calamity her first reaction would be to get a fit of the giggles. She lived a kind of romantic fantasy, usually triggered by music. It was inhabited by all sorts: David Bowie (*Lovely, isn't he?* she'd say, squirming with delight), old music-hall songs (Roy Hudd would provoke much the same reaction) and the reggae exuberance of *Uptown Top Ranking*. When John listened to music (usually Santana or The Shadows) he tapped his feet like a wild thing. When Marjorie did, she was rapt, listening to every word, living the role of the singer, the heartbroken chanteuse, the glamorous unknowable.

When I asked how they had come to move from urban Battersea to the edge of a housing estate in Surrey, Ian, naturally, had a story ready.

'I was seven when we moved up here. To this magical place called *the woods*.' Ian spoke in the same garrulous, expansive, animated manner as all of Marjorie's family. As he talked it was like I was back being a kid again on the floor of our maisonette, cross-legged in the front room, listening to tales of the old days. This was a feeling emphasised by the fact that Ian now lives in an identical maisonette. 'I'd heard about it the year before,' he said. 'We were doing a collage at school. You know, where you get the leaves and stick them on? We had to find our own leaves. Battersea Park was our woods. So I found these great big leaves and asked Dad what they were. He said, *Oh, they're from conker trees.* Really prickly. I touched them and I was like, *urgh!* I got the leaves, held the conkers on the twigs, and took them home ready for school to do the collage. And Nan heard about it, and she said, *Oh, I'm going to see Uncle Bert* – who lived in New Addington – *I'll go over to the woods and get you some leaves.* Well, she came back with an acorn.' He almost jumped out of his chair, startling the dog. 'I'd never *seen* an acorn before, *honestly*, I remember it! Oak leaves. A *proper* horse chestnut leaf and a *proper* conker. And a head of corn out of the field. I'd never *ever* seen anything like that before, and I remember this magical place called the woods where we were going to go to.' He became very still. 'And within a year we'd moved there.'

When they did leave the crowded inner-city land-scape of Battersea in 1969, they were living something that had been enabled by campaigners and visionaries through the ages. No more would Ian walk to school along crowded streets and beside dangerous roads and smoky rail lines. No more would a trip to the country take an hour and a military operation. Instead we were a modern phenomenon: the once urban poor transplanted back to the edge of the city, to the country. One of those circles of which the green belt is surely formed had been completed. Marjorie, John and their two boys were suddenly living life on the edge of the countryside, in a way that Octavia Hill could have barely imagined, but would have surely approved.

2

The Green Door: The Townsman versus the Countryman

'Across the road, which was only a car and a half's width wide, you were on your own. There was no traffic, no other people. It was you, trees, fields, whichever direction you walked.' Paul is my middle brother. Whereas Ian was outgoing and flash, Paul had always been quieter, more inward looking. In football terms that he'd enjoy, conversationally he's a bit of a goal hanger, quiet for most of the time only to nip in and score with some cheeky quick-fire remark seconds before the end of a chat. He was the one of us who spent most time exploring the outdoors. Playing football and cricket, climbing trees, cycling, and, as he got older, taking photos. The three of us were always happy doing our own thing, seldom including the other. It might have been the four- and eight-year age gap between us, or the different circumstances of our growing up. Ian was seven by the time we moved to New Addington, and so had a strong attachment to the city. Paul was three, and latched himself firmly to the country as soon as he saw it. I was born there, and took it for granted.

We may not have shared interests or have played together, but we did make regular family trips into the woods across from us. John pushing Marjorie's wheelchair over the bumps and holes of the dirt track, the chair tipped back on its rear wheels like a cartoon chariot going at high speed. After I was born they used to travel as a convoy: John pushing Marjorie's wheelchair, she pushing my pram. Country walks would be tricky until I learned to walk. Pushing Marjorie's chair was a duty that John took very seriously, when his absent-mindedness allowed. Browsing in shop windows he'd frequently stop and look, leaving Marj coasting along, oblivious. This seemed to happen with great frequency on hills, where Marj had to slam on the brakes to stop herself racing out of control and mowing down hordes of shoppers. *Sorry love* was his standard offhand response. In the woods Paul and Ian used to race each other as John, Marj and I slogged along the path. One time the two boys went sprinting off round a clump of trees. On the far side the path had split and Paul took the wrong one. Being the energetic and single-minded kid he was, he just kept running. After a time he encountered some riders on horseback coming back the other way. They must have been a little bit thrilled to discover a lone tot charging through the undergrowth, their slow Sunday trot along the bridleway given a sudden, urgent purpose. For a moment they were the Croydon branch of the Mounties. The riders led Paul back through the woods, and he was reunited safely with the rest of us. *Where you been?* he remembered them asking. He mimed pointing, and shrugged helplessly. *Er . . . horses!* His laugh was a delighted, filthy chuckle. The woods were an ever-changing game.

Facing those fields on the edge of New Addington it didn't feel like we were part of the estate. I'm not sure we ever felt at one with the countryside either. Instead we were stranded in an intermediate nowhere, like being caught forever on the stairs. Paul was convinced that the people who lived further in didn't have the connection to the countryside that we did.

'Their kids played in *the park*,' he said, sniffily. 'I very rarely went to the park because I was in the woods, always up a tree or up to something. The park was a different world to me. The block was something I cycled round. What was *in front* of me was the fun. I could do anything there. Go and build a camp, go and climb trees, be anybody I wanted to be. Whereas they had a slide and a bit of grass.' My strongest memory of the swing park wasn't of using it, but of waiting with Paul at a nearby bus stop one summer's afternoon. There was no one else around. The little playground housed a climbing frame shaped like an Apollo-capsule, a slide, three swings, a seesaw and a large clanking roundabout, all stuck fast in gritty slabs of concrete. Beyond was Milne Park, acres of football pitches on a flat expanse of green belt, sandwiched between two distant rows of houses. That afternoon the whole park lay beneath an enormous tract of black cloud, the playground illuminated by the kind of eerie light you get just before heavy rain. As we waited there for the 130 bus, a blade of lightning struck the ground twenty feet from us, and skittered along the hard playground floor. We were frozen in place, witnesses to a moment of dazzling divine violence just feet away. In this flat, mown landscape how had that bolt missed the tall, exposed bus stop we were stood next to? How had we dodged that one? After some minutes of awestruck wonder we turned away. *Oh goody*, was all Paul said.

Thunderstorms were a family treat. Marjorie's anxious, superstitious Irish Catholic mother had brought up her children to be afraid of lightning. At the first hint of a storm she'd run around hiding all the metal in the house – cutlery, ornaments, jewellery – and cower under the stairs praying under her breath. Her reaction pre-dated a more reasonable fear of the Blitz, and kept Marj and her siblings terrified. Once they moved to New Addington Marjorie was keen to discard many things: the expectations of her family, the limitations she'd grown up with, and the superstitions her mother had whipped up. And so at the first distant rumble of thunder or flash of lightning she'd throw open the front door and gather us all around her to watch the show. Counting between the flashes and bangs, giggling with delight at the loud cracks, discussing the lightning as if doing so took away the fear. If we were going to live with nature on our doorstep, she must have thought, we might as well get used to the elements.

Even if we were beginners at being green belt folk, my parents found unexpected benefits in country life. In the early 1970s they turned to scavenging. The maisonette had a coal fire. When coal became too expensive around the time of the three-day week, many people from the estate could be found scouring the woods trying to find something that would burn. On a Sunday morning John would head off down the lanes and forage for firewood. He'd spot a fallen tree and he'd be there in a flash, sawing bits off. Ian was the only one of us old enough to remember what Marj and John had thought of all this green space when they moved there, how much they loved it. Back in Battersea they used to go window-shopping on a Sunday, where they were safe from temptation as the shops were all shut. Picnics were a curious novelty. 'You know what Mum and Dad were like,' said Ian. 'That's not a thing they'd necessarily do.' I knew what he meant. They hated sticking out and being noticed. But the scenery made it permissible, somehow, just as the seaside did. Stopping and looking at the trees and flowers, without people thinking anything of it. A chance to be curious without encouraging other folk to be curious about us. Somehow it seemed to give everything a point.

The very earth outside our door had always held a fascination. The thick red London clay of our garden was hard to lift and would stick to a fork in great clods. Yet, just a few yards away, the valley glittered silver with flint and white with chalk. We were on the edge of the Blackheath shingle beds, whose split pebbles gave the fields a frosty edge when they fractured, a silver wash on the slopes scintillating like a watercolour by Eric Ravilious. All around the estate were unexpected landscapes. The heather, oak and pines that make up the plateau of Addington Hills. The regular simplicity of Rowdown Field. North Downs, Addington's first recreation ground, was a reminder that the estate is part of the larger North Downs which stretch from Surrey to the White Cliffs of Dover. There are long strips of woodland to the east separating New Addington from the fields of Bromley. The bluebells of Jewels Wood were a family favourite. Here the trees

– oak, beech, ash, horse chestnut and lime – towered above us, knitting together in summer to form a glorious green canopy.

The green belt doesn't just surround the estate. It's infiltrated it too. Amid all the postwar houses and flats are large open spaces like Addington Vale, a steep, undulating park from which you could see out to the distant skyline of London. As the estate was built, 2,500 tons of rubble were dumped in this valley, and it created the great mounds that form the landscape here. Then there was the peculiar immense mown expanse of Milne Park, where Paul and I had escaped being struck by lightning. It had once been a private aerodrome before construction began on the estate. So many different landscapes, all green belt, and all belonging to the council.

Paul's earliest memories were of playing tennis in the road and knocking down conkers from the big horse chestnut tree that grew facing our house. A childhood of football and cricket followed, usually involving climbing the fence to the school field at the end of our road – another big piece of green belt – and fixing up the nets or cricket stumps.

'We must have repaired them more than the caretakers ever did. We left them in better condition, because that's what we wanted to do.' Okay, so the caretaker of the junior school used to shoot at Paul and his mates with an air rifle, but those were the risks. And not ones I was willing to take, to be honest. By contrast, the caretaker of the high school knew they weren't up to mischief and was on nodding terms as they jumped the gates and sauntered through the playground to the fields. Paul's childhood was full of danger. Coming off his bike on a cinder track in the woods, and hobbling a mile home with the bone of his kneecap exposed. And what he refers to as 'the breaking of the arms', as if it were some kind of solemn rite. His left arm was broken during a game of street football. Sat on the ball at the end of the match, he was taken by surprise when a bigger lad kicked it away. Paul fell backwards, shattering his arm. Six weeks in plaster later, and at the end of the summer holidays, he had the cast cut off. Free at last! He arrived back home to find a gang of his mates had gathered, eager to play outside. Paul ran straight from the car, over the road, through some tall grass and broke his other arm falling over a tree stump. John hadn't even taken his shoes off from driving him back from the hospital. Just as well.

The gateway to the outdoors for Marj in the early seventies was her Invacar, a three-wheeled 'invalid carriage', or as Paul referred to it, *her blue disabled thing*. At the time the Invacar was to disability what running in slow motion was to the Six Million Dollar Man: not the only way to travel, but by far the best. The ice-blue three-wheeled vehicle had first been developed after the Second World War to aid injured veterans in getting about. By the 1960s, with their 147cc engine, these awkwardly functional fibreglass trikes were a familiar sight on Britain's roads. Pointed at by kids, jeered at by fellow motorists and beloved of its many users, the Invacar was one of the most visible signs of 'the handicapped' in Britain. This was the age before political correctness and the Paralympics made life with a disability a little more bearable, and my overwhelming memory of the general reactions at the time to any mention of disability at school were the contorted playground cries of *Joey* and *spastic*. Marj might fold her wheelchair up and haul it for the drive, but more often than not she just left it on the verge outside the house and hoped for the best. There it would sit for an hour or so, an empty grey wheelchair beneath a cherry tree, waiting for Marjorie. The contraption looked so awkward folded up, its grey-painted steel frame, thin spokes, black canvas seat and grey rubber footrests gawky as a bat hanging from a tree. Incredibly, it never got nicked.

Invacar advertised their vehicles as 'freedom for the disabled', and for a woman used to being trapped by circumstance, duty and illness, freedom was what Marj got. She would take the car out to the shops to pick up essentials from the local Co-op, Browns the bakers or Liptons, the delicatessen, places too far for her to walk or wheel in the sprawling estate. Almost every time she left the house in her Invacar, she took it for a spin in the opposite direction too, down the country lanes that stretched in the valley between New Addington and neighbouring Biggin Hill. Somewhere along the way she would stop the car, open the door and look out at the scene before her. A popular view was the vale where the farmer kept sheep. There was just enough room to tuck her car in out of the way of the occasional bits of country traffic. Here she would sit for an hour or so, watching lambs in springtime or shaggy-coated sheep in autumn. She was familiarising herself with this new country environment, just minutes from home. Neither Marj nor John had first-hand experience of the countryside. Now it was on their doorstep – a step which, naturally, John had converted into a ramp.

It was Marj's next car I remember most fondly, a Mini Traveller, with wood panelling on the outside. Often I used to go with her and our neighbour Joan Blood during the school holidays and sit on the tan vinyl bench seat in the back, watching out the window as we headed down those country lanes. Over time the car began to feel as if it had become part of the countryside itself. It stank of damp. Mud and leaves came inside never to leave. The felt runners for the sliding back windows began to grow moss. It was like observing the scenery through the steamy windows of a ramshackle old greenhouse. We went from townsfolk running amok in the country to naturalised green belt dwellers. The lichen on the car proved it.

Bringing urban folk like my family together with the countryside remained an esoteric pursuit until the start of the twentieth century, when the creation of a new type of town aimed to combine the best of town and country. Garden cities were carefully planned settlements, and their influence has spread far beyond the few that were built. The International Garden Cities Exhibition is based in a white-rendered Arts and Crafts house in Letchworth, Hertfordshire, the first of these innovative towns to be built. The broad swathes of green brought into the heart of the city might be confusing for urban folk. 'Newcomers from grassless cities, though they gasp with joy at the sight of green strips in roads, have to be educated not to destroy them by their pleasure in walking on them', wrote planner Frederic Osborn.[1] The exhibition itself was full of proud details of Letchworth's progeny: garden cities around the world, from Welwyn just down the road to Radburn and Greenbelt in the US, Kapuskasing and Don Mills in Canada, Canberra in Australia and more recent developments in Japan and China. It all felt a little bizarre, a bit like Letchworth itself. Could this place, quaint as an afternoon tea (though one imagined by Lewis Carroll) really have influenced new towns in Brazil, South Africa and the Czech Republic? Had the planners managed to export a theme park based on the picturesque products of British colonialism? Disneyland with antimacassars and awkwardness.

If you need a starter kit to help found a new settlement you could do a lot worse than shelling out for a copy of Ebenezer Howard's book *Garden Cities of*

To-Morrow. First published in 1898, this was the extraordinary work that created the idea of networks of verdant new towns. It's a quick read too. At 128 pages this world-changing book is a fifth of the length of that other building block of civilisation, Delia Smith's *Complete Cookery Course*. So, who was this world-changing man? Was he a philosopher, an activist, a town planner? Well, at the time he wrote the book Ebenezer was simply a Hansard clerk, on the fringes of government and the do-gooding societies of the late Victorian era. The garden cities he wrote about so enthusiastically would be built away from existing conurbations, separated from them by agricultural belts. 'How shall it grow?' he wondered. 'Shall it build on the zone of agricultural land which is around it, and thus forever destroy its right to be called a "Garden City"? Surely not.'[2] In one short book he discussed funding, purchasing land, putting up the right kind of homes and the sort of communities that could be forged there. He expounded theories of zoning housing, industry and open space to correct the ills of the Industrial Revolution towns, with solid, practical ideas to back them up. It was Thomas More's *Utopia* as Haynes manual.

It seems incredible that a mere five years after publication of his book, Howard had gained enough approval, acolytes and momentum to be buying land on which to actually construct one of these experimental garden cities. By 1903 a site had been found in

Hertfordshire to build Letchworth. A prospectus laid out some of its advantages. 'Firstly, the provision of hygienic conditions of life for a considerable working population. Secondly, the stimulation of agriculture by bringing a market to the farmer's door. Thirdly, the relief of the tedium of agricultural life by accessibility to a large town.'[3] It was clear that in Letchworth the garden was to be as important as the city. But accumulating enough land to achieve his aims required a poker face and nerves of steel. Frederic Osborn, one of Howard's apostles, recalled that with 'the land being held by 15 owners, not all wishful to sell, great secrecy had to be maintained in the purchase negotiations'.[4]

In 1909 a further landmark was reached. Over a thousand acres between Hitchin and Baldock, to the south of the garden city, had been bought. Only here the Garden City Corporation weren't looking to build houses, shops or industrial areas. Instead it was to be kept as farmland for the town, a protected agricultural ring. In effect, Britain's first piece of green belt. The countryside had been bought as a market garden for the inhabitants. In the original documents, locals would be able to buy food grown in the surrounding countryside, and this self-sufficient attitude infused Howard's thinking and Parker and Unwin's planning. It meant that Letchworth was 1970s self-sufficiency sitcom *The Good Life* scaled up to the size of a town, with, I suspect, more Margos than anyone could reasonably be expected to cope with. Produce wasn't just to be grown by farmers: allotments featured heavily in the proposal too. All Letchworthians were encouraged to have a go. Letchworth would be succeeded by a larger sibling, Welwyn Garden City, and then by over forty postwar new towns, like Stevenage and Milton Keynes. With all of these imitators, Letchworth remains the garden city for purists, keeping those hedges trimmed and lawns mown as the rest of the world goes insane.

As I walked in the green belt to the south of the town the country seemed as neat and polite as an illustration from a 1960s Ladybird book. Immense bales of hay stacked and ready for transportation. The nodding heads of nettles, small purple stars of red campion and great leathery spikes of expired poppies. The biggest thing to have grown here since Howard's day were the electricity pylons, draping swags of wires across the sky like paper chains. As if imitating them, fat wood pigeons took the most elegant of flights up and over the cables, and into the treetops beyond. The hedgerows of hawthorn and hazel were broken up with occasional trees. A large brown rabbit hopped about a few feet from a barbed wire fence and hedgerow, beyond which ran Britain's longest road, the A1, a ribbon of tarmac tied tight between London and Edinburgh. In the corner of a field stood those green belt staples: yellow ragwort flowering at chest height, and the taller pink flower of rosebay willowherb. Following a path through the ragwort I was soon up to my belly like a nervous swimmer. From the willowherb was erupting the most delicate fluff, which, when seen *en masse*, was like a king-size duvet divesting itself of its entire contents across the landscape one feathery shred at a time. I was away from all of the plans, the designs, the maps. Here instead was an eruption of nature, reclaiming a corner of a farmer's field and asserting itself in Ebenezer Howard's market garden, exploding like the last fireworks of the night.

After Ebenezer Howard there were green belt champions everywhere. Take Henrietta Barnett, a follower of Octavia Hill who bought 243 acres of land in Golders Green in 1904 to found Hampstead Garden Suburb. Her mini-Letchworth, with its leafy avenues and Arts and Craft cottages, was designed by luminaries such as Raymond Unwin and Edwin Lutyens. It has long since been one of the most desirable residences in London, slightly undermining Barnett's desire to create a socialist paradise of homes for all. In 1910 she revived the idea of a green belt for London, dusting off Octavia Hill's proposal and expanding on Howard's. Allowing for the growth of the city, she imagined it as a ring five miles from the city centre.

Even the devastating effects of the Great War didn't interrupt the march of progress. The London Society was an organisation set up to encourage people to take an interest in the construction of the city. In 1919 they began to champion the old circular parkland idea.

Theirs was rather narrower than in previous suggestions, and, due to the spread of London, somewhat further out. The following year the society's proposal received the blessing of the great Garden City mastermind Raymond Unwin. London was already quite large enough, he told them. A green belt would provide the people with a place for recreation and fresh air, and protect them from disease too.

In this fervour for all things Ebenezer Howard, the land that would become New Addington almost ended up as a garden village too. Buried in a 1921 edition of a magazine called *Garden Cities and Town Planning* lies the evidence, in the form of a report from E.L. Hudson, the honorary secretary of the Surrey Garden Village Trust. The organisation had been formed immediately after the First World War with the aim of allowing soldiers to settle on the land and take up 'country occupations'. This was as part of the 'Homes Fit for Heroes' movement, whose aims were set out by Prime Minister David Lloyd George as part of a drive to tackle poor education and health, bad housing and transport. Five farms stood on 533 acres of land beside ancient Addington village. The Trust wanted to replace them with a hundred smallholdings. These would be for 'the growing of market-garden crops, fruit and flowers, the production of eggs, poultry, rabbit flesh and fur, pork, bacon and honey, and kindred industries such as the preserving of fruits and vegetables, and handicrafts of all kinds'.[5] Around the smallholdings there would be orchards and a wood along with a new recreation ground. By the time of the article a fair amount of fundraising had been achieved, but the scheme was never realised. Instead, fifteen years later, a developer called Henry Boot bought the very same land to create an even more ambitious – and entirely unconnected – 'garden city', and the beginnings of the modern estate there were born. Would those Croydon locals have been downhearted by the failure of the garden village? Other than the landowners who had lost out on a sale, probably not. As Frederic Osborn noted at Welwyn, the second garden city, 'the apprehension of the farmers was qualified by a deep-rooted conviction that the whole thing was lunacy and would come to nothing'.[6]

The collision between country and town throws up all sorts of issues about freedom. Garden City planners and health campaigners might have been excited by the idea of townsfolk exploring the great outdoors, but media commentators were less keen on the class of people being encouraged into this rural domain. 'I would have every child required to pass an examination in country lore and country manners before he left school', wrote controversialist Cyril Joad in 1938. 'There is something to be said for requiring every townsman who has not succeeded in passing this examination to wear an "L" upon his back when he walked abroad in the country, for, until he has learned the elementary manners of the countryside, he is no better qualified to be at large in a wood than a learning motorist to be at large on a road.'[7]

Joad was a man of his day: Fabian, pacifist, philanderer. He was a forthright philosopher of everyday life, a kind of gobbier J.B. Priestley, and star of wartime BBC radio panel show *The Brains Trust*. At the height of his popularity he was unafraid to tell us how to live, berate us for our shortcomings and urge us to do as he said, if not what he did. Joad is only one of many like minds. The divide between 'townsmen' and 'countrymen' (never women) is played out in countless books, pamphlets, articles and broadcasts throughout the 1920s and 30s. The 'townsman' was a clueless oaf, like the idiot in an advert for soap powder, spilling it over the floor and turning his clothes pink. By contrast, the countryman took on the mythic status of custodian of the land, the spirit of ancient chalk giants or the legendary green man come to life.

Joad was a positive townie collaborator compared to Wiltshire farmer, writer and fellow *Brains Trust* alumnus A.G. Street. He describes the 1930s townsman as 'trespasser, house-builder, thief of blooms and plants and shrubs, creator of noise and untidiness, destroyer of beauty, and possessor of other noxious habits and no manners whatsoever'.[8] And that was just for starters. These weren't just ham-fisted idiots accidentally spoiling the scenery; they were pernicious too. To Street this was a civil war. On one side are country dwellers who safeguard the landscape for generations to come. Against them the townsmen – speculative builders, advertisers, those out to make a pretty penny. Street calls them the 'enemies of society'. His solution? 'I should very happily see some of them – failing conversion – plunged into boiling oil.'[9] It was the land around our biggest towns and cities that was most at risk from this invasion. And for farmers like A.G. Street, the fifth columnist was plain to see: the rambler. Country walks for country folk were a necessity of life, part of an endless, exhausting stewardship operation. These ramblers thought walking was a pleasure! They'd soon learn.

One of the first formal attempts by townsfolk at exploring the country was begun in 1879, when an organisation called the Sunday Tramps first met. It was a men's walking group set up in London by Leslie Stephen, a former vicar soon to be father to Vanessa Bell and Virginia Woolf. He attracted likeminded brain-iacs to the group who would leave the city every other weekend to hike in the wilds. On their first effort they got all the way to Richmond. But they were soon travelling further afield, to the hills of Surrey and the lanes of Kent. So notable was their intellectual chat that novelist George Meredith remarked that the walkers should be accompanied by a shorthand note-taker. What a serious business this exploring the countryside lark was, best left to professors, doctors, lawyers and writers.

Change came in the form of the Sheffield Clarion Rambling Club. In 1900 proto-Labourite G.H.B. Ward formed this working-class walking group in Sheffield. They christened it with an ambitious walk around Kinder Scout in the Peak District, an area which these days is National Park but then was resolutely private. Thirty-two years later a walk at Kinder Scout was responsible for bringing many diverse rambling groups together. Access was a big issue for walkers, with landowners going out of their way to prevent trespass, and severely limiting rights of way. On Sunday 24 April 1932, a mass invasion of Kinder Scout took place, led by communist agitator Benny Rothman. It ended with a punch-up between gamekeepers and ramblers, and five walkers were sent to jail.

Because of that ramble, and much to the annoyance of country folk, the Rights of Way Act became law two years later. Although this didn't actually establish any new routes, it did mean that if a path had been used continually over decades it could be legally established. These days there are over 18,000 miles of public rights of way in the English green belt alone. Protecting them would become an ongoing struggle for decades to come. In her 1969 book, the unappetisingly titled *The Ministry of Housing and Local Government*, Dame Evelyn Sharp, Britain's first female permanent secretary, reviewed progress and was characteristically disparaging about what had been achieved. She wrote wearily that 'the main function of the ministry has been to try and goad the more reluctant county councils into faster action', on the creation and maintenance of footpaths, 'and to placate the more indignant members of the public clamouring for results. The job is an immensely laborious one.'[10] It was fair to say that some of the joy had gone out of the task since the heady days of Kinder Scout.

As my family knew, it wasn't just exploring on foot that revealed the countryside to curious outsiders, and Marj's experience of observing the green belt from her car was certainly not a novel one. From the start of the twentieth century the automobile was seen as enabling the 'townsman' to explore the country as never before. In 1919 influential Scottish town planner Stanley Adshead described how the countryside, 'with the advent of the public automobile, is becoming a real cinema of the people, for from it can be viewed the real panorama of urban and rural life'.[11] Jack Beddington, at oil giant Shell, wanted to associate his product and the motorcar with the wonders of the great outdoors. And as an adjunct to the craze for rambling, in 1933 John Betjeman proposed a new series of travel guides to England's counties. The *Shell Guides* would be written by an eclectic mix of artists, poets and planners, mostly Betjeman's mates from the Georgian and Victorian Societies. As historian Juliet Gardiner has it, the resulting series of beautifully illustrated books 'embodied the selective nostalgia of progressive connoisseurs'. They were also part of an industry helping travellers celebrate the unspoiled countryside while simultaneously spoiling it. Betjeman was realistic about the readership: 'probably not an intellectual in search of regional architecture of the early nineteenth century but a plus-foured weekender who cannot tell a sham Tudor roadhouse from a Cotswold manor'.[12] New books were still being commissioned well into the 1970s, by which time the rise of environmentalism was making the basis of the series more than a little precarious.

As the battle between the Countryside Alliance and Tony Blair's government over fox hunting proved, the war between the townsman and the countryman has never really ended. Britain's most famous landscape architect, Sylvia Crowe, remarked in 1956 that 'the gulf between the townsman's and the countryman's outlook will only be bridged when the townsman has the opportunity of seeing and understanding how the country works'.[13] The ball is in the townsman's court, then. Marj was certainly up for giving it a go. Considering her situation, unable to freely explore the woods, hills and dirt tracks around our home in her wheelchair, she did well familiarising herself with all the wildlife she could from car or house. She could identify all the birds in the garden. She was also the first person I heard mention the parakeets that fly wild in the treetops of South London. Her extensive knowledge led me to believe she had always known this stuff. Now I realise she had acquired it as a mother in her mid-thirties.

For her, country lanes were infused with romance. And when she got her Mini, it was something she was able to share with others. More often than not it was with our decidedly unromantic next-door neighbour, Joan Blood. Long tall Joan in her too-short polyester flares, horn-rimmed glasses and headscarf was a Quentin Blake drawing come to life. She loved to gossip. By gossip I mean do people down. She'd pop round every morning for a swift hour of chain-smoking, gertcha-ing and rehashing the most banal domestic event in micro-detail, to which Marjorie would nod along tolerantly. 'I'm telling you now!' Joan would say. And indeed she was. For ages.

Then they'd head out, these unlikely allies, Marjorie on a cushion in the driver's seat, Joan next to her, like an ironing board in a mac. Marjorie would offer Joan a choice – the quick way or the scenic route. Marj always wanted the scenic route. It's hard to know what Joan thought of her, or of these peculiar jaunts out to the woods. One thing she did react to was Marj's swearing. Seemingly mild-mannered and a bit posh, once behind the wheel all of her street-fighting Battersea childhood came out, and she'd *fucking bastard* her way round the streets, winding down the windows and giving some van driver or reckless motorist a piece of her mind, two fingers and a bagful of bad language. Joan might have flinched at Marj's swearing, but never expressed any interest in the landscape or the country. Instead she brought with her all the anxieties of urban living. She was another escapee from the inner city, some twenty years older than Marj, and had lived on the street for many years before we arrived. Her front room was decorated like a pub, complete with 1950s bar, peeling leatherette armchairs and horse brasses. Her taciturn husband, Frank, remained hidden by stacks of old newspapers, novelty cigarette lighters and tobacco smoke. I'm not sure he'd ever noticed the scenery across the road, let alone ventured into it. And if it weren't for Marj, Joan Blood wouldn't have seen it either.

One of the most memorable relics on the bookcase at home when I was growing up was a large wipe-clean ring binder in a fetching shade of avocado. It sat where the Bible or *Communist Manifesto* might sit in other homes. This was *No Through Road: The AA Book of Country Walks*, an extraordinary 1975 publication containing everything the curious traveller needed to tour the countryside. The folder contained numerous books, maps and sheets that could be removed for a trip, to arm the expectant driver and rambler. There was a large tome describing walking the different landscapes in Britain. Detailed illustrated guides to individual walks could be removed and carried around in a clear plastic pocket, also provided. Then there was an Autocar fold-out map of Great Britain, and for a bit of fun, a small *Country Quiz Book*, containing questions on everything from guessing the names of architectural features to working out which freshwater fish was the odd one out. My favourite component was the little *Walkers' Handbook*, containing descriptions and line drawings of wild flowers, trees, birds, insects and mammals. 'Finding one's way in the British countryside has never been so easy, given care and common sense', claimed the book, going on to explain how to use an Ordnance Survey map, read a compass and understand local signage. To my knowledge the book never left our house. We never unclipped any of those guides, went on any of those walks or spotted any of those medieval barns or teasels. After a brief dalliance where Marj and John would coo over photographs of the Chilterns or a line drawing of Saxon fortifications, its presence became purely symbolic. It was a reminder of what we could be doing at the weekend, instead of watching Paul play Little League football or tuning into opposing families failing to throw a pot on *The Generation Game*. After all, for us a book of country walks was always going to be a bit of a challenge.

Selsdon is the middle-class neighbour of resolutely rough New Addington, and everything about it feels a little precious, like a modernist model village. But it wasn't the housing I'd come to see, but rather its protected semi-natural woodland. It lay at the end of a long road ending in a single-exit roundabout, which creates a perfect exclamation point to demarcate the green belt. Leaves were falling on the damp November day I went to visit. The scale of the place was dramatic, from the mighty oaks up in the canopy to the upward curves of the hawthorn bushes at head height, and the darkening ribbed spumes of the ferns beneath.

Richard Edwards, Croydon's Trees and Woodland Officer, and Simon Levy, a consultant from a contractor called Coombe Forestry, led me through the wood, explaining their work in this handsome patch of green belt. We reached an outcrop of hazel and they stopped to explain a major feature of their work: coppicing. The base of each shrub was a thick knot of old lopped stubs, from which new slender stems shot up, high as our heads. Branches like these had been used for centuries for coppicing, a process of cutting the wood while slender and still pliant, for use in sheep hurdles, fencing and baskets. The old healed wounds in the bark were a reminder that nature here existed at the behest of people. The tradition of coppicing those shrubs affected the entire flora and fauna of the wood. When the hazel was a dense thicket it was the perfect habitat for nightingales and nightjars. When it was cut the clear woodland floor encouraged the sprouting of violets and the flutter of fritillary butterflies. As in much of Britain the woods here had fallen into disuse in the Industrial Revolution, when those traditional hazel products were no longer needed. And so the neglected forest had matured into an even-aged canopy of tall trees blocking out light and killing off diversity. Richard and Simon's aim had been to get it back. And that meant felling a few mighty oaks.

'People wouldn't have batted an eyelid sixty or seventy years ago that trees were being cut down in their woods,' explained Richard, 'because that was what they were brought up with. Simon had a battle for a long, long time to re-educate people to say that this is the right way to manage woodland. Cutting trees isn't wrong.'

'I have to be escorted to public meetings unfortunately,' said Simon. It seems that the re-education of townsfolk still has some way to go.

'Croydon is always considered one of the hellholes of the south,' said Simon Levy, as we tramped through the wood, 'but it's not. We have 500 hectares of woodland, and some of it, like Selsdon and Kingswood, and Rowdown Wood in New Addington, they are as good woods as any you'd find in the south, in terms of ancient semi-natural woodlands.' It was certainly beautiful, if that counted for anything. Simon's enthusiasm for the flora was infectious. As we marched along he hymned wood spurge and bluebells growing low to the ground, signs of a healthy wood. The hazel coppice had been fenced off. Did fencing it off mean it was less disturbed, I asked, trying to sound like I knew what I was talking about.

'Oh no,' said Simon. 'We don't mean to fence it. We'd much rather people went in it. The deer browse everything off.' I gave him a funny look. 'Deer are a huge problem in English woodlands.'

'I've never seen any round *here* though,' I said. Surely they were making some kind of mistake.

'There's tons,' said Simon. How, I thought, have I missed them? I looked about, as if I was now going to see a herd of them breaking for cover. I spoke to Ian about it later, and he recalled friends of his living on the eastern side of the estate having deer in their gardens, and rare lizards they used to go out spotting.

'Come early mornings,' suggested Richard. 'Quite often we will walk through the middle of the wood and then a deer will jump up and off it runs.' I blinked. Deer. *Deer?* In Croydon? Around *New Addington?* What next? Wild boar on the playing fields? Wolves in the underpasses? Eagles on the tower blocks? All the years I'd lived here, how had I not known this?

Richard and Simon had their eye on something bigger than simple woodland maintenance. An attempt to create a more natural ecology in the woods by replicating the effects of long-term change.

'We try to manipulate time,' said Richard. 'In theory you'd have a big, big forest. Our forests are much smaller than they should be because people build houses around them. But in a big place, like the forests in Poland, they can just leave them, and then you'd get a big area blow over. They would rot down and new stuff would come up. We replicate that with our management.' It wasn't easy trying to recreate the changing fortunes of a vast ancient Polish forest artificially in a small wood in South London. Though even Poland doesn't seem inclined to leave its forests any more. In May 2016 they began logging the primeval Białowieża forest, a place left wild for 10,000 years.

Simon and Richard's work in Croydon is having a positive effect. Once they had cleared some of the tall trees so that coppicing could begin again, the nightingales and nightjars came back. They managed the coppicing carefully; few people were allowed to do it so that it didn't get out of hand. On our walk we came across a memorial bench for one of their best workers, a man called Rob Sowter, donated by local volunteers, the Friends of Selsdon Wood. Rob had died the previous year. The kind of townsman so disparaged by all those commentators, he'd been long-term unemployed, but Richard and Simon encouraged him to study with the British Trust of Conservation Volunteers. Pretty soon he was at the forefront of reviving ancient methods of forest management in the borough. Rob had been coppicing and charcoaling all over the woodland in Croydon. Even when he became very ill he continued, such was his love of the work and the woods.

'I didn't realise he did his last block here wearing a colostomy bag,' said Simon. 'Never complained.' Life and death among the trees, something Simon and Richard seemed perfectly attuned to. The cycle, the immense time scales, the small differences that an individual can make in their lifetime. Tramping around the wood in its suburban setting it was easy to feel connected to something bigger than the everyday squabbles between town and country. This must have been the feeling those garden city pioneers had been wanting to create too, of planning a landscape that balanced the natural and the built environment. And here it was, the interface between people and nature, just metres from the edge of a housing estate, where nightingales continued their age-old song and deer browsed in secret.

3

The Bleeding Edge: Suburbia and How to Tame It

The traffic was pretty heavy as Peter Wiles pulled his car over by the roadside. Peter, a dashing photographer in his late sixties, was my guide to the wonders of Metro-land. The windscreen wipers were going, and we could hear rain drumming on the roof. I peered out with what I hope displayed the right amount of interest. Opposite was a nicely kept white-rendered 1930s house. This was the place Peter had grown up back in those early postwar years: a regular suburban semi, recently extended. On this miserable summer morning it presented to my defeated imagination not the open façade of a childhood remembered but the lifelessness of an estate agent's photo, of a house that *boasts* rooms, and *offers spacious accommodation*. Not a home, but a *property*.

'They moved into that house which was new in 34-ish, rented it, and they stayed there until they died,' said Peter of his parents. 'They had a very static life.' It was one they chose to live in Croxley Green, a suburb of Hertfordshire. We peered out a minute longer, neither of us sure if this was what the other wanted to do. Peter took the initiative. 'Baldwin's Lane is a very long road,' he said. 'It goes down towards Watford. But then, if you go *this* way,' he pointed left, 'you go out to the country.' And he pulled away from the kerb and in a spray of mist from the tyres we were off.

I'd taken the Metropolitan Line out to Croxley Green, where I'd agreed to meet Peter that morning, and the journey had been like the presentation of relics from the boom times of the twentieth century. The majority were 1920s and 30s semi-detached houses, when oriel bay windows and sunburst gateposts were the dream. There were some 1960s terraces and flats too, when a more stripped-back modernistic approach suited the fashions and budgets of the era. Between the schools and stations ran a prospect of brick, pebbledash, white render; patched terracotta roofs and dormer windows; immodest extensions and faux-Victorian conservatories. Everywhere, glimpses of estate agents' signs like the flags of a conquering army. Bindweed clung to wire fences like dancers in an eighties pop video. These were tiny patches of green in the commuter scene, where roads of houses stretched out from the city in a continuous flow.

Before they had been absorbed into the tube network in 1933 the Metropolitan Railway Company decided to have a go at building new houses around the stations they were opening. After all, private developers had been doing the same since the early nineteenth century, pouncing on land round new stations, building houses and making a killing. For the ambitious Metropolitan Railway here was an opportunity to be both amenity and developer, a handy two-for-one offer. In 1915 they even started to produce guidebooks using some aspirational new branding to help locals and travellers appreciate the world they had opened up. The marketing department called it Metro-land. It was a romantic place of middle-class country walks, cheery pubs and rolling landscapes. The name has stuck, branding not just the land around the train line but other interwar suburbs of London too.

There was a flash of green belt, and then I'd arrived, in the heart of Metro-land. Croxley Station is on a small high street, with a shop flogging children's dancewear and its neighbour selling Parker Knoll chairs. *That's cradle to grave catered for*, I thought. Opposite, a line of those ubiquitous 1930s houses stood nonchalantly by, like they had been racing me along the tracks the whole way. I could see why people had once become so alarmed by the spread of them. The journey had been a vision of an interwar arcadia, the world that private housebuilders with no particular plan beyond expediency had built intensively on the fringes of London along a railway line.

After my drive around Croxley Green with Peter we headed to Sarratt to visit his old school friend, John Guy.

'It's where people go to be interrogated in *Tinker, Tailor, Soldier, Spy*,' said Peter comfortingly. When we were there and sipping tea he produced a small black-and-white photograph taken in the early fifties and looked at it wonderingly. 'This is my friend Jonathan, that's me, and that's his older sister Bridget,' he said. They look like the kind of trio of children to have burst from any classic children's adventure story. Peter, smartly dressed and solemn, clutching his posy of flowers, could have stepped from the pages of *The Railway Children* or an Enid Blyton. It was the quintessence of early green belt, summoning up images of a childhood playing cowboys and Indians in the woods, cycle rides to airfields to plane-spot, and watching consignments from the local paper mill head off to Singapore and Bombay.

Around Croxley the reality of the green belt is obvious. As the boys grew older the separation between their suburb and the neighbouring towns could be a curse as well as a blessing. Here the nightlife was sleepy, the thrills few. And so the Metropolitan Line became their saviour.

'I always remember walking down to the platform and there would be all the posters for the latest films on in London,' said Peter, 'the James Bonds or whatever, and it would get the adrenalin going. When I was younger I used to go up to London to watch new-wave films and things, and how lucky could one be, really, to be able to do that in one direction and cycle out in the other.'

In 1973 the BBC made a fifty-minute film on Metroland, written and presented by John Betjeman, by then the Poet Laureate, but showing him more in his former Shell Guide mode. It helped put Croxley Green on the map too, particularly his account of the Croxley Revels, the annual pageant which, Betjeman notes with great seriousness, dates all the way back to 1952. Having such an amusing public record of your hometown must grate. The Metropolitan Railways and, later, London Underground, were rationalised by Frank Pick, one of the utopian socialists who lived in Hampstead Garden Suburb. By the 1920s and 30s his ideas on urban design and growth of the network had begun to affect the sprawl of London itself. Pick was a green belt enthusiast. Ironic, then, that his expansion of the functionalist charms of London Underground helped accelerate the need for the green belt, as suburbs swarmed with alarming speed over the open space around new stations.

Croxley was a classic example of unplanned Britain. In the interwar era, rules were lax and laissez-faire. If you had enough money you could build more or less anything anywhere. The new discipline of town planning, it was strongly argued, was the only way to save Britain from the swarm of semi-detached houses alighting along all the major roads and train lines out of every town and city. The 'Homes Fit for Heroes' movement had been co-opted by developers eager to make their mark and a profit, and although these homes were desperately needed, their siting was more of an issue. And so, to address this concern, in the mid-1920s the London County Council's Town Planning Committee were asked to consider whether the preservation of a green belt was desirable. If so, what would that actually mean? Soon Neville Chamberlain, then the Minister of Health, was involved too. He wanted an investigation into London's green spaces, potential satellite towns, and the possibility of an agricultural belt, to 'form a dividing line between Greater London as it is and the satellites or fresh developments that might take place at a greater distance'.[1]

It was time to bring in the big guns. In this instance that meant garden city planner Raymond Unwin. He'd started out as an Arts and Crafts architect in the late

Victorian era, but became better known for his work on those early twentieth-century landmarks Letchworth and Hampstead Garden Suburb. The garden city force was strong in this one. 'Towns must grow by the addition of new satellite parts, industrial or dormitory suburbs, complete satellite towns or garden cities,' he wrote, 'each having its allotted area for expansion and its reserved belt of open space to limit and define it.'[2] Unwin was appointed technical advisor to the Greater London Regional Planning Committee in 1929. Keen on radical solutions (he once remarked that he'd consider 'rebuilding something like half London') his report highlighted a lack of recreational space in and around the city, and suggested that land should be urgently acquired.[3]

In two blockbuster reports over the next five years Unwin presented his radical solution. Over thirty square miles of land should be bought by the LCC to form a chain of green land round London approximately ten miles from Charing Cross. And forget Chamberlain's agricultural belt, it was parkland that Unwin wanted to see. He imagined that the city would have several green belts linked by a series of 'parkways' – linear parks acting as spokes in the wheel. Almost six miles wide in places, it would contain emerging satellite towns like Croxley Green and the proposed garden city at Addington, as well as protected green space too. His visionary recommendations were eagerly approved by the committee, and marked the start of what became known as Unwin's 'green girdle' for London. A pamphlet produced by the committee in 1934 explained that the idea was to link up existing open spaces such as Box Hill and Epping Forest. But the clock was ticking. 'The green belt which was possible round London on a 10-mile radius from Charing Cross in 1910 must now be planned 15 miles out', wrote eminent town planner Patrick Abercrombie in 1935. 'If the LCC is not quick it will be twenty-five.'[4]

It wasn't just London that was facing this problem. The invasion of the English countryside had begun in earnest in the interwar years, with 860,000 homes built in rural areas between 1919 and 1939. Of these, 700,000 were private projects, intended not for locals but for rich middle-class incomers. With land being sold to entrepreneurs to put up mansions, bungalows and the ubiquitous bow-fronted semi, anxiety about the extent of this unchecked construction spread far beyond Metro-land. A letter to the *Manchester Guardian* in May 1935 perfectly encapsulated the feelings of many people about a lack of building controls. 'Already it is difficult to determine where one town ends and another begins,' wrote Chas. P. Hampson on the problems facing south-east Lancashire, 'and yet the tumour goes on spreading.'[5] Six months later a Preston branch meeting of the Campaign for the Protection of Rural England proposed a green belt for the town. The following May Sir Herbert Humphries, former Surveyor for Birmingham, proposed a green belt for the city while addressing the Midland Joint Town-Planning Advisory Council, after which he was asked to go away and prepare a draft scheme. By June 1939 Manchester and District Town Planning Committee had begun formulating a proposal for a green belt within a radius of ten miles from the Town Hall.

Sheffield was ahead of most cities. The council approved a green belt proposal in June 1938, to 'secure the permanent preservation of the city's unique surroundings'.[6] Land had been given to Sheffield by a number of eminent citizens. A typically romantic story concerns Sir John and Lady Maria Bingham, who made their money in the electroplate business and lived in Ranmoor. Their country pile looked out upon the Porter Valley, to the south-west of the city. Well into their seventies, Sir John reportedly asked his wife whether she would prefer a fine set of jewels or to give the 'beautiful gem' of a nearby wooded hill to the children of Sheffield. She plumped for the latter, and he bought the land for the city. Not to be outdone, their neighbour, mail order magnate and Mayor John Graves, donated five large open spaces, including Ecclesall Woods, Tinsley playing fields and Blacka Moor.

Their belt grew from pressure by the local branch of the Campaign for the Protection of Rural England. This branch was dominated by two remarkable figures: Ethel Gallimore, the secretary, and Lt. Col. Gerald Haythornthwaite, who later married her. Ethel was the daughter of a steel magnate, and had been widowed in the First World War. Gerald had been born in Bolton and had trained as an architect. Between them they stoutly defended the wilds around the city from developers, mobilising private landowners and later the council to keep it safe. When in 1936 the council had decided to investigate creating a green belt, Ethel and Gerald were put in charge of marking out just where the boundaries might lie. Ethel had done a similar job on horseback for a proposed National Park in the Pennines.

In Scotland, too, considerable noise was being generated, much of it due to one woman, Jean Mann, a former convener of housing for Glasgow. Scotland built just 300,000 homes in total in the interwar period, and in more urban locations than the suburban semi that was becoming so familiar down south. By August 1935 Glasgow was faced with the need to construct another 70,000 homes to meet population growth and to begin tackling the problem of the slums. Jean proposed a go-ahead scheme: the creation of a satellite town beyond a green belt. Her 'daughter town' would house 300,000 people and cost a cool £30 million in 1935 money. I'm not sure how. Maybe the cost of parquet flooring had spiralled. As she claimed, 'it would be important to have a green belt round the area, so that the two towns would not converge'.[7] Two years later there were calls to extend the city into the neighbouring districts of Lanarkshire, Dunbartonshire and Renfrewshire by fourteen acres. Confusingly, 'green belt' meant land that could be built on – the very opposite of what everyone else was proposing. And this confusion of language and application persisted in discussion about Scottish green belts throughout this period. Nine thousand acres were added to the boundaries of Glasgow in October 1937, referred to as green belt but actually land that could be used for housing. Here it was less a protected space and more a store cupboard essential. Jean Mann, however, was having none of this. By 1939 she was still trying to set up satellite towns and a green belt, now as organiser of Scotland's Garden Cities Association. She became an MP after the war, where she would move from being a marginal voice to the centre of Scottish politics.

Even around London a number of county councils had long since tired of the LCC's laggard lead and had started up their own schemes. At the close of the 1920s, Middlesex County Council, to the West of London, were the first to get going. They commissioned a report by Adams, Thompson and Fry, a thoroughly modern firm of town planning consultants who employed pioneering architects Maxwell Fry and Wells Coates. Obviously they suggested a green girdle should be saved round London. Theirs started at Ruislip Reservoir in the west and ran to Epping Forest in the east, a mixture of forest, farmland, golf courses, private parks and market gardens. The report concluded that

Middlesex should set up a regional fund to buy land and save it from development. In the early thirties, even with the economy in tatters, Middlesex helped fifteen local councils buy and protect regional open spaces.

As in Manchester, Sheffield, Glasgow and Middlesex, if the London County Council wanted to make a go of a green girdle it had to stop talking and start buying up land. Three big figures in the London Labour Party pushed it on: council leader and Lambeth MP Herbert Morrison; Richard Coppock, Alderman of inner-city Stepney and former colleague of Morrison's at the Parks Department; and fellow Parks veteran and Peckham councillor Ruth Dalton. Morrison had grown up in urban Stockwell, and as a conscientious objector had worked for a time during the Great War in a market garden in the new Letchworth Garden City. It was there that he had his first taste of green belt living, and he took that enthusiasm back with him to London. Childhood friend Frederic Osborn was one of the young planners working on the garden city and when they met again in Letchworth it helped cement for Morrison the importance of the idea. He would go on to write several articles in support of the notion throughout the 1920s.

In the orbit of London, Croydon began its own love affair with the garden suburb in 1935. Looking through old copies of the *Croydon Advertiser* for July of that year revealed some choice headlines. 'Treat for cripples'; 'Accidents of the week'; 'Pylon death'; 'Gay

Dogs'; 'Penge Man's Wireless'; and my personal favourite, 'Blamed Lumbago'. All of which would make excellent band names. Beside an article describing a ramble between leafy Chelsham and suburban Oxted, one edition featured an advert that soberly announced a significant event for the town. 'Addington – New Garden City' ran the headline. 'The first turf inaugurating the construction of the above new town will be turned by the Mayor of Croydon on 15th July at 3pm, on the site of Lodge Lane, Addington. All interested persons will be heartily welcome.' The ad was run by the First National Housing Trust, part of the business empire of Britain's most successful interwar private housebuilder, Henry Boot. Great claims were being made for his new settlement on the southern fringes of the district. 'As a building enterprise that will give to the borough one of the largest and best conceived garden cities in the country,' gushed the local paper, 'it will crown the work of Mr Henry Boot, whose accomplishments in all parts of the country place him in the first rank of modern industrialists.'[8]

The land for this venture had been bought from three local farmers, and the ceremony took place in a field that commanded a remarkable view of the surrounding country, land that would soon be covered in diggers, dumper trucks and builders. In his speech that summer's day, Henry Boot described how the combined forces of private enterprise, the local authority, the Ministry of Health (who were still responsible for housing) and the sphinxes of the building societies would make the garden city a reality. To show what a big deal this was, even Sir Harold Bellman, chairman of the Abbey National, was present at a lunch to celebrate the turf cutting.

'I confess, I am a great lover of the countryside,' said Bellman, 'and I never see trees felled without a pang or some cherished beauty spot go to the builder without some heartburning. But we are practical people. We can still be idealistic and retain our practical sense of values. If it comes to whether I would rather see a lovely piece of country laid out as an estate or see people living in unlovely mean streets in the centre of a great city, unhesitatingly I am in favour of breaking up the country and building.'[9] And local councillor W.H. Still was also conflicted by the work they were doing. The paper reported 'he had a certain amount of sentimental regret at seeing the passing of the country over which he had been accustomed to hunt and shoot and watch farming'. This lunch of backslapping politicians, business tycoons and moneymen reads like a particularly clunky expositionary scene in *Downton Abbey*, with old money tutting at the crass commercialisation of modern life while quietly pocketing a hefty fee. You can see Maggie Smith being withering about the upstarts of the garden village and striding imperiously onward. Within three years, and with 260 new houses already occupied, the paper was full of adverts: 'Live at the healthy Addington Garden City.'[10]

The arrival of this enterprise on the border of Kent and Surrey, on a hill where farmers had worked for hundreds of years, came as a bit of a shock for the locals. The sprawl of Croydon had largely taken place in the Victorian era. Here interwar suburban estates had tended to creep up beside existing roads or houses rather than out on exposed hills on the country fringe. A local man wrote to the paper to express his sense of unease. 'To those of us who love the country and regret to see vast areas cut up for building it is of little comfort to be told that the plans provide for a beautifully planned Garden City,' wrote R.G. Bolton in September 1935, 'especially when we believe that the scheme will not be the success that its sponsors appear to anticipate.'[11]

While Henry Boot was living his garden city dream at Croydon, there was an industry of books, articles and lectures tearing into this modern phenomenon of suburbia. Novelist Sheila Kaye-Smith was a typical exponent. She usually recorded rural life in fiction, but in 1938 wrote of proposals to put up 200 houses overlooking Romney Marshes at the Isle of Oxney. It was a venture with echoes of Boot's garden village at Addington. She attended a meeting of villagers and farmers and observed their reaction to pleas from a local man. ' "Agriculture," he said, is the most important asset of the Isle of Oxney (hear! hear!). The next important is the beauty of the countryside (laughter)." ' Kaye-Smith was in no doubt what this reaction represented. 'So in laughter – oafish? ironic? Olympic? – the beauty of England passes away.'[12] These new garden suburbs, often far removed from the idealistic, self-contained vision of Ebenezer Howard, were part of a movement that was being both embraced and resisted. We find it hard to believe these days that such a large project as New Addington could go ahead so smoothly on the edge of a town. And that is simply because in 1935 they had snuck in before the official formation of the green belt.

The pioneers who moved out to interwar – and soon to be green belt – suburbs like Croxley Green and New Addington are the forgotten voices in all of this. Sneered at by the assembled forces of the intelligentsia, they had few defenders in the culture of the day. Which is one of the things that makes R.C. Sherriff's 1936 novel *Greengates* so remarkable. The plot of *Greengates* is so slight as to be almost invisible: the tale of an elderly couple leaving inner London for a new house in a modern estate much like Croxley Green. These homes are being built next to their favourite walking spot, which makes our heroes grieve for the loss of the country. But not enough to resist the lure of the new houses being put up there. They buy one off plan and watch it being built, one Saturday taking a walk around the foundations.

'Funny,' said Edith, 'to think of my chair being right on top of this rabbit hole!'

'And mine,' put in Mr. Baldwin, 'on top of this bunch of thistles!'[13]

Sherriff's instincts are kind and he really captures something of the excitement that people felt moving into these houses. And what of those houses? On their first night in their new home of Greengates Mr Baldwin meets their new neighbour, the diminutive and ambitious Mr Van Doon, ominously from Croydon.

"D'you like it?" said the little man. "I'm not sure whether I don't prefer the Tudor ones myself – but the wife voted for a Regency one because of the high ceilings."[14]

These off-the-peg designs offered by speculative builders in the twenties and thirties are what gives much of suburban Britain – and the green belt – its curiously nostalgic character. Sentimental with a dash of the moderne, wood beams and all mod cons. These little plots on the edge of the city turned townsfolk into country folk, at least until the next wave surrounded them on all sides. Much as many suburban defenders of the green belt might not like it, their homes are the reason it came into existence.

In February 1935, just a few months before the first turf was dug at Addington, the London County Council announced its intention formally to create a green belt around London. It would 'provide a reserve supply of public open spaces and of recreational areas . . . not necessarily continuous, but as readily accessible from the completely urbanized area of London as practicable'.[15] It even sponsored a bill in Parliament to create a Green Belt Act. This was approved by select committee on 21 June 1938. The Act would stop people from either selling or building on green belt land without permission from the Secretary of State. To create green belt the local authority and landowners had to enter into a deed. The Act would affect not just London but more particularly Buckinghamshire, Essex, Hertfordshire, Kent, Middlesex and Surrey, and the boroughs of Croydon, East Ham and West Ham. The great coup for Herbert Morrison and his team was securing £2 million from Neville Chamberlain's Conservative government to fund the scheme. So tied up were the ideals of Metroland and the Metropolitan Railways with this new green belt that the resulting girdle would become known as the Metropolitan Green Belt.

The very first application to the LCC for the purchase of green belt land was made by Hertfordshire County Council to buy Whippendell Woods, on the north edge of Croxley Green, on 26 May 1935. Such was the speed with which the suburb was expanding that they needed £15,000 to buy 162 acres to stop them in their mock-Tudor tracks. A neutered Croxley Green was just the start. A little over a year later and almost thirty square miles of land had been bought by local councils around

London. The LCC's Parks Committee in March 1936 clarified how the blueprint they had put into practice differed from Unwin's earlier versions. 'It was never imagined that the idea of a continuous belt could be realised,' they explained to *The Times*, 'owing to the cost of acquiring land in built-up areas and the rapidity of present-day development.' This didn't stop the media attempting to see what wasn't there. 'London's green belt is now walkable,' claimed an excited *Observer* journalist in March 1937. And it was almost true, if you combined the fifty parcels of land which had already been preserved by the LCC with existing commons and open spaces long made public, and footpaths through private grounds. 'The ring of fields and woods round London was, of course, always there,' the reporter gushed. 'No clearance has laid it open. But now it is possible to walk round the ring with the cheerful certainty that no building or other "development" will ever close it.' The reporter even suggested a route: starting at Runnymede in Surrey, and taking in such newly protected land as Netley Heath, Box Hill, Nonsuch Park, Hainault Forest, Croxley's Whippendell Woods, the Chilterns and Wraysbury, to complete the loop.[16] When you look at a map of the 1930s Metropolitan Green Belt it's a bit of a shock to see how small and isolated those pockets of land actually are. Rather than a continuous sea of green these are tiny islands in an ocean of semi-detached houses. This was not a green belt. This was a handful of confetti blowing around the edges of a model village. Really, was this all that people had been fighting for?

In the autumn of 1978 we moved house. With three kids sharing one bedroom, the eldest being fourteen, the maisonette was no longer practical. And so we reached the top of the council housing list. There was even a choice. We went to visit the first house one evening. It wasn't really what you'd expect a council house to be at all. A rather upright 1930s number with a bay window in upstanding Caterham, a place with none of the image problems of New Addington. It had a step to get in and a narrow front door, which John managed to bump Marj's wheelchair through. Inside it felt lean and constricted too, a storybook house with a skinny staircase rising almost immediately before us. There were small bits of stained glass in the front door and in the top panes of the windows, exposed floorboards dusty and old, banisters fancily carved and ornate. It felt so grand next to our plain municipal maisonette. Where were the brick stairs on the outside for our neighbours to use, or the mown greenery all around? Not even a verge outside, let alone woods. I couldn't really understand it. Up until now I'd grown up with a wall of green opposite our house, where the estate just gave up. Here there were streets and streets all the same. No break, just more houses everywhere. *Did we want to move here*, our parents wanted to know. It was lovely, we all agreed. It was a very desirable house. It was fancy, in a nice neighbourhood, with amenities all around us. It would be a step up. And so we all agreed that no, it wasn't for us.

Luckily the other choice was much easier to imagine living in. Because it was twenty-seven doors away from where we were living. Number 46 Fairchildes Avenue was immediately familiar. Made of the same brown brick as our maisonette, built the same year, all part of the council's aim to extend Henry Boot's garden city. Only this time we would have an upstairs too. And very soon a stairlift, to help Marj get up and down, wheelchairs waiting at top or bottom, announcing where she was in the house. I don't remember ever visiting the place to see what we thought. We'd rejected Caterham, what more was there to say? John got the keys from the council a week before we moved, and he fixed the place up as good as he could, stripping wallpaper, painting, building a makeshift wooden ramp that would run between the step and the driveway at the side of the house. He took the carpets from our maisonette and laid them in the new space – the honey-coloured swirls from the old living room lost in the middle of this bigger lounge. Most rooms wouldn't have a carpet for some time. During this intense week of work he grew a beard, which matched his wild straggly uncombed hair. We moved in a week before Christmas, the house a riot of things out of place, rooms without furniture, everything half-decorated and compromised. It was fantastic.

We were still facing the green belt, but this bit had three schools on it – infants, juniors and high school – set out in a row of increasing size like unpacked Russian dolls. They were classic 1950s affairs, long low buildings out of which rose a clock tower, a tall slender brick column, with blue hands and markers set straight onto the wall. Behind these classrooms lay playing fields, great expanses of green land, marked out with pitches for cricket, football, hockey and rugby, plus a full-sized running track too. All this green space did nothing to shift the school's rough reputation or lack of academic results.

Marj had really let her hair down since she'd come to the estate. In the 1970s her clothes were hippyish, trousers and jumpers in vivid colours, cerise or daffodil yellow, bright scarves in her long dark locks, necklaces of variegated beads and intricate Indian earrings, and huge Jackie Onassis-style plastic sunglasses. The garden was equally colourful. To say that Marj took pride in it might imply that it was systematic, neat and full of prize-winning blooms. It was not, nor would she have wanted it to be. Instead she directed operations to create a cottagey affair, with dog roses, delphiniums and towering daisies in abundance. If her roses asserted themselves through the old picket fence and wrecked it in the process, so be it. Many were grown from scratch in kits from Woolworths, which sat on window ledges in the spring presenting their seedlings like a tray of unappetising canapes. Others were the result of cuttings taken from anything she took a fancy to. Out the back a huge apple tree had grown out of control, but we kept it because of all the bird life it attracted. From the kitchen window, through the chip-pan splatters on the panes, you could see all manner of finches, tits, jays and even the odd wood-pecker darting about. The tall fences were covered with bindweed, which clung on like an unwelcome infatua-tion. The beautiful white trumpet flowers emerged late that first summer, the large heart-shaped leaves twist-ing to create a horribly efficient net around the garden. We took to digging it up, but the snaking roots, or rhizomes, of the plant criss-crossed the garden, every fragment leading to new growth. When I was eight or nine I spent so much time tugging at these pale ropes of roots, like grabbing a snake by the tail, that I began to dream about them. Dark, disturbing nightmares of strangulation and imprisonment. Even the Latin name – *convolvulus* – makes me shudder, summoning up images of tendrils wrapping tightly around the body, and of the convulsions brought on by their attentions. It still fills me with a strange creeping horror, the memory of those white tendrils running under our feet. Chasing them pulled me from the sunlight into dark corners of the garden, where who knew what creatures lurked?

Revisiting these old haunts can have unusual effects. A walk in the woods opposite our old house should be a doddle, right? Well, in April 2016 it didn't feel that way. Heart beating hard, I'd walked onto Fairchildes Avenue, past the low blocks of flats on my right and the red brick semis on my left. Ahead of me, beyond the flats, was the wood. The trees and the fields beyond, the valley and the hills. It was absurd that after all these years I still felt anxious when I came back here. The street where a lifetime of standing out had done me no favours whatsoever. And now here I was, standing out again. What if someone saw me behaving oddly again? A grown man – without a dog, mind – walking into the woods from the estate, just like that. An old familiar sense of dread was rising. But in reality there was no one around to point me out, to judge me. The whole length of the street was deserted. Just me. I crossed the road, found the track, turned and followed it round. As the estate was lost from view and the canopy closed above me I felt myself relax for the first time that day. And then the steep descent began.

Fairchildes Avenue came into existence in 1951. Only a small portion of the garden city at Addington was finished before the outbreak of the Second World War, when Henry Boot's builders had been dispersed among the armed forces. But that didn't mean everything had stopped. Croydon Corporation took the opportunity to buy up patches of farmland and bluebell-drenched country nearby, such as Jewels Wood, purchased in 1944. It hadn't been a happy experience for the sellers. Crippling death duties loaded on the Daniels family, the owners of Fairchildes Farm, had ended their centuries-long connection with the estate. What were the council going to do with all of this new land they now owned? Patrick Abercrombie thought he knew. 'The recent purchase by the Corporation of the Fairchildes Estate should prove a useful contribution to the open space needs of the Borough', he had written in the bible of the postwar city, *The Greater London Plan*.[17] But as I discovered, it wasn't a given that the borough agreed.

Great lumps of flint and chalk moved underfoot and skittered down the slope ahead of me as I walked into the wood. Silver birch, oak and beech were bursting into leaf – and the shade was welcome on this unexpectedly sunny spring morning. Thick walls of hawthorn blossomed on either side of the path. Among them grew brambles, their old leaves blackened, fresh new ones a rich green, stems like the tangled tracks of a rollercoaster. At the bottom of the hill there was a sign, erected by the London Wildlife Trust. Hutchinson's Bank Nature Reserve ran the heading with a map and photos and descriptions of some of the plants you might see there. Things to look out for, it told me, included glow-worms, marbled white butterflies and the greater yellow-rattle, whose flowers resembled fat canaries. I looked but couldn't see any of them. To my knowledge I never had.

The tiny hamlet of Fickleshole lay beyond the wood. It consisted of a pub, The White Bear, whose status as the go-to place for blokey rowdiness back in the eighties was unrivalled, and which now was all wasabi peas, pulled pork and expensive wines. And there was Fairchildes Farm too, with a gate plastered with *beware of the dog* signs. I rang an old steel bell and from the far side of the garden I heard someone call 'Hello!' A big man in his sixties with a broad smile was peering through a hedge. I introduced myself.

'I'm just taking delivery of some hay,' he said, and disappeared. This was Malcolm Mott. I'd come to ask him what it was like to farm in the green belt, but also out of personal curiosity, to find out just what had been going on in those fields opposite our old house all those years. Malcolm farmed them all.

A few minutes passed and we were sitting down for tea in his garden. I was thinking about the big trees that stood in the middle of the cornfield in the valley facing our house. My dad used to spend an enormous amount of time taking photos of sunsets through them, every year he could. 'You don't often see trees in the middle of farmers' fields any more,' I said. The land had belonged to a grand lodge called Fairchildes House, explained Malcolm, which had been accidentally burned down by Canadian troops in the run-up to D-Day. The landscape he farmed had originally been set out as parkland.

'It was all to do with vision from the big house where they drove in,' he explained in his gruff, no-nonsense voice. Suddenly it made sense. The reason that landscape opposite our house had been so beautiful was because it had been set out as such. Not as a farm but a garden. We'd been the unknowing beneficiaries of some nifty eighteenth-century landscape gardening all these years. There aren't many council estate families who could say that.

Back in the 1950s Fairchildes Farm had been a dairy. When I was a kid two decades later it had been turned over to wheat, oats and barley. These days Malcolm's dropped the barley and replaced it with green beans. He says that the residents, far from begrudging him his land, complain if he leaves fields fallow, because they like to see crops growing. I'd assumed he'd been born a farmer, but he hadn't. Instead, he was a child of suburban Norwood, later adopted by a family who moved out to New Addington in the early days of the estate, 1953, at the time of the Queen's coronation.

'I remember getting the mug and all that, as we all did.' It was another shock to discover he'd been brought up about ten doors down from our house, albeit two decades earlier. At that time his road and mine were still being built, the schools we were to live opposite having just opened.

The council had owned all this land since the 1940s and yet had built right up to the edge of the valley and no further. The maisonette in Fairchildes Avenue was finished not by Henry Boot's company but by the council. They'd bought what had been built of the new estate outright with ideas of ditching the 'garden city' trappings and expanding. Malcolm is convinced that if it weren't for the introduction of the green belt, houses would now stretch from the edge of the estate right up to his farmhouse, over all those landscaped fields. Croydon's ambitious postwar council, reluctant custodians of wood and farm, had held onto the land not out of some sense of duty to the country but in the hope that one day they would be granted permission to build on it. Instead, the green belt policy came in.

This explained how Fairchildes Avenue came to be the outskirts of the outskirts: not really London, not really Croydon either, barely even New Addington. Yet was Malcolm right, was there a council housing plan from the forties where our road was in the middle of a much larger estate, the fields before us built over all the way to his farm? 'The high downland S of Addington has been buried under boring modern housing', complained the *Shell Guide* to Surrey.[18] But as the beneficiary of this 'boring modern housing' I have to offer a heartfelt 'fuck off' to such snobbery. No matter too that shoving the poor to the furthest reaches of the borough might have been a stroke of genius for the council, getting us out of sight and out of mind. I'm sure more local authorities would love to try that now, if it weren't for green belts stopping them. With few amenities and bad transport links the countryside became an unexpected friend to the residents, a place we could escape to. When I finally came into the world in October of 1970, my chubby face coloured by jaundice, it was to these curious boundary lands that I was taken. The developer's proposals had been scuppered by the war, the council's by the green belt, and an uneasy truce brokered between the isolated estate and country surrounding it. From such compromised places do many of us hail, the tensions generated giving rise to unthought-of freedoms and unpredicted anxieties.

Some people, like Malcolm, became expert at crossing the boundaries between these two worlds.

'I'm so used to people walking their dog,' he said, when I asked how he got on with locals from the estate. 'If I wanted to say this is no footpath, private property, I'd spend my whole day 24/7 moving people. There's a quarter of a million chimneys down the road, and it's so busy, so you have to accept a bit of that.' But how had he done it, a council estate lad jumping the fence and now running the farm he'd looked out onto as a child? Surely very few people made that transition so effortlessly? He'd started work as a lorry mechanic, like my dad. By the early sixties he was called in on numerous occasions to fix the tractors on Fairchildes Farm. Within a decade he'd been reeled in, working there as a mechanic and farm-hand. Malcolm bought it outright from the council in 2005. As he talked about it he seemed as increasingly baffled by the course of his life as I was.

'I've got so used to living out here now,' he said; 'forty years I've been living here.' And his horticultural skills, his love of it? 'I dunno where it come from,' he smiled. 'I haven't got a clue.' He shook his head and laughed. 'I don't know who my real father is, he might have been a farmer, wandering about somewhere!' That might be so, but it's hard not to think of Malcolm as an archetypal green belt man, just as at home in the suburbs as on the back of a combine. He's a reminder that the barrier between the two worlds isn't insurmountable. Most of it is in the mind.

Perceptions of change in the green belt are similarly slippery. Back in Hertfordshire I asked Peter Wiles and his childhood friend John Guy what their parents might have thought of the Metro-land suburb of Croxley Green today. At first they didn't quite get my drift, and so I described them stumbling through a wormhole by the Parker Knoll shop in the 1950s and time-travelling forward to today. Peter thought it would have been very recognisable to them, although his parents had moved there in the thirties when all of the big changes had started. Back then they had lived in one of the end houses, beyond which was the country. By the fifties the new estate, shops and busy road had arrived. But that was as far as it went. John's parents had come from Watford, now much changed.

'We were always very pleased that Watford wasn't part of London,' said John, 'and that there's a gap between the two. When you go down to the canal just beyond Ricky' – that's Rickmansworth to you – 'towards Harefield, past the gravel pits there, it's all fields. Suddenly there's a sign saying Borough of whatever it is' – Hillingdon – 'and London comes right up to the other side of that canal.' All around Croxley Green the reality of the green belt is obvious, keeping the boundaries and separating it from the surrounding big towns. They both agreed the area was remarkably unchanged, just like the fields around Fairchildes Farm. Still cosy after all these years. And that really is one of the curious things about these places – how they remain frozen in time, Pompeii in the Home Counties. This is the green belt effect.

4
Protect and Survive: The Wartime Vision of Patrick Abercrombie

I stood in the clearing and was engulfed by it. The stench of death. Its laughing face, the tiny white flowers a simulacrum of happiness. Pillars of them on every side. The may tree in bloom, in legend the gateway to other worlds, home of fairies and dark magic. This was white hawthorn, in its warrior's weeds of dense flower. I was caught up in their mayday dance, tangled in their ribbons. That pungent fishy odour was the product of triethylamine, a chemical distilled from the flowers of this ancient tree. When the human body begins to decay, triethylamine is produced. It's this echo of putrefaction that gave the tree sinister overtones to survivors of the Great Plague. The chemical and its familiar funk is also found in semen and vaginal secretions. Triethylamine is just one of many couplings of sex and death in our collective subconscious. Here it was being released liberally into the Hertfordshire green belt.

I'd been walking in Rusheymead, a lightly wooded area of the River Lee Country Park to the north-east of London. All day I'd seen hawthorn in flower and inhaled its powerful scent. But nowhere had I seen such a concentration as in this clearing, where May was urging on the may tree with its crowded flowers on thorny branches. Of death there were reminders enough in the park, without the associations the hawthorn brought. I'd only that minute stepped over the scattered white feathers of a gull, dispatched most likely by a fox, and before that dodged the grim remains of a crow, wings fanned like a discarded umbrella. The clearing was just off the beaten track, a quiet dell away from the busy river path where life continued on its boisterous way. The monochrome remains of the dead birds lay scattered away from the canal boats, mallards and cyclists, all kitted out in their colourful patterns of display and competition. The may tree was a symbol of hope, too, its flowers signalling the start of warmer days. Hope, sex, magic and death, all woven together by the hawthorn.

In 1935 a law was passed to protect landscape 'whose preservation on account of rarity, beauty, distinctiveness or on account of scientific, ethnic, forest, or hunting significance lies in the general interest'. This was the German Imperial Conservation Law passed by the Nazi government. 'It was only the transformation of the German man which created the preliminary conditions necessary for an effective system of protection of natural beauty', declared the law. In Britain it was warmly recommended by the Lord of Penrith, Esme Howard. Writing in 1938 he said, 'whatever we may think or feel about Nazi political philosophy' this was a law 'which I hope will in many things become a model for the rest of the world'.[1] Promoting thoughts of an ethnic purity of landscape brought about by a transformed German man, the law enshrined the same kind of hierarchies that Nazi social policies were policing.

These hierarchies of landscape appealed to some of the green belt's proponents. In 1944 Cyril Joad, in typically provocative terms, described his disgust at the reality of Marlow Bottom in the Chilterns, an area now in the green belt. 'To my horror,' he wrote, 'I found not an empty valley but a muddy road running through an avenue of shacks, caravans, villas, bungalows, mock castles, pigsties, disused railway carriages and derelict buses, scattered higgledy-piggledy over the largest possible area of the Chiltern hillsides.' But for Joad worse was to come. 'Each dingy little abode in this rural setting was distinguished by some dreadful appellation as, for example, Eretiz, The Nest, The Splendide, Kosy-Kot, Mon Abri, Linga-Longa or U-an-I.'[2] His combative book, *The Untutored Townsman's Invasion of the Country*, whose very title suggested an alien attack, also railed against petrol stations, advertising hoardings and rubbish dumped on the edge of towns. With Joad and many of his contemporaries it's hard to unpick the petty snobbery from the genuine grievances. In fact, there is a faint whiff of 'the transformation of the German man' about the book title and his remarks, towering as Joad appears to over his tawdry fellow countrymen. Maybe it was a hangover from his brief sojourn as Director of Propaganda for Oswald Mosley's fascist New Party a decade before. The green belt idea could attract some unpleasant fellow travellers.

The stench of triethylamine would have been familiar in Britain's industrial cities in wartime. In the Great War the protagonists – those soldiers, sailors, airmen and medics – had been away on far battlefields. In 1940 the war came to Britain, and suddenly anyone could be hero or victim. With the country under its most urgent threat in recent history, everything was under examination to wring better performance from every aspect of workaday life. And there were people bringing forward remarkable schemes for better times beyond too. They would be tackling the scandal of healthcare and the slums, a backwards-looking education system, poverty and Blitz damage. The emergent NHS and Welfare State would become constant reminders that life is fleeting and should be made as good as it could be. The green belt was part of the solution to Britain's problems too. It was about making the best of the peace. As with the hawthorn, it would be a reminder of the cycle of life.

One of the experts drafted in to help make these vague hopes a reality was Patrick Abercrombie. The monocled pioneer was Professor of Town Planning at Liverpool University; his younger brother, Lascelles, a successful poet who moonlighted as a quantity surveyor (or perhaps it was the other way around). In the biggest job of his life the elder Abercrombie was invited to work up an outline for a future London. In it he considered many things: housing, industry, transport, resources, recreation. A later postwar planner, Peter Hall, thought that 'it is hard to resist the conclusion that the objectives were not rational in a strict sense. They were mystical. In the special circumstances of a major war, that is perhaps understandable.'[3] One of the things at the front of the queue, as far as Abercrombie was concerned, was the green belt.

For Abercrombie the green belt was the culmination of a lifetime's work, not as town planner, but as protector of the countryside. In 1926 he'd set up one of

England's most successful and enduring crusading organisations: the Council for the Preservation of Rural England (now the Campaign to Protect Rural England, and still, helpfully, the CPRE). It was born out of a leaflet written by Abercrombie on the challenges of dereliction and development facing the wilds of England. He managed to pull together the might of organisations as diverse as the National Federation of Women's Institutes, the Country Gentleman's Association, the Royal Institute of British Architects, the National Trust, the Automobile Association, the RAC and the Society for the Protection of Ancient Buildings. During the 1929 general election he even pulled off the coup of getting all three main party leaders – Stanley Baldwin, Ramsay Macdonald and David Lloyd George – to co-sign a letter to *The Times* urging support for fundraising for the CPRE, advocating 'the preservation of our countryside in its rich personality and colour'. So successful was Abercrombie at mobilising the great and the good that a survey fifty years later revealed that chairmen and women of CPRE's county branches still showed an elite bias: among the double-barrelled names, 19 per cent were members of House of Lords, 31 per cent were retired military officers, and a significant number of the rest were Justices of the Peace. These eminent folk took on many of the issues of the day: the evils of unscrupulous developers, the ramblers' desire for justice and access, the fear of the ever-sprawling suburb eating up the landscape, and the protection of the natural habitats of plants and animals.

In just over ten years the CPRE went from marginal group to creating a central role in imagining the new Britain. They even made a short film in 1938 to be shown at cinemas across the country: *Rural England: The Case for the Defence*. The tone is active and militaristic, against houses sprawling over the broad acres like an invasion. In clipped tones the narrator bustles us along so briskly we barely have time to process what's going on. 'Are you going to allow such scenic loveliness to be despoiled because you won't fight to preserve it?' he barks. And then it was an ice cream and onto the main feature, *The Lady Vanishes* or *Bringing Up Baby*.

Yet perhaps one of the CPRE's most lasting contributions had been the 1934 *Code of Courtesy for the Countryside*. It was full of tips for the 'townsman' blundering into a realm they did not understand. It was formalised by the government as *The Country Code for Visitors to the Countryside*, published by HMSO in 1951, a pamphlet that went through annual revisions until the mid-sixties. It revolved around ten commandments:

> Guard against all risk of fire.
> Fasten all gates.
> Keep dogs under proper control.
> Keep to the paths across farmland.

Avoid damaging fences, hedges and walls.
Leave no litter.
Safeguard water supplies.
Protect wild life, wild plants and trees.
Go carefully on country roads.
Respect the life of the countryside.

Each was illustrated by a beautiful woodcut by James Lucas. 'We regard the Country Code as a core around which will grow a body of information about the countryside', wrote the National Parks Commission in September 1951. 'As knowledge spreads, there should be much less of the damage often done by sheer thoughtlessness in well-intentioned people. By all these means we hope there will be a deepening respect and friendliness between countryman and townsman.' The booklet cost 4d, which meant that most people never saw a copy, although it was distributed to schools, and the RAC and AA began printing the ten commandments in their membership packs. These days it's a downloadable PDF on gov.co.uk. 'Respect. Protect. Enjoy.' runs the headline, in which you can hear an unfortunate echo of the 'Protect and Survive' nuclear war safety campaign of the 1970s. One of the big changes these days is that the code now offers as many rules for landowners as it does for visitors, from providing clear paths, stiles and gates to helping keep the public safe from electric fences.

Abercrombie's peacetime task had been the protection of the countryside. In wartime it would be to replan the damaged capital. Around him unlikely collisions of class and sex, urban and country, were occurring in those turbulent six years of war. They fundamentally changed both the dynamics of society and the way we used our land. Parks and open spaces across Britain were dug up for farming and allotments, including acres of the LCC's new Metropolitan Green Belt. Farmers who had been pushed from their land by the Green Belt Act were now asked to stay on, in sufferance, to continue work to meet wartime demand. Tightly packed city streets were being opened out by craters and fire damage. On urban bombsites on roads where no flowers had bloomed for decades, bursts of bright colour – the pink spikes of rosebay willowherb, the tousled yellow of ragwort – were seen sprouting between fallen bricks, cracked pavements and dislodged walls. Meanwhile townsfolk were discovering the outdoors – not ramblers this time, but city kids evacuated to small villages and towns. Land Girls, those spirited urban female volunteers, were sent to work on farms. For some this came as a baffling shock, for others it was the start of a new life that they continued after the war.

As the bombs fell, committees met to change the country: Lord Justice Scott's on rural land use; Augustus Uthwatt's on compensation for land purchased by the government; and Anderson Barlow's on the distribution of Britain's industrial population. For each of them the green belt was a pressing issue.

Scott described green belts as 'a tract of ordinary country, of varying width, round a town ... where the normal occupations of farming and forestry should be continued so that here, as elsewhere in rural land, the farmer is the normal custodian of the land'.[4] Barlow sought to lower the density of the working-class areas of London, and proposed housing a million out beyond this 'tract of ordinary country'. And Uthwatt wanted to know who was going to pay for it.

Abercrombie recruited a band of researchers for what would become *The Greater London Plan*. His team included Harry Stewart, a technical advisor to the LCC; Gordon Stephenson, who went on to shape the new town of Stevenage; and Peter Macfarlane, who worked on another, Crawley. A fourth ambitious comrade was Peter Shepheard, a young man who would later design Gresley House, the modern block that my parents lived in throughout the sixties. I met up with his son, Paul Shepheard, in a busy little café in Kentish Town, to try to get a picture of what it must have been like to work with Abercrombie. He spoke quietly between long, thoughtful pauses and outbursts of despairing giggling. My first surprise was to discover that his father had been Patrick Abercrombie's godson. My second was to realise how rudimentary their research methods had been.

'He had to find out where the edge of London was,' explained Paul, 'which involved driving down streets in your location and saying, *Okay, the houses stop here, so we put the mark on the map*. And they went all the way round doing that. Just driving out to the edge and making marks. And this was all done from the back of a car.' We laughed at this low-tech solution, a Wallace and Gromit version of those Google Streetview cars that cruise around creating a virtual record of the urban landscape. Abercrombie's conception of a 'green belt ring' would hoover up the tiny scraps of the already established Metropolitan Green Belt into a much more substantial continuous loop of land, five miles wide, around the suburban edge of Greater London. It would even swallow large, densely populated towns like Romford, Dartford, Sevenoaks, Potters Bar and Watford. In Abercrombie's version of the green belt, much of it wouldn't be green at all. In fact, some of it seemed a wilful projection on stubbornly unrural areas around the city.

But Abercrombie's team wasn't just young men out to make a name for themselves. Paul recalled seeing a photo of four of the team, including his father and an unnamed woman.

'The caption on the photograph goes, "from left to right: Gordon Stephenson, Hugh Casson and Peter Shepheard". *But who's she?!* And she's the one doing all the talking.' My guess is that she was one of the mapmakers. Eight were engaged in the project, seven of whom were women. Miss B. Chubb, perhaps, or Miss M. Greenhill. The London County Council, like many organisations of the time, employed many women cartographers but few architects. It might have been the men doing the fieldwork, but it was these women who mapped it. Of those listed I'm most curious about Miss R. Caro who was 'kindly lent by West Ham Council', like an unhappy striker hanging out for a transfer deal.

'He was gripped by the crusade of it, the rightness of it,' recalled Paul. 'The zoning and the land value and the planning acts. Getting everything straight so that after the war life would be worth living.' Peter had told his son that the war took away all of his anxieties about the future. 'You just had to do what you were told and everyone was working like stink all hours of the night just to get this stuff done. I think he was exhilarated by it, by being a part of it. Being in the Home Guard and doing this work with the Planning Office, and it just having to be done, and it all being so *modern*, so *revolutionary*.'

Abercrombie's influence wasn't just felt in London and the Home Counties. He was drafted in to write the 1946 *Clyde Valley Regional Plan* too. And not a moment too soon for Jean Mann, that steadfast advocate for Glasgow, who told the *Scotsman* in 1941, 'we have lost our countryside. Our lovely babbling brooks are now only glanced at by officials considering a method of culverting and concreting. We now go right out to Paisley. We have no green belt.'[5] Yet Abercrombie's proposal was a tough sell, and much of the persuasion was left to a charismatic garden city veteran, Frederic

Osborn. The old smoothie worked tirelessly behind the scenes to win over influential Scottish politicians, planners and architects. He did a great job. Robert Grieve, who was working on the Clyde Valley blueprint, remarked of Osborn, 'How I adored that man!'[6]

It wasn't just Abercrombie making the running. *The Manchester City Plan*, 1945, produced by R. Nicholas, the City Surveyor, intended to make the place more liveable for its inhabitants. As in London, the green belt proposed was larger than the built-up area it contained. 'Is Manchester prepared once again', he wrote, 'to give the country a bold lead by adopting standards of reconstruction that will secure to every citizen the enjoyment of fresh air, or a reasonable ration of daylight, and some relief from the barren bleakness of bricks and mortar?'[7] It is almost impossible to read this without hearing Tony Hancock's voice as the heroic jury chairman in his spoof of *Twelve Angry Men*: 'Does Magna Carta mean nothing to you? Did she die in vain?'

In the immediate aftermath of the war the pressure on industrial expansion and housing was immense. People on the edge of many of the industrial cities north of Stratford-upon-Avon were living a shared experience, and little of it was green or pleasant. An industrial din echoed around the bluebell forests of what is now the East Midlands green belt, observed in 1928 by Mellors, the randy gardener in D.H. Lawrence's *Lady Chatterley's*

Lover. To the west, planners and politicians calling themselves the West Midlands Group published a hefty tome in 1948 called *Conurbation* to discuss Birmingham's problems. To illustrate them it contains four pages of photos cataloguing a train journey taken from urban Birmingham, through the industrial wastelands of the Black Country, to Wolverhampton. The images are depressing, bleak and relentless, showing 9,000 acres scarred by quarries, mines, spoil heaps and tips. 'The River Tame winds through a landscape of slagheaps and pitmounds' reads the commentary. 'Open land stretches towards Rowley Regis. Houses advance across land evacuated by industry.'[8] But the group could see a way ahead, imagining new public open spaces on this derelict waste ground. At the time they rejected a conventional green belt, fearing that cunning speculators would simply rush to build beyond it. Their preference was for a more flexible 'green setting' around the city and in wedges or strips of land snaking into the towns of the Black Country. There was even an idea that 'bad' building might be left in this green setting to slowly dissolve, like a tooth in a glass of cola.

Some land had already been bought and protected here. The picturesque Lickey Hills had been preserved since 1889 by the Cadbury family. And *Conurbation* included incredible pictures of hundreds of holidaymakers streaming there from their houses for a not-so-quiet stroll in the country. The Forestry Commission recommended indigenous trees be planted in the area: birch, mountain ash and Corsican pine for the knolls; sycamore, plane and wild cherry for the slopes; and poplar, alder and willow for the lowland areas. The landscape of the Black Country could be transformed, if there was the will.

Paul Shepheard was in no doubt as to the radical nature of Abercrombie's work, obscured as it was by his tweeds and preservationist ways. His father, Peter Shepheard, had taken that radical dual stance a step further.

'One of the things that impressed me most about my dad's take on it, because he was surprisingly left wing as well, was that he was the one who pointed out to me about planning permission, and the Town and Country Planning Acts being an *attempt* to nationalise the land. You couldn't nationalise the banks and you couldn't nationalise the land, because that's what they really wanted to do, but you could nationalise the right to *develop* it, so no one had a right, even though they owned it, without the consent of the community. I'd grown up among architects – *bloody planning permission*, you know, *making you do this, making you do that* – but it is the consent of the community.' He smiled. 'It's a beautiful idea.'

We may not have had the Blitz when I was growing up but that didn't seem to stop everyone from being constantly on the verge of death. There were the initial skirmishes. Marj in her wheelchair, living through the painful effects of operations from the 1950s. Paul diagnosed as diabetic at the age of thirteen, getting used to pummelling his leg to inject insulin with wickedly long needles. And John catching bronchial pneumonia one winter in the early seventies, a disease which never really let go. Life was not so much a free run as an obstacle course, and we were very slowly making our way through the tyres.

When I was eleven Marjorie woke one night swamped in her own blood. John carried her to the Mini and rushed her to hospital. In the next bedroom I didn't even wake up. On his way, John got nicked for speeding. Although, when they saw what was happening, the police acted as a handy escort to the hospital, clearing a path through the early-morning streets of Croydon. An emergency case, Marj was immediately given transfusion after transfusion. She got through seventy pints of blood that night. No one knew the cause of her bleeding, or how to stop it. When I awoke the next day it was impossible to get any handle on how serious it was, because everyone was being so cagey with me. Talking to me very quietly, as if I were a timid creature captured for its own safety. Paul found the same. *You're a child: you don't need to know.* Life or death, we were excluded.

'I think Mum being ill did change a lot,' recalls Paul. 'Especially for Dad. I think that really shocked him, because Mum was Dad's world. There was nothing else.'

Some of Marj's brothers dropped by, full of the usual banter. At first I thought they'd rolled up because that was just what you did. Later I realised they had come to pay their last respects. Marj with the endless treatment on her spine in the fifties. Marj with the wheelchair. Marj who'd been marked for death all these years. And there she was, at the centre of it all, an immobile form, small and unresponsive in the big hospital bed in the corner of a big ward, connected to plasma, saline and monitoring equipment. Her skin was a papery silver, coloured only at the edges of her eyes and lips by the sickly pink of seventy pints of blood, as if she'd not properly digested them.

I carried on at school as if everything was normal. Not being the most sociable of children, I didn't have anyone to talk to about it, and so nothing was ever said. After a few weeks of this strange double life I casually mentioned my secret to the closest I had to a friend there, my English teacher, Mrs Ross. I had been proud of not making a fuss, and it seemed almost boastful finally to acknowledge what had been going on. Her reaction – startled, concerned, compassionate – confirmed what I'd refused to grasp. My mum might die. And so it was suddenly shocking, seeing my situation reflected back from Mrs Ross's big sympathetic eyes. This was not a fire drill, where we stood around bored in the playground waiting to be ticked off on a register. This was the real thing. Yes, we were doing all right; no, we didn't need any help, thank you. After that chat, anxiety flooded in. No chance of sleeping through another tragedy, I thought. Sleep was now a precious commodity. For the first time I was scared by something that wasn't spiders or daleks or unnamed creatures under the bed. Not that anyone would have noticed. A quiet boy being quiet. Not much to go on.

We visited every night. The house was forgotten, we were only there to sleep, or to eat the food John hurriedly prepared – burgers, sausages, mash. An attempt to cook a roast dinner was a particularly legendary affair, with burned bullets of unhydrated Paxo rattling around on a baking tin like shrapnel. Marjorie remained critically ill for several weeks, but the end people had been expecting didn't come. Instead she confounded everyone from the brink of death. After a month she turned a corner. Gradually machines and drips were taken away. Recovery would take the most phenomenal effort, and would leave her more disabled than she had ever been, but she would cling on. Better than that, she came back to life stronger than she'd ever been. Marj stayed in hospital for ten weeks, but was home for Christmas. She slept downstairs on the sofa for months and didn't walk now because she couldn't. All those weeks in hospital it had been assumed she was on her way out, and so physiotherapy had seemed, literally, a pointless exercise. By the time she was ready to leave it was too late to save her legs from atrophy. Her tendons had seized up, never to be straightened out. Her legs would now be stuck in a slightly awkward, twisted sitting position, Marj forever turning a little to the left, one knee higher than the other, both feet twisted inwards. No more walking short distances. No more sitting comfortably, even. A new beginning with new problems.

With Marj banished to the sofa, every small mishap seemed to spell danger. A morning spent playing out among the trees across the road came to an abrupt halt when I realised I'd locked myself out. It wasn't as if it was easy to misplace my keyring, a large hollow tin globe. I flapped open the letterbox and could see the little metal planet discarded on the chest freezer next to the door. Ingenuity was the order of the day, and so I found a wire coat-hanger, unravelled it and pushed it through the letterbox, attempting to hook the keyring onto the end.

'Are you all right?' called Marj from the sofa. Ingenious I might have been, but stealthy I was not. Luckily she couldn't see what I was up to. 'Have you forgotten your keys?'

'No.' Rattle, scratch, curse. This was harder than it looked. I tried again.

'You sure?' she called.

'Yeah.' The coat-hanger was shaking in my hands. There it was, the little tin planet with my keys held in orbit, lost across the infinite icy reaches of the chest freezer. Fishing around through this slot in the front door it began to dawn on me that this *was* a big deal. Mum was trapped inside, immobile on the sofa, with no one to help, fetch a drink or check she was okay. And I was stuck out here in the cold in my navy parka, with the wind in the bare trees and the fallen leaves on the scrappy turf, fiddling around through the letterbox with some wire. What a relief it was when I finally hooked the end of the coat-hanger through the ring, dragged it to the edge of the chest freezer and finally pulled it through the letterbox. I felt like Bruce Willis in *Armageddon* before the fact.

'You all right?' asked Marj suspiciously when I burst open the door and hurried inside.

'Yeah!' I said, breezily. I had just saved the world, after all.

It was around the time of Marj's illness, in the early days of Margaret Thatcher's first recession, that John was made redundant. He was an HGV mechanic, repairing lorries for a printing company owned by Robert Maxwell. In his scruffy engine-oil-stained blue anorak, with his wild mid-length hair and untidy brown beard, John looked like Paddington Bear down on his luck. Always somewhat sketchy on the ways of a responsible adult, his already limited plausibility was now paper-thin. He kept absent-mindedly getting into the wrong cars down the shops, back when Mini keys were almost interchangeable. He failed even to spot a Great Dane in one, until it put its head on his shoulder. To sign forms at the bank he'd produced a pen from his coat. Only it wasn't a pen, it was a penny whistle he'd brought home for Ian, making John look like he'd stepped from the pages of a particularly sentimental Edwardian novel. And on a trip to Bejams he'd been unable to close the lid of a chest freezer, only to discover this was because he had trapped an elderly woman in the other end of it, her grey hair now covered in frost. *Sorry love* his cheery apology. He staggered through his days dazed and adorable, giggling at every misfortune and allowing himself to be the butt of the world's jokes because that seemed to make life easier for everyone. Eventually he found unstable work filling in at various garages around Croydon. He'd bring work home: oily sumps sitting on the twin tub, piles of half-destroyed Haynes manuals stacked about the place. John was the engine whisperer. Whispering swear words, mainly. *Pissarse* was a favourite. Usually did the trick.

It was *Only Fools and Horses* that did for John. Two years had passed since Marj's mystery illness, and by December of 1983 she'd recovered and he was the one in a bad way. The hard physical strain of fixing lorries and cars was getting to him. We'd find him stood still about the place, trying to smile reassuringly at us because he temporarily couldn't move or speak. *Puffed out*, Marj used to call it, so as not to increase his anxiety. Soon it reached the stage that every time he laughed he'd have to go upstairs for a lie-down. Until, one night, sat on the sofa watching his favourite sitcom he couldn't even manage that. Wincing and swearing under his breath, he began complaining of chest cramps and shooting pains in his arm. Soon it was like an elephant standing on his back, he said. The pressure was unbearable. An ambulance was called. Marj tried to keep him calm, telling him to take deep breaths and concentrate, like she'd taught him many years earlier as a way to relax, to self-medicate, to keep calm.

'My feet!' he cried. 'Get me a bowl of hot water.' I did as I was told, filling the yellow plastic tub he often soaked his feet in as he watched the telly. I returned with it, and he was pulling his shoes and socks off.

'Don't worry about that,' said Marj. But he had the fear in him, something instilled from childhood, to be clean for the doctor, even if he was caught in an accident. He stuck his bare feet into the water, still grimacing, gasping, desperate. The ambulance arrived, and there he was, having an angina attack with his feet in a bowl of water while canned laughter burst from the telly.

He was taken to Brompton Hospital in West London. Within a week he'd had a quadruple heart bypass operation – in 1983, not a straightforward procedure at all. Sometimes Marj drove us there, but mostly we went by Dial-a-Ride. We'd arrive, cluster round his bed, and for several days he was unable to speak. His face was purple and red. A wicked scar ran down the centre of his chest. There was nowhere to look that wasn't upsetting. Meanwhile all around him the equipment glowed and beeped and hummed like a spaceship from an ELO video.

Christmas as we had known it was changed utterly. On 23 December Marj had no choice, and sent Paul and I off to our local toyshop, Playbox. Paul, I guess, must have had some idea what was going on. I didn't have any. When we arrived the kindly shop assistant, a middle-aged woman with big Mrs Slocombe hair and a fancy blouse, handed over several bags of wrapped presents. She gave us strict instructions: we weren't to look in them, shake them, or even try to guess what was inside. It seemed like some kind of magic. How had she got these presents ready? How had they been paid for? And so we walked back to our house with them, alongside the bleak wintry turf of Milne Park, those seventeen acres of mown playing fields declared green belt in 1963. We trekked from the centre of the estate out to our house right on the edge of it all, where people could be perilously ill and no one knew. We arrived home, having lugged our presents like two inexperienced elves drafted in because Father Christmas was indisposed. Too much brandy and mince pies will do that to you. Not that any of us had ever believed in him: there was never the slightest effort made by our parents to make us swallow that nonsense. But, equally, there was never an attempt to show us the workings of the Christmas we *did* have: tinsel tree by the front window, foil decorations on the ceiling, a Bernard Matthews turkey roast in the freezer, presents in abundance on the day. All year they never had any money, and then suddenly they'd make presents materialise.

Even, it turned out, if Marj or John were hospitalised.

We spent Christmas morning at home unwrapping them with Marjorie watching on. And then we spent the rest of the day in the hospital ward. John was barely with us. The nurses, in paper hats with tinsel over their blue uniforms, kept our spirits up with mince pies and cheery banter. It had that strange feeling hospitals have of being utterly exceptional while also monumentally dull. Still, Paul and I managed to see the *Top of the Pops* Christmas special in the television room. There wasn't anyone I could talk to at school about what was going on at home. And so I fled, far away, into fantasy: worlds created on paper, Lego and in the woods, set in space, the past and the future. Easier not to discuss it than try to process it. So this was what life was like: on the edge of a housing estate, where your parents were in mortal peril all the time and no one ever made a big deal of it.

It must have been such a frightening time for Marj, not that she ever let on. She remained cheery and upbeat, chivvying us along and keeping John calm. Ian had moved out with his girlfriend, so here she was, left with two kids in a house she could barely manoeuvre around. If John died what would happen? Would she be able to cope bringing up two boys by herself? There was never a chink in her armour. Neither John nor Marj let us see how scary this was for them, or how badly things might end up. Forget Santa. This was proper magic.

A gull swooped and pulled a live crab from the river. It didn't seem to know quite what to do with its catch, and the crab hung from the yellow beak, hopelessly wriggling its pincers and legs. The River Lee in Hertfordshire has been the site of a battle between two aggressive invasive species, the mitten crab and the signal crayfish, and luckily for the gull this looked like a pretty small feller. Along the opposite bank lay the reason for the green belt in the first place – some handsome 1930s semi-detached houses, built near the station at Broxbourne, and a voracious invasive species in their own right.

Like a niche concession in a department store, 1944's *The Greater London Plan* was all about belts. London would comprise four of them: the inner London belt, a suburban belt, a five-mile-wide green belt, and beyond that a country belt ten miles deep, into which many of the new towns like Harlow or Stevenage would be slotted. The green belt ring would, in Abercrombie's words, 'separate the threatened countryside from the threatening town'.[9] And it would protect scenic areas from London's sprawl too, such as the approach to the Chilterns or the North Downs. He had a bone to pick with what he called 'upstart communities' – the straggling new estates around Upminster and Orpington. Places like New Addington, for example. The Green Belt Act in its current form could save parks and playing fields, but preventing agricultural land from being built on would require a different approach. Here, councils wouldn't buy up the land; they just needed to stop farmers selling it off to building firms. Abercrombie also thought that derelict industrial land could be brought back into use as parks. The gravel pits of Lee Valley in north-east London, for example, could see its streams and reservoirs turned into a mini-Norfolk Broads. And this would be part of his extension of the green belt into the city, linking parks, footpaths, riverside walks and bridleways to the country beyond. For him the green belts weren't just a barrier, they were a place of escape.

The first bit of the Lee Valley Country Park I came to was certainly more barrier than escape. A great crush of yellow mustard and blue flowering alconet grew around a gate which had been obstructed with a block of concrete. Signs read *Contaminated land* and *No admittance*. Beyond, there were piles of logs on a great expanse of scratty tarmac. At the suggestion of Abercrombie, Lee Valley is full of ground that has been reclaimed, either from marshes or gravel pits. Lots of it has been filled, some of it with rubble from the Second World War, the rest with domestic or industrial waste. The resulting terrain had been landscaped and this forms the country park. The only trouble is, no one is quite sure what was in that domestic or industrial waste. And so this chunk of land had been closed off until investigations could take place into its safety.

It wasn't quite what I had been led to expect from pictures in *The Greater London Plan* – images painted by Peter Shepheard.

'My dad could draw,' said Paul, 'so he did a lot of the big polemical drawings. And he did the big water-colours of the Lee Valley and those sorts of things. They are all amazing. It wasn't just sheer nepotism; he had some quality to bring to the table.' In the book this area is described as a recreational centre in London's green belt. In a panoramic view of the scene Peter shows a steam train powering along the line, the various winding watercourses of the River Lee set in a landscape of green fields, tree lines and the occasional building. An aerial view shows re-sited bungalows, glasshouses, an open-air theatre, a grand swimming pool, games pavilions, amusements, lakes converted from gravel pits, a stadium, hotels and a boathouse. All of this was extremely ambitious for the site. Yet as I found and roamed along the banks of the river what felt remarkable was that they managed to replicate, if not the detail, then the spirit of that plan.

If it were written today *The Greater London Plan* would promise that private enterprise would create a *vibrant public realm* and chuck up the odd *iconic* structure. It would use hyperbolic language and establish something far more modest. But this huge country park was created in an age of public, not private development. Abercrombie plays the romantic in part, but the majority of *The Greater London Plan* could have been written by a bank manager. In the midst of our modern obsession with vision and enervation there is something reassuringly boring about it. Yes, it's full of fold-out maps and Peter Shepheard's beautiful illustrations, but for the most part the prose is surprisingly low-wattage. Communities weren't about being vibrant in 1944. They were far too busy being bombed out, overcrowded and displaced.

In a beer garden beside the River Lee there were middle-aged men in Lycra comparing war stories of ill-advised cycle rides. Some barely disguised business units abutted the river. One of these was a stack of metal shipping containers that made up Broxbourne Self Store. The side facing the river had been covered with some tarpaulins printed with a deeply unconvincing ivy design to lessen their visual impact. Half of one tarpaulin had come loose and had flapped up in the wind and onto the roof, exposing the rusty metal container beneath. It was a reminder of the mixed use of the green belt, how leisure and industry, woodland and water all co-exist within a few feet of each other.

I took a left through a gate into a cattle field, where a herd of young animals in stylish black and white lay basking in the sun beneath some electricity poles. Seventy or so iridescent starlings were feasting on the riches fostered by the cowpats, and took to the air in a noisy squadron, settling on a tree. Through the shorter grazed turf lay the pretty silver fronds of ferns and the sultry pink bristles of flowering clover. At the back of the field ran a small brook spanned by a little wooden bridge. I stood very still for some time, hoping to see a vole or frog between the reeds, but was disappointed. When I moved off again into the meadow beyond, a tiny silver dragon fly nipped by and rested on a blade of grass, its weight not even enough to cause it to sway. Further along, and another buzzed around me, a beautiful prehistoric relic beneath the pylons. Cow parsley was all out in flower, those simultaneously robust and tremulous stems suspending clouds of white flowers up to my chest. A dark shape fluttered ahead of me, and as I got nearer I could see it was a dazzling blue damselfly. It alighted on a reed, wings folded neatly behind, and I thought of a young woman I'd seen earlier at Broxbourne Station, holding her hair back and applying makeup.

I took a path through spindly limbs of garlic mustard and wan purple comfrey in the shade of tall ash trees. Ahead of me, where an old gravel pit had once stood, was a lake ringed by dense woodland and the occasional house. A line of mighty three-tier pylons strutted along the far shore. I stood on a small wooden jetty and looked around me. A couple of indignant-looking ducks were being chased away from a nest by a coot. Further out, a great crested grebe came up with a fish, which it swallowed down in one gulp. Above, a cormorant made a lazy crossing of the lake, keeping an eye out for dinner. I thought of landscape architect Sylvia Crowe's judgement of Lee Valley back in 1956. 'The ugliness and squalor, of which there is plenty, are almost all unnecessary', she wrote. It wasn't that she was set against modern industrial structures; far from it. For example, she spots 'a magnificent group of cooling towers'. What made the East London scene sordid? 'It is the shacks, the dilapidated houseboats, the uncared-for waste land and an unnecessarily ugly type of power line posts following beside the towpath.'[10] The clean-up operation since then has been miraculous.

On the way out of the country park I noticed one of the direction signs had a tagline: *Lee Valley – For Nature, Sport and Discovery*. I couldn't help thinking that despite a lack of the predicted games pavilions, amusements and hotels, they had largely achieved what Peter Shepheard had illustrated back in 1944, and what Abercrombie had dreamed of since the twenties. Here was a country park full of wildlife and day-trippers, locals and explorers. A landscape reclaimed from industry and dereliction. The green belt, Abercrombie style.

5
Making It Happen: Green Belts for Everyone!

On 25 April 1955, six months into his new job as Minister for Housing and Local Government, Duncan Sandys made a surprise statement in the Commons.

'I am convinced that, for the well-being of our people and for the preservation of the countryside, we have a clear duty to do all we can to prevent further unrestricted sprawl of the great cities,' he began. Sandys praised the Home Counties that had already created the Metropolitan Green Belt around London, some seven to ten miles across. He praised, too, other authorities around the country who were attempting the same, even though they hadn't made it official in the way London had. It was to these counties he turned his attention. 'I regret', he continued, 'that nowhere has any formal green belt as yet been proposed'. And so he asked county councils for 'proposals for the creation of clearly defined green belts wherever this is appropriate'. The next stage – the belting of Britain – had begun.

One of the reasons that people became so attached to their local green belts was the amount of time it took actually to gain them. By February 1956, twelve years since the publication of *The Greater London Plan*, only two counties, Berkshire and Buckinghamshire, had had their blueprints confirmed. The rest of the Home Counties were mired in tortuous inquiries, as local people had to have a chance to have their say on them. Grass was growing more quickly than the green belt was progressing. Meanwhile, in Birmingham and Sheffield, despite all the land bought or donated, dreams of formally creating green belts seemed as far away as ever. Sandys decided to formalise the process and help speed it along.

Duncan Sandys packed a lot into his career, so much so that in his obituaries the green belt barely gets a look-in. An old Etonian, he was the son of an MP and son-in-law of Winston Churchill. Close friends with Enoch Powell, he was an old-school reactionary railing against immigration and independence for former British colonies. As Defence Secretary he oversaw the merger (and collapse) of much of the British aircraft industry, the halving of the military and the end of National Service. Yet it is his penis that has achieved the most enduring fame. In 1963 the high-profile divorce proceedings of the Duchess of Argyll were getting ugly. At trial it was assumed Sandys was the 'headless man' in a Polaroid that surfaced, where the Duchess had been pictured blowing a man at an orgy while another masturbated in the background. Only a visit to his doctor to compare the bearing of his penis to those in the photo removed him from the frame. Next to all that, the green belt, the creation of the Civic Trusts and the introduction of the Clean Air Act seem a little tame.

Appropriately enough, green belts were championed in a circular. Four months after Sandys' surprise parliamentary statement, a letter from his department began to make its way around all county and borough councils in England and Wales. These two sides of foolscap would prove to be the single most significant document in the history of the green belt. And, unlike so many government circulars, this one offered hope, if not for ambitious urban makers then for the preservationists to whom Sandys and his Conservatives were then natural allies.

'I am directed by the Minister of Housing and Local Government to draw your attention to the importance of checking the unrestricted growth of built-up areas, and of safeguarding the surrounding countryside against further encroachment', began under-secretary B. Valentine.[1] He explained Sandys' desire for all counties to consider inserting green belts into their development plans, and gave three reasons:

a) to check the further growth of a large built-up area;
b) to prevent the neighbouring towns from merging into one another; or
c) to preserve the special character of a town.

The belt should be several miles wide so as to fix a 'rural zone' around the town, and permission to build there would only be granted under 'very special circumstances'. Those would include agriculture, sport, cemeteries, institutions standing in large grounds, but not housing, unless that was for 'rounding off' an existing town or estate. Annoyingly for the ministry, permission had already been given to build on some of this land, and now they would have to revoke it. As senior civil servant Dame Evelyn Sharp wrote, 'without these powers it would never have been possible to establish the London green belt in its present form'.[2] And certainly these sweeping new prerogatives went much further than the now rather timid-seeming 1938

Green Belt Act, which had only very limited effect.

The circular gave the green belt an entirely towny definition. J.R. James, one of the most senior civil servants in Sandys' department, made that very clear in a 1959 talk to the CPRE. 'May I say at once that the designation of the green belt is not a measure for the protection of the countryside.'[3] Sandys' successor, Henry Brooke, made the case for the belt's primary purpose quite plain. 'The very essence of a green belt is that it is a stopper. It may not be all very beautiful and it may not be all very green, but without it a town would never stop, and that is the case for preserving the circles of land around a town.'[4] Those idealistic Victorian notions of protecting the best of the country with green belts were nowhere to be seen.

In all of this Sandys' most formidable opponent existed within his own department. Dame Evelyn Sharp, the perennially ambitious civil servant, was an expert in using the levers of power to get things done, and to derail those things she was less keen on. The Dame, as she liked to be addressed, had deeply held concerns from the off. It was all very well creating this *cordon sanitaire*, she thought, but if there was to be no construction within the green belt, where would it go? It was easy to say that new towns and the like would jump the belt, but would that be enough to stop big cities striking out into it of their own accord? She doubted it. More than that, her fears were that the likely population increase in England and Wales between 1959 and 1974 would be around three million, double the figure that all the plans had been based on. And that wasn't even taking into consideration the desire for better, more spacious housing, or for smaller numbers of people in each home, as the number of single people rose. She lobbied hard but Sandys got his way, and the circular went out with none of her concerns addressed. Conservative Lord George Douglas-Hamilton expressed similar worries in June of that year. 'We shall reach the stage in a very short time when there will be no room left for building houses inside the green belt at all,' the *Manchester Guardian* reported, 'and that stands for all our large conurbations, whether it be Liverpool, Manchester, Glasgow or London.'[5]

An element of pragmatism entered the policy when a second circular the following year introduced the idea of 'white land'. This was unbuilt ground that lay on either side of green belt boundaries. Crucially, it could be built on in the future. Given today's obsession with brownfield sites, it's important to realise that white land was nothing like that either. Not only was green belt not always green, but white land was sometimes greener than the green belt. It just happened to be the bit between where a town or village currently stopped and where the green belt started. White land might be just the thing to save the policy from almost immediate failure. But when it ran out, as The Dame worried, what would we all do then?

Those proto green belts from the 1930s hadn't had a particularly easy ride. Sheffield's, for example, existed as some of the most beautiful countryside in Britain: the foothills of the Pennines National Park. Before the war the council had promised this land to the local branch of CPRE, run by Ethel and Gerald Haythornthwaite. But soon the council regretted it, and in the 1950s plans for 50,000 new houses were drawn up for that area to ease the city's housing problems. 'It is incomprehensible that a city which has for fourteen years pursued a magnificent policy of preserving for all time these great national assets should suddenly reverse its policy and disintegrate its plan,' the redoubtable Ethel told an inquiry in October 1952, to no avail.[6]

But that was nothing compared with the struggles that were about to hit the city in the 1960s. By then, Labour's new Minister for Housing and Local Government, Richard Crossman, was finding the green belt one of his trickiest responsibilities. Late December 1964 he wrote in his diary that one of his civil servants, Jimmy James, 'has made me see that one can't really preserve all these green belts intact; if one tries to, seepage occurs. The best thing to do is to allow planned incursions into them in certain concentrated developments, with model villages like the Span village or a New Town, and then to keep the rest truly green.'[7] Private developers Span were attempting to create a modernist village near Hartley in Kent, called New

Ash Green. Birmingham was pushing to expand into ancient Chelmsley Wood. And in Sheffield the council were determined to build at Stannington. 'I've decided to give Birmingham a huge area of housing in their green belt,' he wrote:

> . . . and last week there came the announcement of my decision to create Hartley, the Span model village, in the green belt in Kent. I'm moving the same way on another big decision whether or not to give Sheffield a large amount of housing land in their green belt area. I'm making these three planning decisions quite deliberately because I've decided, if rigidly inter-preted, a green belt can be a strangulation of the city . . . I know this will cause me my first major row but I'm pleased about it.[8]

He didn't remain pleased for long, the formidable Dame made sure of that. His diaries, published in 1974, became one of the main inspirations for the satirical sitcom *Yes Minister*, and locked Crossman and Sharp together forever as the prototype Jim Hacker and Sir Humphrey Appleby. Three days later, in classic Jim Hacker mode, he wrote: 'Dame Evelyn tried to shove me into a snap decision to violate the green belt round Sheffield, but by now I had reflected carefully and said, "No, that's going too far." I have decided to go there and see for myself.'[9] His firm belief and desire for a major row, when pushed by Sharp, became a case of mild political panic and backsliding. The next day, at a meeting of the Labour Housing and Local Government Group, a fight broke out about one of his big three proposals: to allow New Ash Green to be built on the green belt at Hartley in Kent. You can hear the deep sigh as he wrote, 'I began to realise what a sacred cow the green belt has become in progressive circles.'[10] Three days later he'd entirely switched around again. 'I've made a bad start with planning permissions – I shan't say this to anybody, but the green belt decision in Hartley was a mistake.'[11] It was exhausting.

He rode into 1965 burned by his decision in Kent, and forced the housebuilders, Span, to construct lots of local authority housing in penance. With the other two green belt decisions pending, Crossman's main desire now was to get through them without it all exploding in his face. He told *The Times* in January that 'we have to face it that many of the plans made as recently as eight years ago were based on false premises. They neglected the population explosion. We now have figures of population growth that would have seemed incredible 10 years ago.'[12] It was clear that Dame Evelyn Sharp was finally being listened to. In June Crossman was met by a delegation from the CPRE. 'They were led by a bustling little business man and a great smooth lawyer, and they placed before me a very offensive memorandum about how badly I had behaved in granting compulsory purchases in the green belt. After they had gone out J.D. Jones [deputy secretary in charge of planning] said to me, "You didn't realise but that chairman is a consultant who is constantly advising developers on how to get permissions granted for building in the green belt." '[13] And so the final element of Crossman's *Yes Minister* green belt farce was in place.

And what of the Haythornthwaites and their Peak District wranglings? Were these doughty Sheffield campaigners put off by their failure to preserve the green belt in the fifties, or by the exhausting process of public inquiry? Not a bit of it. They continued agitating for decades. In a BBC radio broadcast in 1966 called 'My Case for Preservation' Gerald explained his philosophy. 'The most noticeable characteristic of the nineteenth and twentieth centuries, and especially the twentieth, is ugliness. Like it or not, beauty is subject to rules. If the rules are not obeyed, beauty will not emerge.' And rules, such as the green belt, were the very thing to help him and activists like him protect landscapes from being built on all over the country. A rather different programme from the same year would have a much more immediate impact. Ken Loach's film *Cathy Come Home*, on the plight of a mother trying to keep hold of her children after being made homeless, highlighted the lack of affordable homes available despite all of that rapid postwar building. It was a grim reminder of the terrible circumstances that a great number of people found themselves in, and of the fact that for many, arguments over housebuilding were not abstract issues of aesthetics or politics.

For ardent preservationists, green belt policy proved to be a rather abstract and imperfect saviour. Salvation came to us twice weekly in the rather more practical form of Mrs Grant in her blue Datsun Sunny. Maybe because of our out-of-the-way location we didn't get many visitors to the house. District nurses were the most common. The effects of syringomyelia and a lack of physiotherapy meant that Marj had lost sensitivity in her legs. She'd knock her ankles against doorframes and furniture and the resulting wounds, ankles raw and sickly red like sliced beetroot, wouldn't heal. There were a number of district nurses who came to visit her, some kindly, others not, with their starched uniforms and antiseptic aroma generally more Joan Sims than Barbara Windsor. But if we were lucky, the health centre's complicated shift system would bring Mrs Grant, a large, loud nurse from Jamaica, to tend to Marj's post-operative wounds. Most of the nurses were like us: shy, awkward, giving the impression they'd rather be somewhere else. With her ready laugh, warmth and quick tongue Mrs Grant disrupted all of that. If we were a little absent, she was startlingly, formidably, overwhelmingly present. Even John's silliness seemed muted next to her technicolour brightness. The time he and Marj met the Queen Mother (don't ask) didn't cause so much of a flustered sense of occasion as that brought on by the arrival of Mrs Grant and her gauze dressings. Her frequent short visits were like being whirled around the floor by an expert dancer, in whose arms you felt giddily exhilarated.

Mrs Grant was just one of the factors that shook up Marj's post-operative world. It was a different woman who began to emerge from the cocoon of illness. Her long, straight, chestnut hair was falling out, growing back as thick mid-brown curls. Gone was the faded hippy, now came the Jan Leeming look beloved of so many women in the 1980s: perm, bat-winged jumpers and tie-necked blouses. As a child I'd just accepted that my parents were how they were. The thought that they might have been struggling never occurred to me. Marj seemed happy enough to me in the 1970s, tiny as I was back then, but it was only when she left hospital that I began to notice a change. There was a burst of energy, a feeling of light-ness. It was as if a cloud had lifted. She found things funnier, laughed louder, began to positively assert herself as never before. Now she wanted to live a little. Perhaps Marj had been more subdued than I'd realised, because now she was shedding that old life and beginning afresh. Ian wondered if all of those seventy pints of blood had a memory. And I knew what he meant. It was as though she'd remembered what living was like – except these weren't *her* memo-ries. She had channelled them from somewhere quite different. For Paul it was like a different person had been transplanted in her place. And this new woman rapidly began to leave us all behind.

I began to see that the garden and the outdoors had been Marj's saviour in the depression of the 1970s. But now it was the town that brought her back to life. She'd been persuaded to attend Waylands, a day centre for people with disabilities. Until that point Marj had a strange relationship with her affliction. She'd never really accepted it, and refused to be defined or stopped by it. In fact, she used to relish the opportunity to humiliate anyone who attempted to talk down to her because of it. Paul and I cringed at the memory of the sorts of encounters we'd have down the shops, people talking to John over Marj's head, asking about her as if she wasn't there. I remembered one woman bearing down with a full-on pantomime *Are You Going on Your Holidays?* For one terrible moment it was as if the entire street – the trees, the cars, the buildings – took a deep breath. Marjorie smiled up at her. Ten minutes later the woman was staggering off down the street a broken, mortified wreck. Never has a nuanced, precise and uninterrupted account of a week in a caravan on the south coast been wielded to such devastating effect.

And so, in many ways the day centre seemed like a defeat for this capable, clever, independent woman. But pretty soon the wisdom of going there became obvious. It started with small things. Raffia. Fimo. Embroidery. I suppose these days we'd call it mindfulness. One day she returned with a lamp she'd made. The base was clay, glazed to a high-gloss sheen, a leafy stem painted onto it. The shade was a tightly wound canopy of green thread, wrapped around a wire frame. It was what she had missed all that time in hospital. A tree.

The day centre had a rather woolly users' group. Marj hadn't been rehabilitating there long before she'd been asked to join it. She became frustrated with it almost immediately, and within a few weeks found herself running it. A former PA at Arding and Hobbs department store, she had all the relevant skills rusting in a drawer: typing, organising, taking minutes. She'd soon whipped the shambolic group into a functional team. Before we knew it she'd been co-opted onto the board of Croydon and Sutton Dial-a-Ride too, and within a couple of years she was chairing that as well. Given what chaotic, ego-fuelled nests of vipers voluntary boards can be, her reasonable tone and practical suggestions went down a storm. It helped that she was an incorrigible flirt. There always seemed to be a band of men who doted on her wherever she went, and who rushed to attend to her every whim. Certainly the fact she was married, with three kids and a wheelchair, never got in the way. Instead, with renewed energy came a well of industrial-strength charisma. Thinking about it now she would have made an excellent politician – a local councillor or even MP, if accessibility issues in council or parliamentary chambers weren't a problem. Not that she could be fussed pushing herself forward. She did these voluntary roles not because she wanted recognition, but because it annoyed her to watch them being done badly. She was not a patient woman. Her work was a testament to that age-old motivator: *oh, just give it here*.

During all of this upheaval Marj and John didn't have much of an idea of my twisted childhood desires. One parents' evening that would change. I was tediously good at junior school. Quiet, studious, no fuss. My parents were used to blandly positive reports. A week earlier, class 2B had been asked to complete the sentence 'I wish . . .' on thought bubbles drawn on coloured sugar paper to be cut out and pinned to the wall of our classroom. That evening Mrs Bone pointed out the one I'd written to Marj and John. Here it was, on the board, alongside all the others: desires for toys and sweets and adventures. Mine read: 'I wish I was more quiet beaucause I give my mum a head ache.' It was a lesson ripped straight from the pages of *The Ladybird Book of Passive Aggression*. I expect Mrs Bone had her head at that *is there something you want to tell me* angle. They came home and mum asked me if I remembered what I'd written, but I didn't. So she told me, and we laughed about it because that was easier than explaining or listening.

The truth was, I found Marj quite tough at times when I was growing up. She was clever and funny and constantly creative, but when she was in a dark mood I was afraid of her. She was easy to disappoint. Offhand remarks could be pounced upon, and her verbal dexterity and clarity could be a bit much for an over-sensitive child to take at times. I certainly didn't concern myself with why she was like that; that she was so obviously depressed. For one thing, I didn't know what that meant, and I'm not sure Marj did either. For another, she would have flatly rejected the idea. She was too proud to acknowledge any more medical complications. And what would have been the outcome anyway? Being smashed off her face on Valium for decades? No thanks. So she decided to endure it. And that meant we had to tough it out with her.

Generally, as a family, we were very quiet. I sometimes suspected that, had we removed sitcoms and cats from the conversation, we would have barely spoken. Successive waves of cats made conversation both possible and also oddly redundant. Even with them we took the notion of 'companionable silence' to an almost wilfully uncomfortable degree. But they did allow us something to look at, to remark on, to project onto and to fuss over that wasn't human or might actually need attention. The cats walking along, or not walking along, would be the topic of 50 per cent of conversation. Look at what the cat was or wasn't doing. Did you notice the presence or absence of certain behaviour? Meowing? Purring? Swishing of the tail? It would be funny if they did it, and funny if they didn't. *That cat hasn't moved all day* was as noteworthy as *this cat has just jumped on my shoulders*. But equally, the cat that moved about a bit would become a tale of how hard it was to settle, how fussy the cat was, how difficult to please. We may have thought of one another in a similar way, but we would never have said so. And comedy, too, allowed us to say and do things we wouldn't be able to directly. Quoting obscure lines and behaviour replaced having to have any of our own. And so conversation was a hall of mirrors, operating on so many layers of artifice and irony that any real content became impossible to decipher. Strangers entering our highly coded world found us unbreakable. Even Alan Turing would have struggled.

Marj and John brought with them to the estate a mysterious use of language. Some of it was straightforward, if opaque. They had both been brought up steeped in the joys of Cockney rhyming slang. Alongside the more familiar phrases, *dicky dirts* (shirts) say, or *Lily the Pink* (drink), were *round-mes* (round me houses: trousers). Often these phrases were embellished into entire ritualistic sentences, John being unable to hear the word tea, for example, without automatically saying *a cup of Rosie Lee sarge* or relaying the jingle of *a Double Diamond works wonders* at any mention of either the word double or diamond. Marj's love of polari, picked up largely from Kenneth Williams and Hugh Paddick on the radio comedy *Round the Horne*, meant that *trolling along* and *bona* were frequently employed. But they were also quite happy to make up their own slang. It's telling that the most common was a pet name for Disprin – *nellies* – a product that none of us for one moment thought it odd to give a slang name, or such a camp one at that. Much of it was wilful. In the nineties John got a fish tank and the fish were only ever referred to by everyone as *the birds*.

Most infuriating was their adoption of the word *ticket* to mean more or less anything. Going shopping, Marj would ask John, *have you got the ticket?* This would cause him to stop in panic and start patting down his many pockets. What he was looking for was a mystery. It could mean money – notes *or* coins – a cheque book, a cheque card, the disability allowance book, a permit from the car park, a shopping list, a wallet or purse, a token, a loyalty card, a receipt, a letter or postcard, a book of stamps, a tax disc, a driving licence, sometimes even the product they were buying. Even the car keys became, in the end, a ticket. Going shopping with them was like some kind of baffling logic game with no clues or, indeed, logic. This perfectly summed up how insular we were as a family. We were happy with our own language, even if between us – *inside* us – we couldn't agree what these words actually meant.

A few years passed since Marj's illness and depression, and in the age of Perestroika and Glasnost she came back from the dead. John too made a spectacular recovery, and ended up as a handyman at Waylands, the day centre Marj had attended. It was another one of those circles from which our life on the edge of the green belt had been made. This one was the most surprising, and the most enduring too. A cycle of hope. My difficult relationship with Marjorie would be saved by a shared sensibility. The two of us spent hours absorbed in wordy songs, plays at the Fairfield Halls and TV sketch shows. She often remarked on how she saw life as if it were a Dennis Potter play: full of musical interludes and, I presume, bleak uncompromising darkness. We played post-school games of Scrabble on the table looking over the garden, and took books out there in the summer. Visits to the British Home Stores canteen in Croydon were enlivened by references to Victoria Wood skits – 'Can I crash by, I'm a diabetic' – or Alan Bennett monologues – 'Lemon wedge, that sounds nice, doesn't it Graham?' Hours of giggling at running jokes and sharing pointed observations. While other teenagers might have been smoking, doing drugs or drinking to oblivion, I was on endless day trips with my mum round the edge of London, to gardens, parks and castles, often with friends she'd made from the day centre or her voluntary work. Over those years she went from being a force I was wary of and desperate to impress to my best and most inspiring friend.

1 January 1951 saw the start of the biggest green belt drama of them all. *The Archers* debuted on the BBC Home Service, a soap set in the fictitious village of

Ambridge. It was supposedly based on Hanbury in Worcestershire, a village which within the decade formed part of the green belt. But the way of life in Ambridge was rather steadier than the reality, as those West Midlands green belt counties of Worcestershire, Staffordshire, Warwickshire and Shropshire would discover. It is curious that the moment green belts began to be established as a desirable thing for cities to have, they also faced some of their gravest threats. Ambitious Birmingham had raced to hand in their development plan to the minister and, ominously for the outlying counties, Duncan Sandys said it 'struck me as particularly good'.[14] Because only a third of land round the city was classified as agricultural, there was pressure to build on it. Birmingham's desire to cash in was matched by some of those farmers round and about, whose efforts were undermining the surrounding counties' attempts to fight off city expansion. The flimsiest of pretexts would do. There were dairy farmers describing their land as *milked out*, and farmers flogging off *exhausted* land to construction firms. And so the counties rushed to get their proposals in too, as a way of defending their territories from the city through a new green belt.

In the decade leading up to 1963, 86,000 people had moved out of Birmingham and there had been an increase of 100,000 living in the proposed green belt. New towns, estates and extensions to towns and villages were things the counties around the city were all too aware of. And so in order to put a stop to what was to them an alarming trend, Warwickshire, Worcestershire and Staffordshire proposed a green belt up to fifteen miles wide in places, larger than the one around London, to contain the giant. Birmingham's pugnacious and ambitious planning mastermind Herbert Manzoni was enraged by this provocative act, curbing the city's growth, and so the fight was on. Manzoni pushed ahead with proposals to build on a proto-green belt area of Bromsgrove called Wythall, to the east of the city, creating an estate for 54,000 people, using it as a kind of overflow car park while they rebuilt areas of the city closer in. Never mind that Wythall had been given to the county council by the Cadbury family on the strict proviso that it should not be built on. This didn't seem much of an obstacle for Manzoni. But to his dismay the then minister, Henry Brooke, turned down his blueprint in April 1960. 'I have decided to reject the application', said Brooke, 'on the grounds that the development would mean a serious incursion into land which ought to form part of the green belt round Birmingham.' Instead he wanted to put up new towns further away, beyond the protected land. On the whole, city politicians and planners hated new towns, which were imposed by central government and diluted their local power base. Pugnacious Harry Watton, Alderman of Birmingham, wasn't happy with Brooke's decision. 'I feel disappointed and somewhat dismayed', he said. 'I have difficulty in reconciling the minister's decision to turn us down on the ground that this land should form part of the green belt with his statement that the decision does not imply that the land ought necessarily be included in the green belt.'[15]

Given the moratorium on construction round and about I was surprised to see how many mid-century structures there were at Wythall – bungalows, ranch-style homes, and even a private road filled with the kind of pitched-roofed flats and houses favoured by developers in the 1990s. This was infilling, the only kind of building allowed in villages in the green belt. Three big signs warned that one stretch was a private road, and so I obviously took a detour into it, sitting on a bench in the shade watching a beautiful green grasshopper make its way across the lawn in short determined jumps. Careful, I told it, this is a private road. No hopping in their parking bays. Walking through the village I kept expecting the ribbon of houses to peter out, but it just carried on going through this rural landscape. I asked local planner Adam Mindykowski about the kind of building that had been going on here, and how it might be affecting the green belt. He talked about how the neighbouring village, Hollywood, had been massed into a rather dense 'block' which contained many more houses than Wythall. But the villages were about as long as each other.

'Small ribbon developments that accrue over time create a more urbanised character,' he told me, 'because of the way they frame highways, even though they may be only one property deep, so to speak. There is a tinge of irony in that wayside, and not block development, was the established form of settlement in this landscape. So, while there is likely to be a perception that places like Hollywood have imposed the greatest change to the landscape it is actually the cumulative effect of modern wayside development that is challenging the green belt character.' The ribbon in Wythall may once have been threadbare, but now every inch of roadside between existing buildings has been claimed by a house. Unless you approached the village from the air you would never know that this feeling of being built-up was so shallow – just one house deep.

Soon I stumbled across another, even newer estate, computer-generated unmarked yellow brick boxes plonked here as tightly as they could be. I could hear children playing, and a man emerged from one house with a bag of golf clubs which he dumped into his car. No one seemed to have a garden, although there was a communal area around a large dried-out dew-pond overgrown by bulrushes. As I made my way round it, under telephone wires and electricity pylons, I could hear the raucous chirping of the insects making merry in this little corner that was neither farmed nor built on. One thing that had struck me walking around here was how little of the green space was actually accessible. None of the fields seemed to have rights of way, and there were no public parks. Besides, the houses ran next to the railway line, the rails banked up on grey shingle higher than the houses at one point. At least here they were making good use of some derelict land beside the railway line, and had created a patch of public open space too. I had to commend them for that. Incredible to think that the Cadbury family had left Wythall to Birmingham as a gift. Much as with their own business – Cadbury is no longer an independent manufacturer with Quaker roots but instead part of a (legal) tax-avoiding multinational* – there seems little of the Cadburys' legacy that hasn't been extravagantly pissed on.

A retired Worcestershire planner, Mick Wills, was there when the Wythall decision was being made in the early sixties. 'There was a constant battle between Birmingham,' he explained, in his deep voice, 'who were always looking for opportunities to develop in the shire counties, and the shire counties, who were against unplanned development in this county coming from Birmingham.' He explained how Birmingham, a powerful authority, would bend the ear of the current minister, who would then inform the surrounding counties that they must accept the city's demands for more housing and greater industry.

---

* Cadbury's parent company Mondelez paid no corporation tax on the confectionery subsidiary in the UK in 2015 despite making profits of £96.5m in 2014. This led Labour MP Margaret Hodge to remark to the *Sunday Times* that 'multinationals like this are deliberately exporting their profits with artificial company structures to avoid tax. The founders of Cadbury who set it up as an ethical company will be turning in their graves.' (*Guardian* 6 December 2015)[16]

Wythall was taken to a public inquiry. 'People in Birmingham could not be allowed, through no fault of their own, to live in disgusting conditions merely to preserve every acre of peripheral land for green belt purposes', thundered Alderman Watton.[17] But still they lost. Fellow Alderman W.T. Bowen was outraged on behalf of the 47,000 Birmingham families living in unfit conditions and the 31,000 lodger families with no home of their own. 'People would not be content to live in some of the worst slums in the country to preserve land which is miscalled green belt', grumbled Bowen.[18] But the minister still thought a better solution was providing homes in faraway new towns such as Redditch and Dawley. Confounding both the shire counties and the government, the city chose a third way. It dropped proposals to expand into Worcestershire's green belt at Wythall, and instead did something totally unexpected. It asked the incoming minister, Richard Crossman, whether it could build on the Solihull green belt instead, which was then part of Warwickshire. This would involve chopping down Chelmsley Wood, a fragment of the ancient Forest of Arden. Crossman agreed. In 1966 Birmingham compulsorily purchased the woodland and began building almost 16,000 new homes on the site.

Chelmsley Wood is the closest thing to New Addington I have ever seen. Sat in the Solihull scenery surrounded by green belt, the houses here are classic 1960s municipal modern – red, brown or black tile-hung terraces and flats, the odd high-rise thrown in to show that they meant business. The familiar elements are all here: oddly shaped greens, traffic-free snickets occupied by sulky girls and noisy boys, and a complex layout of paths and roads making it tricky for a stranger to navigate.

There was little sign of the ancient wood, nor of the social problems people reflexively name at the mention of Chelmsley Wood, just as they do with New Addington. One former resident was the journalist Lynsey Hanley, who catalogued her time there in her book *Estates*. For her it represents the political failure of the likes of Crossman, with its identikit houses and crime born of boredom from a huge estate with few amenities. On this sunny day it just seemed oddly quiet. There was even a conspicuous lack of the kind of dereliction that may once have overtaken the estate in its ASBO heyday.

Gone too were the ancient oaks. The trees here were sixty-year-old ash, growing out of mown corners, and at the southern end near Marston Green they became more ornamental species carefully placed beside the play park and health centre to add a bit of flash. It was hard to believe that back in the sixties this had all been ancient woodland, and green belt to boot. But politics had intervened, and houses that might have been better sited in the scrappy fields of Wythall had been dug into the earth where the roots of an ancient forest had stood weeks before. The Pyrrhic victory for the burghers of Wythall is typical of green belt stories.

All of the confusion and pain caused by the construction of estates like Chelmsley Wood and the protection of areas like Wythall was pounced on by Wyndham Thomas, director of the Town and Country Planning Association, who later that year said, 'if the government and the county councils succeed in preserving the green belts around our large cities over the next 10 years, without having taken strong and effective action to guide jobs and people together to many more new and expanded towns, they will have worked the biggest confidence trick since the South Sea Bubble'.[19]

By the end of the 1960s, every self-respecting town wanted a green belt. It was greenbeltmania. In England there were proposals from Middlesbrough and County Durham, the Hampshire coast, the Wirral, East Sussex and Gloucestershire. In Scotland, Aberdeen, Ayr, Clackmannanshire, Dundee, East Lothian, Edinburgh, Falkirk and Grangemouth, Greater Glasgow, Midlothian, and Stirling. Northern Ireland's were initially focused on Belfast, where many of the people who wrote the Clyde Valley plan had imposed their ideas, and on the coast. Wales didn't propose any at this time. But almost as soon as these ideas were put forward the Ministry began to strike them out. Ideas for belts around Scarborough and throughout Essex and County Durham were killed off by a rule that stated they shouldn't be applied to small towns. Swindon and Salisbury lost out because there was no pressure for growth there. North Tyneside faced uncertainty about the possibilities of future construction, and so waved goodbye to theirs. Hampshire's coastal belt was crushed because it was too large, although, to be fair, the county never seemed all that keen on the idea either. And towns with a green belt still needed room to expand, which did for Amersham, Beaconsfield, Chesham and Marlow in Buckinghamshire. Surrey was the most wily of all county councils when it came to pitching for green belt. It submitted controversial proposals, designed to preserve as much of the county as possible and push any construction pressure onto their neighbours' patch. It thought it was being subtle, but it was as obvious as snow.

Planners made a decisive intervention in the map of Britain in the postwar period, and the green belts were just part of it. The effect of human behaviour on our landscape was beginning to be appreciated, from spreading cities to sprawling industry, destruction of wilderness and spoiling of the country. And so they devised a series of new categories to protect different sorts of landscapes. Ten National Parks had been established across England and Wales in the 1950s. Like some kind of clickbait troll, E.M. Forster got in early, dismissing them over a decade before they were created. 'Does your heart leap at the idea of National Parks?' he wrote back in 1938. 'Mine doesn't, because the England I care for is composed of oddments and trifles, which decline to be scheduled – the light thickening, the crow flying into the wood, here a bush and there a sheep, the England of Cowper and Crabbe, Tennyson and Housman.'[20] He liked the new town built next to his beloved village of Old Stevenage even less.

The map was now showered with acronyms: AONBs (Areas of Outstanding Natural Beauty), SSSIs (Sites of Special Scientific Interest) and AGLVs (Areas of Great Landscape Value). These different classifications are the ones whose purposes are most commonly confused with those of the green belt. With AONBs, AGLVs and SSSIs it is the quality of the landscape that is being protected, for its beauty, usefulness or diversity. In the green belt none of these apply. The landscape here can be as ugly, useless and barren as you'd like. But then, does all landscape have to be beautiful? Should it be reduced to the lascivious gaze of the male Wimbledon tennis commentator when faced with an attractive female player? One of the things I like about the green belt is that it protects the ugly, and sticks two fingers up to the narrative that all landscape should be pretty. There is no point telling the green belt to *cheer up love, it might never happen*, because it already has. Towns have been built, pylons erected, residents have trampled it and dumped mattresses and burned out cars. If you want a pretty bit of skirt, go and wolf whistle at an AONB or practise your Sid James act in front of a Site of Special Scientific Interest.

AONBs were like mini National Parks. As the Ministry of Housing and Local Government put it, 'while not having the outstanding scenic qualities of a National Park, the landscape [of an AONB] is of more than local value and significance'. Set up in 1949 was the Nature Conservancy, which advised on the important environmental stuff: SSSIs, research and protection. AGLVs were the most nebulous category of all, countryside that was not up to being classified as either outstandingly beautiful or scientifically special. Areas that are 'All Right I Suppose' might have been a better description. 'Areas that Are Not Too Shabby'. In Scotland, where the government had encouraged the creation of National Parks, nothing was done. Instead the Scots relied on an AONB equivalent, National Scenic Areas, which account for a whopping 13 per cent of Scottish land.

None of these designations were compulsory and their use was as political and competitive as the contemporary rebuilding of town centres or the construction of large council estates. While one county might consider an area an AONB, its neighbour might not agree, and so natural beauty would stop dead on a boundary, regardless of topography or sense. Then there were counties like Middlesex, which didn't bother proposing any AONBs, AGLVs or SSSIs at all. Two AONBs would end up overlapping London's green belt: 160 square miles of the Surrey Downs south of London, and the Chilterns in Hertfordshire to the north. Sites of Special Scientific Interest within London's green belt include Epping Forest, Burnham Beeches, Staines Moor, and Ashtead and Esher Commons.

When it comes to preserving a landscape, woodland can be as saved as it is possible to be. Tree Preservation Orders became law in 1947, and cover anything from an individual tree to an entire wood. It is possible therefore for a tree to have been subject to a preservation order while being in both a Site of Special Scientific Interest and a green belt. Many of these protected woodlands are hangovers of old landscape gardens. In the London Metropolitan Green Belt they include Black Park, Broxbourne Woods, Epping Forest and Pollards Park.

With all of this complex and invisible work going on, in 1962 the Ministry of Housing and Local Government decided to celebrate England's town planning achievements. They published a rather beautiful thirty-two-page booklet, *The Green Belts*, available for four shillings from HMSO. It was good value for money: a pocket at the back contained a fold-out map, showing the green belt laid around London like a rather threadbare holly wreath. The cover depicted couples picnicking on Box Hill, and images inside the book ranged from maps of Raymond Unwin's 1930s green girdle to a photo of newly planted trees outside a sewage works in Rickmansworth. After some generalised rubric, London's green belt takes up eleven pages of the booklet; the rest of England's warrants just three. Which was representative perhaps of the amount of fuss caused relative to each. But in the coming decades, as housing pressures would build, and dereliction around towns would increase, that was going to change. This booklet represents a high-water mark for the green belts' universal popularity. Sure, more acres would be designated after publication, but the concept and now the reality would never again receive the easy ride it had up until that point.

As that first generation of green belt masterminds began to retire or die off, their idea was left in the hands of younger people, and the way in which it was viewed would begin to evolve. With the battles to establish the green belts fading in our collective memory, it was harder to understand just why people thought we needed them, or how we had ever managed without them before, depending on where you stood. In popular currency the notion of the green belt towered over all other achievements of planning of the period. It was part of the fabric of the new Britain, the modernisation that was going on: the building of new roads and scrapping of old railway lines; the reconstruction of town centres, shops, offices and civic buildings; the spread of council houses; the construction of new towns. It sat pre-eminent above all of those, and of the other landscape designations too: National Parks, AONBs, AGLVs, SSSIs, country parks and nature reserves. It came to represent all of these things, without ever actually meaning to. It had the simplest function of the lot: to stop towns spreading. And it would end up embodying the most complex web of hopes and ideals. Boundless leisure, bounteous nature, timeless beauty. Things the green belt had never hoped to stand for, and could not possibly hope to protect or create.

Like the internet, green belts sometimes seem to make a handy stand-in for God. They seemingly offer answers and wisdom, surrounding us with the hope that, with such a vast presence, everything might just be all right after all. Welcome to the Garden of Eden, where the snakes have been tamed and the apples have been nationalised. But what the green belts actually were, and what they would become – these were things that the originators might not have been able to recognise. Once we had them in place, then the real struggles would begin.

Part 2

Reaping

6
Ever Decreasing Circles: Or, Enter the Nimby

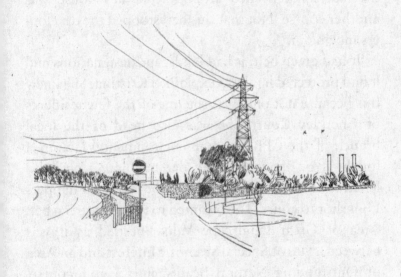

'Do you know how many golf courses there are in a fifty-mile radius from here?' Kristina Kenworthy asked me as we sat in her house high in the North Downs. I shrugged. 'Six hundred and twenty-seven! I kid you not!' Three of them were immediately next door to the land she lived on, the grounds of Cherkley Court, a country house once owned by Canadian tycoon Lord

Beaverbrook, wartime proprietor of the *Daily Express*. Astonishingly, Surrey isn't even the most over-golf-clubbed county in England. It lies third, behind Merseyside and the West Midlands. And compared to Scotland, forget it – it's reckoned to be the nation with the most holes of golf per head of population. Still, Surrey isn't doing too badly on the golf club front. And the last thing needed around Kristina's house was another course. Not that this had stopped the developers moving in.

'It had green belt, it had landscape designations and it had protected habitat,' explained Kristina. She knew this because not only was she one of the few residents of Cherkley Court, she was also head of the local branch of the CPRE and an environmental lawyer. 'I fought it on landscape and habitat, not green belt.' Kristina was telling me how she took developers Longshot to court. They wanted to turn this green belt Area of Great Landscape Value, nestled as it was between a Site of Special Scientific Interest and an Area of Outstanding Natural Beauty, into a golf course. Kristina's husband, the sculptor Jonathan Kenworthy, had lived in the grounds of Cherkley Court for decades, originally in a Nissen hut which had been Beaverbrook's wartime radio transmitting station. He and Kristina built a new house on the site of the hut in the mid-1990s, and it was here I met her. Perhaps it was Jonathan's animal sculptures, but with her cheesecloth shirt and sunny, no-nonsense disposition, Kristina reminded me of the kind of intrepid bohemian played by Virginia McKenna in a 1960s film about lions or elephants. Up here it felt like the wild plain too, looking down on the busy and curiously named commuting towns of Leatherhead and Dorking.

Nearby, there were men busy putting up a clubhouse and facilities for a golf course, an underground spa, pool and cookery school. She sat on the sofa barefoot and recounted the most incredible story.

'Before they bought it, the Longshottians had a public consultation to which they did not ask me and they did not tell us about it.' However, her friends at the local branch of the Campaign to Protect Rural England told her what was going on, and so she rang up and booked a place as their representative. When she arrived at the consultation one of the employees wagged his finger and said, 'You're a very naughty person Mrs Kenworthy for coming to this meeting. And I said, "Why, I'm a local resident, I'm a neighbour, and you need to get on with me."' Not only that; part of the company's original scheme saw the Kenworthys' garden turned into a fairway.

It got very unpleasant very quickly. There was a huge groundswell of opinion against the company when they put their planning application in, but they were resourceful and well connected.

'I was warned early on, this is very political and they've got good contacts high up in the Tory Party. And I thought, well, even if they have, that shouldn't matter.' The local decision went against Kristina by one vote. She fought for, and gained, a judicial review, where the judge, Justice Haddon Cave, overturned the judgment. Kristina won on all four grounds: green belt, landscape, need and rationality. 'You couldn't possibly look at this and say this was a development that was needed,' she told me, 'or that it was an improvement.'

When we stepped from Kristina's house I saw that the field next to their house had been obliterated. This was to make way for a spa and swimming pool. It was hard, looking at such large and entirely frivolous incursions into the green belt, to understand how permission had ever been granted. Kristina had been shocked how pro-business the government had turned at the expense of all else following the 2008 financial crash. Its effects had been felt everywhere, even on this rural hillside on the North Downs. The work was visible all the way from the house right to the very edge of the estate, a good half a mile away. On the crest of the hill stood the big clubhouse, a mysterious form shrouded in scaffolding and plastic sheets. Facing it was a marquee, put up overlooking the spectacular view of the Dorking Gap and Mole Valley. Blue sky was stuffed with fluffy white clouds, mirroring the many full tree-tops we could see down in the valley. It was here that a soft launch event had just been held, to encourage more backers for the club before the facilities were finished. The road was demarcated by blue rope tied to steel poles, and as we walked we were passed by rich business types and builders in big cars, while massive earth movers and JCBs rumbled about. Occasionally we saw them sticking out of fields like oil derricks. Beyond the hedges the greens had all been created, the landscaping smooth and blank as a dust sheet over an armchair. We spotted people in blue pinstripe shirts being shown around.

Longshot's director, Ian Todd, told the *Get Surrey* website in 2014 that 'Our opposition said we are only supplying a golf course for the super-rich; this could not be further from the truth. The Cherkley Court building, the hotel and other facilities will be open to the public. We want to open Cherkley Court to the public, to give it back to Mole Valley.' This seemed a very generous statement: all of these rolling fairways, greens and facilities, open to all? 'The only thing that will not be open to all is the golf course,' he added, 'which will be members only, like many other golf courses in the country.' So what are these public areas that can be enjoyed? Maybe he was referring to the public rights of way which criss-cross the site. That said, they've planted big trees and shrubs – holly and yew, oak and beech – where once low fences stood, to ensure that any non-members trying to catch a glimpse of the famous landscape (or of an even more famous celebrity teeing up) will be disappointed. Many of these new trees were already brown. The chalk soil was unforgiving, water draining away from the roots almost immediately. I estimated that at least one in ten trees were dying at the height of summer. A few countryside stewards were there, pulling up ragwort from the borders, poisonous if it got into cattle feed, but of little consequence as the hayfields were now fairways. Blue and yellow hosepipes curled about on the ground by the entrance to one of the holes, like outsized rubber bands from the blueprint that had been unrolled and was in the process of being imposed onto the landscape. There were old houses being turned into some form of hotel and a cookery school, while facing these a big concrete bunker was being built to service the growing entertainment complex. There were lots of new structures here on the green belt. No one apart from Kristina seemed bothered.

After Kristina's win at the judicial review it all looked to be going well, until Mole Valley council got together with the entrepreneurs to put in for an appeal. The appeal judge overturned all of the decisions, on what Kristina characterised as 'very weasely grounds'. He ruled that the landscape might well be improved by the work, despite Natural England's evidence that golf courses within AGLVs cannot be considered natural beauty. 'Because you cannot call a golf course naturally beautiful,' said Kristina. 'We said, "How can it be an improvement if it strips it of one of its designations?" It's now only got green belt. As for habitat, they didn't give a damn about that.' The Kenworthys were ordered to pay costs.

The name for Kristina's form of activism has a tradition leading back some forty years. It can first be identified in relation to the Hooker Chemical Company in the district Love Canal, Niagara Falls, which sounds like a series of names designed to be caught in an email spam filter. Hooker came to public attention in 1978 when it began dumping toxic waste in the district in an attempt to dodge the expense of disposing of it responsibly. Pretty soon this working-class area saw some grisly side effects, not least a soaring rate of miscarriages and birth defects. In response, resident Lois Gibbs began the Love Canal Homeowners Association, a group of people for whom 'fighting for their own backyard is what democracy is about'. The PR departments of petrochemical companies came up with a term to discredit Gibbs' supporters. It was the acronym Nimby – Not In My Back Yard. Soon it had jumped the Atlantic, with Tory MPs Rhodes Boyson and Nicholas Ridley both claiming to have created it. By 1989 it had even become an answer in that ultimate bastion of propriety, *The Times* crossword.

Nimbys, you might think, are never self-declared. The conjugation goes: I am a conservationist; you are a protester; they are nimbys. Kristina Kenworthy was having none of that.

'So many times when I'm with my CPRE hat on,' she told me, 'they say, "We're not nimbys you know", and I go, "It's all right. I am! And what's more, I'm a note." And they go, "What's that?" and I say, "It's 'Not Over

There Either!"' She laughed. 'And proud of it. Everyone's a nimby; we should be, we should look after our planet. It's everybody's back yard.'

It is this thought that informs Kristina's nimbyism, even though it might not be what many of us would associate with the phenomenon. The more infantile forms of nimbyism hide behind the skirts of environmentalism, claiming special protection out of fear of change and outsiders rather than having a genuine interest in conservation. Kristina had quite looked forward to new neighbours up on the hill when it had been mooted that the old buildings would be converted into flats. But when the golf club came instead it was the senseless loss of natural habitat that got to her.

'I don't understand how the green movement – one almost doesn't dare use the word environmental any more – how it's got such a bad rep when it's more important than ever,' she said, a note of despair creeping into her voice. 'With these people here when they first came they started writing us pompous letters, and they even said to my face, "We own the land, we can do what we like now." I said, "Well, you really have no idea of planning or countryside or landscape or anything." We are stewards of the land, and that's all we are. And if you're lucky enough to own a big chunk of land, if you don't have that sense of looking after it for future generations . . . It's *not* yours, we're just here a short while, all of us, and how *dare* we think it's ours and we can do what we like with it. The arrogance of it is stunning.'

When we think of nimbys we're more likely to conjure up the image of a rather different child of the Mole Valley, Martin Bryce, the obsessive busybody from 1980s BBC sitcom *Ever Decreasing Circles*. Martin, as played by Richard Briers, was desperate to embody suburban perfection, from cricket club to neighbourhood watch. His world was threatened by the arrival of a handsome, worldly new neighbour, Paul, and undercut by the exhausted melancholy of his wife Ann, played by Penelope Wilton. In one episode Martin fights to use a local footpath through a wood, which only leads to the discovery that another runs through his back garden. Via a rant about Turkey's supposedly imminent joining of the EEC and an imagined uprising against his Norman overlords, Martin erects his own sign and stile for the footpath, so determined is he to obey the letter of the law. Eventually the council make him take them down because some shady dealings between them and the estate's developers mean that the footpath has long since been moved. It's a beautiful little vignette in which 'not in my back yard' and protection of the countryside are twisted 180 degrees and back again. In many ways Briers' character in *Ever Decreasing Circles* is the polar opposite of his in *The Good Life*: one rebelling against suburbia and corporatism, the other a staunch defender of both. In the situation comedies of John Esmonde and Bob

Larbey we find the attitudes and snobberies of suburban life skilfully, almost heartbreakingly, satirised.

Demands for economic growth trump environmentalism in planning cases, be it fracking or high-speed rail. It was ever thus. A telling example of 1970s pre-nimby protesting took place in Potters Bar, Hertfordshire. It kicked off at 9 a.m. on New Year's Day 1975 when workers arrived to fell trees on leafy Santers Lane. Housebuilders Wates were intending to put up 163 homes on part of Wrotham Park Estate, land owned by a nearby manor. A resident spotted men with tree-felling equipment and alerted neighbours, who then spent the rest of the bank holiday obstructing the workmen. The following day they posted a watch on the woods from 7 a.m. while a Tree Preservation Order was being rushed through the offices of Hertfordshire County Council. Over a hundred people were involved in scuffles with police and woodsmen, and resident James Hurd was cut in the fight and charged with breach of the peace. Retired Lieutenant Colonel Alec Ball rode in on his electric wheelchair to the rescue of his wife Elsie, who he saw being carried from the battle scene. Nicholas Cole, a spokesman from the Wrotham Park Estate Company, spun *The Times* a line. 'The work has nothing whatever to do with the appeal that is coming up in April concerning the proposed development for part of the estate,' he said. 'It is an absolute coincidence that forestry work has been going ahead, because of the state of the trees.'[1] At 9 a.m. on New Year's Day?

Kristina's attitude was that she had to fight every case she could on the green belt to stop the concept becoming devalued through the courts. One case that had been troubling her concerned a field owned by Merton College, Oxford, which was green belt separating Leatherhead and Ashtead. The council granted permission to build on the field. Through it runs a bypass.

'The councillors were seriously saying at one point, "That's the green belt now, that's the barrier between the two settlement areas."' She was flabbergasted. 'What, *the road*? Rather than having green fields either side? And they were saying, that's perfectly all right because you've still got a separation. *But it's a motorway!*'

She was determined to show me the disputed forty-acre field which had kicked off all of the arguments between campaigners and developers. I wasn't sure what state it would be in when we got there, and when we turned from the lane and rested on the five-bar gate, bark chippings underfoot, the finality was shocking. What had been the chalk grassland Kristina had fought to protect was now an immaculate golf course. Bunkers, flags, greens and fairways. Clumps of trees and tall grass remaining, but none of the very tiny plants of the ancient habitat.

'This used to be full of the kind of bees and wasps that would have given an ecologist a fit,' said Kristina.

'In a *good* way.' But now the ancient scrubby grassland is dead, suffocated beneath a pristine glossy green shroud. A sinister act of green-on-green violence. The unique habitat has been carefully packed over with peat and sand and rolls of turf to create this artificial landscape. 'We lost that one,' said Kristina. 'We shouldn't have, and we'd even won it for a time.'

The trees on this chalk hill had been felled in the Iron Age, and sheep and goats introduced to graze there. But because the soil would have made poor agricultural land it was never ploughed up and planted.

'That continual grazing of that land created these tiny plants and everything that is chalk grassland,' said Kristina. 'This soil is so special and it takes thousands of years to evolve. And when you destroy it and destroy the contact with the chalk it doesn't come back. It's gone. And so it's been destroyed on Cherkley for the most part, and that's very upsetting to me.'

Still, she is remarkably philosophical now, as we talk, looking over what had until recently been an Iron-Age survival, and was now a single pantone green terrain for a few rich businesspeople to idly hit a ball with a stick.

'This is only a golf course and it is only chalk grassland habitat and most people don't understand what that means,' she said. 'But it is still open and green, and that's a good thing. I can't complain personally, I'm not prejudiced; if anything my house value's gone up! I don't care about that. There are much worse things and there are many more important cases to fight.' And then we walked back to the house.

There have always been smaller-scale, more personal battles in the green belt too, of course. My own trauma was mainly psychological, inflicted by boys with more to lose and girls whose smiles were all pet lambs and innocence. There was I, buck-toothed, boss-eyed, effeminate, posh-sounding, clever, bad at sports, never a joiner, always a loner. At a rough comprehensive on the edge of a big housing estate I was the easiest target going and got what would have surprised no one. I never mentioned being bullied to my family or the teachers. It was clear that this was what it was. I knew early on I was playing a long game, that sometime in the future things would get better. Not that I held out much hope of better treatment from adults either. I was too good, too clean, too weird for them. Everyone loves a snotty-nosed ruffian or a perfect princess. Play up to the narrow gender stereotypes from adverts and you've got it made.

Remarkably I only got into one fight, with a boy whose stammer and specs suggested a fear of becoming me. He declared one break time that we were fighting. We weren't. I was sitting there reading an Agatha Christie. No matter, he'd said the magic word and we were immediately surrounded by a baying mob screaming *Bun-dle!* I was at least self-aware enough to realise that no one would imagine I was the one involved in the fight. So in the chaos of the mob I fell to my knees, crawled backwards through the legs of the boys and girls crowded around, stood up at the edge of the circle, dusted myself down and wandered off. I could hear him furiously screaming my name, having humiliated himself in a crowd. Oh well. All the other boys wanted to be Ian Rush or Rambo, and here I was, strolling to the library, adjusting my imaginary bowler hat and brolly like John Steed in *The Avengers*.

Like a lot of shy children I never felt I belonged with other kids. It's a shame that none of us realised there were others who felt the same way, embedded as we were like Cold War spies in the suburban scene. With the open fields for company I had an advantage at least, because here I didn't have to make any effort to fit in. Instead I had acres of space in which to indulge my abnormalities. Not that they were allowed to stand as they were. An operation corrected my squint. Orthodontistry was making a token effort with my teeth, not that you'd notice. And as for the effeminacy, well no amount of bullying, humiliation or repeats of *The Sweeney* could beat that out of me. In the distance people seemed to be having the kind of knockabout schooldays catalogued by Madness in 'Baggy Trousers'. In contrast I seemed to be locked in some junior psychodrama, a *Play for Today* on the *Play Away* set.

When I was younger I did have one friend. Mary was my constant companion throughout infant school. She was everything to me: my confidante, my best mate, my co-explorer. She had only one fault: Mary was imaginary. I was aware of how strangely my older brothers and the grown-ups looked at me whenever I referenced her, the glances they exchanged with each other, the teasing, the amused references. I wasn't stupid, I knew full well that Mary didn't exist. But I just wanted someone to play with. And then one day even Mary was gone. Adults would ask about her and I'd not say anything. It was probably a relief for them: little John had stopped hanging out with his unmanly friend; that must mean he had real ones now. Instead I was lost in my imagination, talking to the trees and hawthorn bushes and hearing their replies. Loneliness hidden in plain sight.

Mary disappeared about the same time as I realised I fancied boys. Suit yourself, Mary. As a child I was best left to get on with exploring things by myself: Lego, cartooning, homosexuality. I had rather more success with the former. It was amazing how little I had to base my sexuality on. Sure, there were handsome male teachers and a few effortlessly sporty classmates, footballers in the paper and those tantalising glimpses of male crotches in the underwear section of the Littlewoods catalogue. But in the desert of a 1980s adolescence the leaps I had to make to transmute these glimpses of contraband into the stuff of male-on-male fantasy showed I was definitely keen. Given the available inspiration it was more likely I'd want to grow up to be Metal Mickey than gay.

I studied *The Importance of Being Earnest* for O-level English. I'd told my teacher, Carol Kay, that I'd been getting into the plays of Joe Orton. She thought I'd like Oscar Wilde too. There was a production of the play at Croydon Fairfield Halls by a local amateur dramatics group called the Croydon Histrionics. It was a marvellous affair, with bells ringing before people had reached them and actors choking on sandwiches. Afterwards someone in my class asked me if the actor playing Jack Worthing reminded me of anyone. 'No,' I said. 'Who?' 'You,' she said. My classmates laughed.

They were right, I thought at the time, though not perhaps in the way they meant. Living on the edge of the estate, being secretly gay and obviously gay at the same time, I felt myself to be, like Wilde's hero, Ernest in town and Jack in the country. As a metaphor for hidden gay lives it has never been surpassed. How transgressive of me, and how nice of my classmates to notice. But with the best will in the world I knew that wasn't really what they meant. The man playing Jack Worthing spent the entire production clomping up and down the stage delivering Wilde's witticisms with the subtlety of a heavy bomber. It wasn't the character, it was the actor and his ponderous, galumphing campness that reminded them of me. Here was I with the sophistication of a child dressed in their parent's clothes, and the élan of a photocopier engineer explaining the finer points of toner.

By the time I was thirteen I could draw Paul Rutherford, the gay clone from Frankie Goes to

Hollywood, with the ease with which I had once drawn Dangermouse. I blame Paul Rutherford for a mistaken sense of empowerment I'd felt, back then, when faced with four boys determined to do me down. This row of lads followed me out through the school gates one lunchtime, and I could hear their muttered jokes about me, which was a not unusual occurrence. One, the boy who'd once attempted to fight me, called out, 'John, are you queer?' Mild laughter. I thought for a moment, and then decided, fuck it, what was there to lose? 'Yes,' I said. Cue knee-bending, gurgling, incoherent hysteria. I decided immediately that it was not going to be worth the fuss. 'Yes,' I said again. 'Queer teeth.' One of the few advantages about having so many weak spots is that it is easy to transfer hurt from one onto another. My orthodontically immune bucked teeth were the weak spot from another age, back in junior school before jokes at the expense of my sexuality were suddenly in vogue. *Queer teeth* might have seemed a poor comeback, and it was, but I knew it would work. Because the general consensus was that I might well be queer, but I was also too naïve to know it. Only my worldly peers could possibly understand. Poor John. Well, as I sat at home knocking out another drawing of a naked Paul Rutherford, I thought about how it suited me to play the innocent. Because if they knew just how utterly, wholeheartedly, filthily queer I really was, then God knows where that would have ended.

Like most suburban gay kids of my generation, and
a good few of the rest, I have no childhood memories
of flirtation, first kisses or romance, of practising for
adult love and heartbreak. Instead, at the age of seventeen I still hadn't even held hands with anyone. I guess
the spectre of AIDS was at the back of my mind, but
given what a specimen of physical unloveliness I
presented, sex seemed about as likely to me as space
travel or eating tomatoes. And so my first encounter
was unexpected. I met him on a 130 bus one evening
after my Thursday-evening shift in a Croydon bookshop. A young black guy I'd never seen before sitting
too close, talking to me, from the start to the end of
the line. It was a long way into the journey before I
realised I was being chatted up. I couldn't believe my
luck. And on a packed bus too, people all around
engrossed in their Rosumunde Pilchers, listening to
their Walkmans or smoking. My stop was the last on
the route, from the centre of town to the edge of New
Addington, with just my street and the trees beyond.
And he stayed with me. When we got off I wasn't sure
what I was meant to do next, and stood around
awkwardly, saying goodbye but hoping it wasn't. He
beckoned me to follow him, and we slipped down an
alleyway next to the Chinese takeaway at the end of
the small parade of shops. In the dark we ended up in
the takeaway's overgrown back garden. I was terrified
someone would find us, but too excited to say no. It
was hard to enjoy myself while keeping an eye out for

stray takeaway customers or the chef on a fag break. I doubt they'd have approved. Not in their back yard, anyway.

This became the shove I needed to come out to my parents. I decided to do it during an advert break in *Taggart*, because I knew that afforded me a short window as everyone would want to be concentrating on the TV again rather than wanting to go into more detail. Marj didn't bat an eyelid, and said, *Oh, is that all* while smiling supportively. John started to mumble something about *phases* before Marj told him to shut up. And that was that. It was barely ever mentioned again, partly because a distinct lack of boyfriends for the following two decades made it a rather barren topic.

Finding campaigners to speak out against green belt development is relatively straightforward. But what about the other side of the story? I visited Barton Willmore, Britain's biggest private planning company, who are doing the kind of work local government used to do. Ian Tant, a cheery round-faced man who'd worked in planning since the 1970s, was putting to me the argument from the other side of the fence from Kristina. Barton Willmore has worked with all of the major housebuilders in Britain. Ian knew a fair bit about how they worked and what they were after.

'From a private developer's point of view green belt is a tricky thing to do,' he explained to me. 'It's high risk. For instance, a developer comes to us and says, "I've got the opportunity on this greenfield site. It's on the edge of a town that happens to be in the green belt. What do you think the prospects are?" ' Not great, was Ian's feeling. That bit of green belt might not be under review. Even if it were, the chances of their proposals succeeding were slim. And would the company be willing to shoulder the risk? Generally not. And so Ian's experience was that the green belt really was putting off the majority of developers. 'There aren't armies of people marching out there looking for pieces of green belt land, which is what I think the CPRE perception is. It's targeted and it's intelligent.' Ian's attempt to make it seem less sinister slightly backfired; he made it sound like a drone attack.

We got talking about the origins of the green belt, and the postwar Act that made it all possible. Ian felt the whole process in those early days was fundamentally flawed. The main problem was they hadn't factored in the vast timescale it took to get any of this work done, and the disruption that it would cause in the meantime. His remarks reminded me of Richard Edwards', the tree officer for Croydon, who spoke of the vast amount of time it took for forests to regenerate and for his work to be seen. Both urban planners and foresters were working to a timescale well beyond the expedient demands of local politicians. The plans and reviews, the strategies and policies, could only protect so much. At some point life takes over.

The kind of slackness and anarchy that ensues in this time gap was railed against by a famously angry young man in 1955. A year before John Osborne brought the phenomenon to the attention of the nation in his play *Look Back in Anger,* a young critic was giving a practical demonstration in the pages of *Architectural Review* magazine. *Outrage!* by Ian Nairn took up the whole of the June 1955 edition and painted a picture of an England where the countryside had been reduced to 'a limbo of shacks, bogus rusticities, wire and aerodromes, set in some fir-poled fields'.[2] Nairn laid into the suburbanisation of our outdoors. His co-conspirator, Gordon Cullen, took photographs of the interchangeable straggling edges of towns: Stratford, Warrington, Northwich, Stafford, Newcastle-under-Lyme, Oxford, Romsey, Bolton-le-Sands, Birmingham, Southampton, Carlisle. In them we see near-identical thirties semis, overhead telephone wires and ugly lampposts looming over lifeless acres of tarmac. Nairn termed this landscape 'subtopia'. It was everyone's back yard, and Nairn didn't like it.

He even came up with a checklist, for the reader to spot the worst outrages in their own subtopian fringes. It begins: 'How many Things in Fields are there in your parish? Are they indispensable? Have you any idea why they are there at all?' Half way through and he's begun channelling an inner J.B. Priestley. 'If there is an arterial road, has it brought a trail of cafes and garages strung out from one parish boundary to the other?' – a question that brings to mind Sheila Kaye-Smith's observation from 1938 that Britain's beauty spots were living off of the 'immoral earnings' of cafés and gift shops. Finally, Nairn asks, 'What does your visual profit and loss schedule since 1939 look like?'[3] I wonder how many people actually did this: stood on a village green or layby, marking down the results on a postcard to send off to Nairn. One thing that may have made *Outrage!* more topical was that by 1955 the Conservative government was beginning to generate a boom in private housebuilding, and with it came a real fear of a return to 1930s-style ribbon development.

Nairn's truculence was an inspiration to a generation of young architects and planners. In May 1956, for example, Liverpool University's Architectural Society put on an exhibition of photos and sketches of these subtopian landscapes. Also called *Outrage!*, it was held in the bomb-damaged Church of St Luke. Nairn came to the opening and provided some typically tough words. Planners, he said, 'dump an amorphous pudding of two-storey houses just four fields' width from the edge of Liverpool'. Soon 'there will be no countryside to gallop into, and the planners, like lost sheep, will ask where the green belt is'. This apocalyptic vision hung over much of his work. Writing in the *Observer* in 1965 he called the green belt 'a tourniquet which stops the bleeding but doesn't heal the wound'.[4]

There were people trying to tackle the source of all this outrage. One such was Duncan Campbell, who had started his career in the 1960s as a woodsman at the Forestry Commission, an organisation which you might think was conservationist, but which was instead more famous for the blanket planting of 'useful' non-indigenous trees wherever it could get away with it. By the early sixties the government had informed the Forestry Commission that it needed to pay more attention to appropriate planting. This led to the appointment of Sylvia Crowe, the mother of landscape architecture in Britain, to the organisation. Crowe had become Britain's foremost landscape architect following her work on the 'green wedges' in Harlow, one of the first new towns built after the war. After a couple of years with the Forestry Commission she began to realise there was too much work and she couldn't keep up with it, and so the Forestry Commission decided to train its own landscape architects to help. Duncan Campbell was the first.

'She was my mentor, if you like,' said Duncan, 'or I was her protégé, however you want to call it. She was fantastic. She had a very fine sense of humour, and she could get hoary old foresters eating out of her hand in no time at all. But she could explain very simply the very important issues that were the order of the day, whether they were planting or harvesting coups, or the design of a new road or recreation area. She was able to put pictures into words which was a real gift.'

In her 1956 book *Tomorrow's Landscapes* Sylvia Crowe addressed the same problems Nairn had brought up, and instead of journalistic hand-wringing offered practical solutions. 'For the regeneration of the English landscape, there are two outstanding needs', she wrote. 'One is to make good the depleted tree population, the other is to reclaim the waste lands.'[5] She was obsessed with tree planting, and so had been an ideal recruit for the Forestry Commission, even if her attitude to landscape conservation was rather more modern than that of the militaristic organisation. 'The planners' attitude to any space near a town', she wrote, 'should be "Can I plant trees on it? If not, why not?"'[6]

You can see the shadow of Nairn, too, in a 1965 book by modernist architect Lionel Brett called *Landscape in Distress*. He particularly focused on Oxford, whose green belt had been put in place to help preserve the character of the small city by containing it. Around the outside he found 'a beauty-spot with scots pines and car parks'; 'roadside squalor'; the 'industrial blight beside the railway'; and 'an old car dump' which 'no doubt hoped to evade discovery'. Then there were the smallholdings, or, as he describes them, 'the whole shackery, with an old tyre dump, poles and wires ad lib, a crude water tower – all exposed on the bleak and treeless crest'. Coming to the end of his trip he finds 'as wretched a row of builder's allsorts as we have seen anywhere. This, appropriately enough, was a final slap in the face.'[7] If only county-sized organisations could see places like Oxford as a living whole, he argued, we wouldn't need these 'immature' ideas like green belts and AONBs. Here is John Lennon's 'Imagine' reworked by a policy wonk.

Brett reserved his greatest upset for Nuneham, to the south-east of the city. Here there were woods planted by Capability Brown, but Brett could only see slow decline. The great house, occupied during wartime, had been sold to Oxford University, who'd leased it to an absentee landlord. The gardens had been neglected, and a prison created on the site along with huge national grid power lines. The 1960s and 70s saw Britain embrace progress, while also being repulsed by some of the effects. As Nan Fairbrother, the brilliant landscape historian, put it: 'loving the country now means loving the pre-industrial country, and it is bitter to realise that most of the landscape we still enjoy unreservedly is where the twentieth century has not reached'.[8]

The realities of protecting this sort of land were more complex than anyone had quite realised. By 1960 there were fourteen green belts mooted in England, and they appeared in the back yards of forty different local councils. Each one had its own public inquiry. Take, for example, the Lancashire green belt, created in the hope of preventing the many large towns in the county from coalescing. At a local inquiry for East Merseyside in March 1960, lawyer T.H. Pigot, who did a lot of work for the local farmers, spoke up with business interests in mind. 'The green belt is not some sort of shrine at which one must bow and worship in uncritical and ecstatic adulation', he said. What the local people in East Merseyside needed were new houses, not some semi-derelict land protected by some distant Lancashire county planners. New houses on the land could be profitably sold, too, if it wasn't for that pesky policy. And he had another bone to pick with the scheme. 'We must not regard the green belt as green in this part of Lancashire', he told the inquiry. 'This part of Lancashire has been disfigured for generations and there is much sterile land. Yet apparently some of it is included in the green belt', he scoffed.[9]

E.H. Doubleday, an official from Hertfordshire, claimed that no planning document had ever been so popular with the public as Sandys' 1955 circular. Well, it's not like there was much competition. Doubleday mentioned it at a meeting of the Town Planning Institute in May 1957 to demonstrate the gulf between Sandys' fine words and the reality of putting them into action. He spoke of devious people who were already trying to get round it, inventing fictitious smallholdings in order to build a house, or claiming to expand for agricultural needs and selling the resulting houses to rich incomers. The new rules allowed farmers to put up homes for their employees, but a survey showed that fewer than one in ten ended up occupied by farm workers.

An anonymous planner followed Doubleday into print in *The Times* in March 1963. Here city executives were described as fighting tooth-and-nail to gain a foothold in the green belt. 'Once secure,' wrote the official, 'they bar the passage to all who would follow them and henceforth are the loudest champions of green belt inviolability.' But once there, these executives are shocked by what the countryside actually contains: the planting of new forests or tractors working round the clock or the noise of chickens or dogs. And so the townies begin their protests. 'Their whines went unheeded,' noted the planner 'when directed against beef silos, pylons, reservoirs and power saws.'[10]

If green belts were causing headaches for local authorities then it was the virginal 'white land' on the edge of these belts that got housebuilders into a lather. The very existence of white land had created a boom in land prices fuelled by speculators. It had been for that very reason that Patrick Abercrombie had said that white land should never have been shown on maps. Worse, because white land didn't have a limit on compensation as green belt did, the costs could spiral ever upward. Councils were finding that they couldn't buy it to stop the developers even if they wanted to. And so this land, which had been intended to be banked and only built on when absolutely needed, was being panic-bought by both speculators and councils as they attempted to outmanoeuvre one another.

All of this organisation of land in the mid-twentieth century, from green belts to National Parks, had been the result of modernity. But by the late sixties, in the heat of that space-age moment, the vogue for all things modern was on its way out. The buildings, the cars, the style, the technology. There were some people who had never taken to it, like the folk music revivalists of the fifties, singers like Ewan MacColl and Peggy Seeger, who displayed their love of rural traditions in song. The green belt and new town heartlands of Hertfordshire and Bedfordshire were the places to go to hear them. They performed at The Cock or The Peahen in St Albans, The Spinning Wheel in Hemel Hempstead, or in Luton Folk Club. This rejection of modernity grew through the next two decades, and is central to Margaret Drabble's 1977 novel *The Ice Age*. She tells the story of 1960s property developers who have moved to the country for a more 'authentic' life, away from the urban decay they have helped create. At the close of the decade, Howard Newby, in his non-fiction study of rural Britain, *Green and Pleasant Land*, records an affluent middle-class commuter exodus to the houses, barns and villages in the green belts around prosperous cities. With it he spots a trend for artefacts that represent a rejection of progress and embrace instead the hand-crafted values of John Ruskin and William Morris. Newby lists the suspects, 'from Friends of the Earth to Laura Ashley fabric designs, from the vogue for wholemeal bread to that for corn dollies, from the enthusiasm for "self-sufficiency" to that for turning 1960s tourist shops into 1970s craft centres'.

Yet for all of this romanticised rustication, the reality of the countryside of the 1970s was more likely to be asbestos barns, pesticides, artificial insemination and battery farming. Newby pointed the finger for this mismatch between reality and fantasy at the Hampstead Fabians, who had directed the protectionist policies of the postwar era, led by sentimental notions of the great outdoors. Instead, a cabal of farmers and landowners ran the place, with a vested interest in preserving the status quo. Green belts played into both of these realities: rules on construction would restrict the change of land use in the country, and would provide the perfect backdrop for those middle-class escapees aiming to live the good life. It is a reminder that, despite superficial appearances, green belts are as much products of modernity as the jet engine, flat roofs or polyester slacks.

A growing interest in Britain's rural heritage was reflected in the rising membership of countryside charities. In 1952 the RSPB had fewer than 7,000 members. By 1977 there were a quarter of a million, and by 1998 they'd quadrupled that. The National Trust, too, had just 10,000 members in 1945, and 200,000 by 1972. This tripled in just six years during that environmentally minded decade, and now stands at well over four million. And they weren't the only people venturing out into the country. In 1970 there were five million campers and caravanners in Britain, three million anglers and a million golfers. Disappointingly for the CPRE, only 5 per cent of people visiting the countryside were recorded as using the Country Code.

Just as Ian Nairn might observe, the reality of our postwar countryside might have come as a shock to incomers. A farmer's wife was overheard by Sylvia Crowe to express her delight at all the green space in London compared to her rural home. 'Lovely to have all that grass to walk on in the parks. At home you couldn't set foot off the road.'[11] The timeless image of village life was also brought into question by Nan Fairbrother. While the village might superficially appear unspoiled, she observed that it could only exist thanks to the wider industrial economy, from power stations to factories. She condemned this as a form of environmental cheating, 'preserving one landscape at the expense of another'.[12] Nearly five decades on and that illusion still pervades much of life. Fairbrother had a knack of skewering the pastoral dreams of townsfolk too. 'Planners (like us) may dream of wheat waving gold to our doorsteps and of mild-eyed cows gazing over our garden fences,' she wrote, 'but we are all of us urban generations, out of touch with any practical knowledge of cows and wheat fields.'[13]

The ink was barely dry on the Ministry of Housing and Local Government's 1962 green belt booklet when new minister, Keith Joseph, wanted it re-examined. The son of the owner of one of Britain's biggest building contractors, Joseph saw his mission as constructing houses rather than protecting land. With pressures already growing, his 1963 White Paper turned all of the planners' hard work on its head, asking local authorities who were still trying to confirm where their green belt boundaries actually were which bits of it they could now lose.

Joseph became the first minister seriously to suggest building on the green belt. His White Paper claimed that not all of the 840 square miles of green belt round London was essential and by November he was saying that 'some changes may have to be considered'.[14] He was in tune with people like Harold Bellman, Chairman of Abbey National, who said that while he wanted to protect green belt, 'the whole South East of England is becoming overcrowded, uncomfortable and unduly expensive to live in'. His solution? 'There is an urgent need for more house building land. There is still more urgent need to move the magnet of employment to new fields away from the present large cities, so that families can live and grow up away from the depressing restrictions of megalopolitan Britain.'[15] Northern Powerhouse, anyone?

One of Joseph's last acts as minister before the Conservative government was kicked out in 1964 was to commission a study into the state of the congested south-east of England. His ultimate aim was to provide for population growth, relieve the pressure on London and make enough land available to end the housing shortage. Predictions of an explosion in both population and car ownership meant that the government had to think big. Even if all the new towns that had been planned were built, they still expected 400,000 people to be made homeless by 1981. And the report suggested some alternatives to the rigid green belt agreed by Sandys. Maybe the inner edge could be pushed out half a mile all round to give lots more land for construction? Or how about a 'star-shaped' halo of green wedges, where more country would be pulled into the city with building pushed out around it. 'All land in the green belt should have a positive purpose,' went the report, 'whether it be its quality as farmland, its mineral resources, its special scenic value, its suitability for public open space or playing fields for Londoners.'[16] The green belt's easy ride was over. Now it would have to work to justify its position.

By the mid-sixties, expansion had begun again in towns and estates around London. Waiting lists meant that New Addington needed to grow, with eighty-seven acres to the north suggested for building. The land bordered Kent's green belt, and the county argued hard against the plans. Two months later the proposal was approved, and a densely packed extension to New Addington, called Fieldway, was waved through, much to the disgust of its Kentish neighbours. They had another battle on their hands with housebuilders Span, who were intent on constructing a modernist village in the green belt near Dartford. Span was an example of an exemplarily responsible developer, against the (occasionally unfair) cliché of the big bad wolf. Span insisted on incorporating large amounts of green space in its carefully designed and innovative estates, and its work is infused with a gently utopian vision of a more open, egalitarian future. None of that cut any mustard with Kent County Council. A report by its planning department in 1963 showed that there would be a worrying doubling of long-distance commuting by 1971. It predicted that all of the county's newcomers would be commuters, needing to travel through the green belt to work.

It was into this environment that Span made a typically idealistic application to put up what it called 'a complete environment for country living'.[17] By late 1964 Richard Crossman had allowed it to go ahead, much against the wishes of the local authorities. 'Every time a little bit [of green belt] is nibbled away it encourages others', complained Sir William Richardson of Kent County Council. 'Any extra development in the green belt or just beyond it aggravates the commuter problem, which is already at saturation point.'[18] The first of these contested houses were completed in 1967, and opened by that ghost from the past, Keith Joseph. So, had Eric Lyons, Span's architect, ruined the green belt? Ian Nairn, that hater of all things suburban, didn't think so. 'The establishment may not enjoy him,' he wrote in the *Observer*, 'but the landscape is in his debt.'[19]

Ash, the neighbouring village in Kent, was home to one of the green belt's most celebrated modern legends. Clive King wrote his 1963 novel *Stig of the Dump* as an antidote to the sleepiness all around. Inspired by the nearby chalk quarries that were being slowly turned into landfill sites, he imagined a prehistoric society left undisturbed in the Kent woodlands. One day a boy called Barney falls into a chalk pit and through the roof of the makeshift home of Stig, a young caveman. From those first few pages I was hooked. Everything about *Stig of the Dump* felt irresistibly right. It was as if Clive King had access to the contents of my head. The setting might have been my back yard, the edge of a built-up area beside scrappy woods filled with old rubbish. I could see how a landfill site could be home to something fantastical. I understood the appeal of an imaginary friend, of course. And the idea of a secret society of cavemen living over in the woods didn't represent some threatening invasion, it was magic. *Stig of the Dump* took the fantastical imagination of E. Nesbit and John Masefield and placed it in a realm I understood: an unremarkable boy on the edge of the green belt discovering something amazing.

Shadows in Spring: Grief in the Green Belt

When the wind comes in from the right direction you can occasionally hear strange cries in the Bedfordshire hills. That wheezing call is an antelope. That deep roar is a lion. That trumpeting, an elephant. What are those displaced creatures doing here, on the tail-end of the Chilterns, near the National Trust tearoom of Dunstable Downs or those other familiar green belt standards, a private golf course and a chalk quarry? As I investigate the history of Whipsnade, Britain's biggest zoo, some heavily signposted parallels hove into view. It was created in 1926 on the site of a derelict farm and founded as an overspill to its sister in Regent's Park. Animals from the cramped and overcrowded urban jungle of London Zoo were moved out to this bigger site in the green belt over the years. The elephants left their modernist concrete dwellings in London, designed by Hugh Casson in 1962, for the green expanse of Whipsnade in the mid-1990s. I wonder how they have adapted to their new life? Pretty well, it would seem. They move as a small herd as far from the visitors as they can manage, or at least they did on the day I visited. It's easy to sympathise with the elephants – their desire for some quiet time away from the crowds, picnicking in the country, trying to fit in inconspicuously with their neighbours, the camels and hippopotamuses. I wonder what they remember of their time in the city?

A chalk lion was cut out on the nearby hillside in 1933, advertising the zoo to the many passengers on the busy London to Birmingham train route. Nearby stands another, less well-known but no less remarkable, collection of specimens of the natural world. But this one is a more sombre attraction, and of remarkable flora rather than fauna. From a car park on the edge of the woods, Whipsnade Tree Cathedral looks like any other small country park. The handy National

Trust information board tells a different story. Rather than the managed landscape you get at, say, Lee Valley, with copses, meadows, glades and trails, there was nothing faux-naturalistic about the woodland here. The diagram shows a formal, schematic layout: long avenues of trees, shrubs planted in circles, symmetrical patterns and right angles. The plan is a recognisable one, a great cruciform projected onto the woodland floor: a medieval cathedral made from living trees. Whipsnade Tree Cathedral is a memorial to the dead of the First World War.

Walking through the porch, a grand structure of sturdy oak trees, I went to investigate the many circular features: the chancel, formed of slender silver birch; the vivid leaves of beech and field maple in the autumn chapel, all burning away in vibrant reds. In March 1918, at the fag-end of the Great War, a young soldier named Edmund Blyth experienced the loss of two old friends, Arthur Bailey and John Bennett, killed in action. Years later, on a trip to see Giles Gilbert Scott's then-unfinished Liverpool Anglican Cathedral, Blyth and his wife pondered ways in which they could commemorate the fallen. Something as permanent and monumental as Gilbert Scott's endeavours appealed, and they even owned twenty acres of land on the chalk hills of Bedfordshire to help make it a reality. But the idea of creating a cathedral not just in the woods, but of it, came to them on their return journey. 'We talked of this as we drove south through the Cotswold Hills on our way home,' recalled Blyth, 'and it was while we were doing this that I saw the evening sun light up a coppice of trees on the side of a hill. It occurred to me then that here was something more beautiful still and the idea formed of building a cathedral with trees.' And so they set about it, taking the elements of medieval cathedral cruciform layout – towers, chapels, a nave, cloisters, transepts and chancel – and rendering them in living trees and shrubs.

It was slow work. Throughout the thirties Blyth and associate Albert Bransom, a local man whose son Frederick had been killed in the Somme in 1916, planted all of the major features that form the cathedral today. But the coming war stopped progress, and at the end of it Blyth found himself working far away, for the military government in occupied Berlin. When he returned in 1947 the landscape had become overgrown, and he began the work of restoration. The cathedral wasn't just a gesture; by 1952 it would hold ecumenical services, and it remains little changed to this day. Blyth's family even help keep the tree cathedral going, alongside hardy National Trust volunteers.

That clear autumn afternoon I walked respectfully through the living church. On the perimeter enormous ash trees replicated the cloisters, casting long shadows along the leaf-strewn floor in the low sunlight. At the centre, loo-brushes of Norway spruce formed the Christmas chapel. There were families with small children throwing fallen leaves into the air, and the occasional walker pursuing their dogs through the intricate network of hedges and shrubs. With the trees so denuded it was sometimes hard to make out the cathedral's more complex patterns and enclosures. Was this circle of twigs and damp bark the Lady Chapel, or simply an unmanaged copse which had grown up without anyone noticing? But the grand avenues and curves were unmistakable. Here the annual cycles of the trees were a kind of grief, a celebration of ongoing life in the spring, an acknowledgement of frailty and mortality in the autumn, a perfect memorial. A classic green belt curiosity, the perfect site for reflection and acceptance of the way of things, and a great place to hang out and feel a bit sad.

The rings of countryside around our towns, be they managed or neglected, are themselves caught in a cycle. Living death, or dying life. Here the cycle is – like the belt itself – a gesture. In farmers' fields crops are cut down not by the turn of the seasons but by the great mechanical scythes of combine harvesters. Wild flowers live on here at the whim of green belt policy, the ground they grow on the unconsidered, abandoned scraps, not the choice parcels divided up for roads, industry or agriculture. As the seasons turn and the decades pass, the only change here seems to be decay, the repetition of the gestures of the previous year, once more with less feeling. Signs of human activity in the neglected areas are slowly reclaimed by creepers and roots, electricity junction boxes and wire fences buried by the quiet forces of nature.

These acres of green belt fields, away from the country parks or areas of outstanding natural beauty, don't feel like a riot of abundance or a celebration of the bounty of life. Instead they have the sombre tone of widow's weeds: black veils and subdued emotion. Mourning the disappearance of ancient forests, unable to gather enough momentum to grow back before the human hand comes to attend with another new thought, to strim and dig and dump and fill. They are an attempt at creating stasis, commemorating a cycle and fixing it for years to come in a state of subtle decay. The massive tracts of farmland that make up the majority of our green belts are the custodians of those zombie vestments. And it was only through the application of some of the twentieth century's most insidious markers of progress that we would reduce our farmland to this undead way of life.

On 22 November 1944 Professor I.M. Heilbron, chair of organic chemistry at Imperial College, gave a talk at the Royal Society. He explained how the shirts of soldiers serving overseas in such inhospitable landscapes as the jungles of Burma and the deserts of Egypt had been impregnated with a new chemical which successfully removed lice and bugs: *dichlorodiphenyltrichloroethane*, or DDT. *The Times* covered the talk, reporting that 'the discovery of DDT heralded a new era in man's ceaseless fight for mastery against disease'.[1]

Very soon the same newspaper was running adverts from Shell Chemicals on the efficacy of another new pesticide: aldrin. 'Many farmers have used aldrin this year with outstanding success' ran the copy of a 1954 effort. The following year Shell claimed, 'Aldrin is fast becoming recognized as being the best of all soil insecticides. A little goes a long way and lasts a long time.' The final ad in this series ran in 1960, by which time it was reported that there were 50,000 pesticide spray kits in England and Wales alone, being used on five to six million acres of our countryside. By this time the tone of reportage on the subject had begun to change. 'By the end of the season they will have been "raining down a ghastly dew" on five or six million acres at least to the risk, as some think, of human life and health and the destruction of wild life and game', ran a report in *The Times* in July 1960. 'Their users see them merely as a means to an end for cleaner crops and less work.'[2]

The following year, 1961, saw the emergence of some troubling statistics: a growth in bird deaths at a rate of four times those of the previous year, affecting forty species. 'Birds that were dying were often reported as standing about shivering' went the RSPB's *Bird Notes* newsletter. The creatures were spotted gasping, floundering and overbalancing. Concerns began circulating in government that pesticides were causing this worrying pattern of avian mortality, so much so that in July 1961 the Ministry of Agriculture, Fisheries and Food announced that there would be a springtime ban on the use of the pesticides aldrin, dieldrin and heptachlor. Yet for politicians, concerns about the damaging effect of the wheat bulb fly that those pesticides were being used to eradicate were just as pressing. The chemicals were still cleared as safe for sowing that autumn and winter.

Wider public concern was raised when a book from the US, *Silent Spring* by Rachel Carson, was released in Britain the following year. The eerie title was inspired by Keats, and Carson used it to imagine the effect of pesticides on the countryside in years to come. 'There was a strange stillness. The birds, for example – where had they gone? . . . It was a spring without voices.'[3] In the US she was attacked by the corporate scientific community, but defended by academics and, as the reputation of the book spread, by the reading public. She revealed that since 1940 some 200 chemicals had been created to kill insects, weeds and vermin. The British edition contained fascinating additional information on the plight of our own wildlife. A powerful introduction by Labour politician Edward Shackleton told the tale of Tumby in rural Lincolnshire. Surveys there had seen a massive increase in the number of dead birds counted at the turn of the sixties, with 6,000 in the spring of 1961 alone. Pheasants were particularly badly affected, and not only were there fewer hatched, but a significant proportion of those that did soon died. An analysis of the pheasant eggs found traces of *benzene hexachloride* in them, a chemical found in many pesticides. Then there were the peregrine falcons, which by 1962 had mostly vanished from the south of England, and which in the North and Scotland were suffering from an infant mortality rate of one in two, again linked to chemical compounds found in their eggs. In a further introductory essay to *Silent Spring*, ecologist Julian Huxley remarked on the sudden disappearance of butterflies, and the cuckoos that eat their caterpillars. Bringing us right back to Keats, Huxley quoted his brother Aldous, who'd remarked on reading the book that 'we are losing half the subject-matter of English poetry'.[4]

The same year that *Silent Spring* was published in Britain, the Ministry of Agriculture, Fisheries and Food released a leaflet, *Chemicals for the Gardener*, which recommended some twenty-six DDT-based products for the home. In 1965 it was recommended that the damaging chlorinated hydrocarbons DDT, aldrin, dieldrin and heptachlor should be withdrawn from sale in Britain. Yet aldrin and dieldrin weren't withdrawn until 1973, and 1974 in fact saw an *increase* in the use of DDT. It wasn't banned until 1986. In Britain pesticides have been responsible for the decline of everything from skylarks and turtle-doves to harvest mice and great crested newts. In his 2012 book *Silent Spring Revisited* the naturalist Conor Mark Jameson recorded forty bird species that had disappeared from a single estate in Buckinghamshire since 1963, including the whinchat, cirl bunting, wood warbler and corncrake. While living in Cambridgeshire in 1994, Jameson became involved in surveying a random square of the local landscape for the national Breeding Birds Survey. His account is heartbreaking. 'I gave up on walking these fields. I found them to be so lifeless and soul-destroying. Even a sunny morning couldn't redeem them.' The local farmer whose fields he was walking was interested to know what wildlife he'd found living on his land. 'I didn't count much. There wasn't much to count. The highlight was a large covey of grey partridges . . . I found the exercise in general dispiriting.'[5]

As these old pesticides were slowly being phased out or banned, a new form, the neonicotinoids, was developed in the 1980s. Based on nicotine, these insecticides seemingly resulted in a less toxic legacy than the chlorinated hydrocarbons. Yet they have been a major factor in a decline in bee populations, disrupting the way their brains work. Affected bees are observed to be much slower than normal and unable to feed, exhibiting tremors and convulsions. It seems that the pesticides don't kill them, but they do affect the colony's ability to feed themselves. Given the seriousness of the problem, in May 2013 the European Union placed a temporary ban on neonicotinoid use while research was carried out. The British government voted against the ban.

~

When I approached Fairchildes Farm I was greeted by a hand-painted sign by the gate. *Fairchilds Farm* it read, the misspelling jarring like the Fawlty Towers sign. Before it, on a small green, there was an awkwardly placed pond, perfectly round, lined and filled with water. Malcolm Mott, the farmer, told me it was a bomb crater. After all, we were very near Biggin Hill, an important Battle of Britain aerodrome. The landscape here was full of the accidents of human intervention, by-products of farming, war and legislation. One of the things Malcolm had most noticed is the way that the processes of farming have sped up since he first came here to work in the 1960s. The sixty-seven-acre field he farms down by Kent Gate Way used to take three days to plough with two tractors, he told me. Now a single tractor can do all that work in half the time. Not that he needed to plough these days, as the drill he owns can work the seed straight into stubble.

'You can drill it and roll it in one, and it's jobbed,' he said with great satisfaction. Malcolm farms 600 acres and used to employ eight men; now it's just him and one man, Tony, a sixty-four-year-old tractor driver who retires next year. 'What happens next I don't know,' said Malcolm. Apprentices, I suggest. 'We used to have apprentices from Hadlow College for the summer. We had a couple of good ones but in the end we gave it up. You're spending your time helping them and showing them, which is all right but you're not doing what you normally do, and get on and do it and it's done.' He worried about what would happen to them in the years when the farm was financially stretched. 'We're here to make money,' he reminded me. 'That's the basic problem. Well, it's not a problem, it's life!'

The speed of progress in farming, the march to constant obsolescence and tight margins, dominates Malcolm's life. Not least in the way that he controls pests. He uses weed killer on the fields – 'otherwise you wouldn't get the yields of crops' – but long gone are the old insecticides. Mainly because he keeps bees on the farm. There are seven hives near where we are standing, and another eight down by that far Kent Gate Way field.

'I love 'em pollenating the beans,' he said. 'So we don't use anything that would touch the bees and we haven't lost a beehive in twenty years.'

His main crops are wheat, oats, beans and grass for hay. The field opposite my old house was fallow this year, due to a collapse in corn prices, and the valley was covered in a soft green pelt. The neighbouring one had been taken for meadow as part of a green steward-ship project.

'I haven't touched it,' said Malcolm. 'It's there for wild birds and all that sort of thing.' 'Is that working?' I asked. 'Well, they pay me for it,' he said, bluntly. 'It's nothing to do with the government; it's the EU. For what they call *greening*.' This was a couple of months before the referendum. Since then I've wondered what will happen to those uneconomic fields, without that guaranteed funding to encourage wildlife. When pushed, Malcolm didn't seem particularly fussed by the creatures being attracted or the success of the scheme. More urgent was the effect it was having on the locals. 'You have to leave six-foot margins from a hedge. Which is a problem here, because if people see a gap of six or ten foot, it's a *lovely* place to put rubbish.'

A 1957 Worcestershire County Council report remarked upon green belt parcels too small for modern farming, and too near the urban land to do it successfully. Once upon a time these areas had been thought of as desirable building plots, but the creation of the green belt killed that too. Unloved by farmers and unattainable for developers, these areas soon became neglected and in need of management. Further out in the big fields the effects of aggressive management were being criticised too. The pace of change would continue to accelerate. By 1970 there were half a million tractors and 60,000 combine harvesters in Britain. Government grants were in place to help farmers create bigger, more productive fields by combining them, at the expense of hedgerows. By 1980, 140,000 miles of hedgerows had been removed since the war in England and Wales.

In the midst of these rapidly changing times two conferences were held in the sixties, called Countryside in 1970, imagining the future of the British landscape. With a panel of farmers, environmentalists, ramblers and country dwellers, the conferences pontificated on everything from leisure to agriculture. Their thoughts helped formulate the 1968 Countryside Act, which decided, among other things, on the creation of country parks to take the pressure off the larger National Parks. Country parks were recreational areas accessible from dense suburbs, with amenities such as toilets, car parks and a café added to the wild landscape. Because of their need to be near towns and cities, the majority of Britain's country parks are in the green belt, from the Pollok Country Park in Glasgow to Wandlebury Hill Fort in Cambridgeshire. The Countryside in 1970 conferences fed into a bigger project still: European Conservation Year 1970. A kind of environmental Eurovision, the Conservation Year brought issues that had hitherto been thought of as the fringe concerns of hippies to the mainstream of government and respectability. The tone had shifted since the war. Cheery patriotic visions of a countryside fit for all had given way to a rather more bleak assessment of the future. 'The brief authority, prestige and dominance of the man-made wilderness of the great cities is collapsing', wrote the naturalist and government advisor Max Nicholson, in 1970. 'It may be that the rot has already gone too far. Human numbers and material demands may be destined hopelessly to outrun the most that ingenuity can now achieve towards restoring the equilibrium through the sensitive and healing use of the natural environment.'[6]

This bleak pronouncement was being echoed in the work of a British science fiction writer of the time. John Wyndham was born in what became the Warwickshire green belt, and in a brilliant series of imaginative novels he managed to articulate our fears about the side effects of progress when it collided with nature. In his 1951 smash hit *The Day of the Triffids*, aggressive alien plant life bred on a research station takes over after a freak astronomical event. *The Chrysalids* (1955) deals with fears of post-apocalyptic mutations. In *Trouble with Lichen* (1960) the anti-ageing properties of a rare plant present a dilemma for a group of scientists. They are often seen as metaphors for the Cold War, but it is curious that in each of the novels it is specifically the morality of tampering with nature that is explored. Wyndham also seems obsessed with zones of safety and danger, from the village behind the force field in *The Midwich Cuckoos* to the Isle of Wight haven in *Triffids*. He deals with the same anxieties that drove *Silent Spring* and the conservation movement, and his novels release our darkest fears into often-mundane rural locations. Through the prism of John Wyndham it's easy to see our relationship with nature recast as a cold war of sorts, and the tension between town and country as a form of paranoid arms race.

Rachel Carson's popularity was a threat to corporations and governments charged with accelerating a rush to environmental catastrophe. It was time for the PR departments to spring into action. Petrochemical corporations strove to choke off government interference and regulation by being seen to be taking the initiative and leading the debate. As a result, a flurry of corporate-sponsored documentary films were made in time for European Conservation Year, flagging up issues and offering solutions. There was *The Choice* by chemical giants ICI, *Environment in the Balance* by oil companies Shell-Mex and BP, and *The Air My Enemy* by the Gas Council, all shown at earnest film festivals. The most famous and hard-hitting of these films was BP's *The Shadow of Progress*.

'*The Shadow of Progress* is not a film you should enjoy. But it is one you should see', went the ad, which could easily have been the film company's tagline for *Star Wars: The Phantom Menace*. The narrative was straightforward enough. The elemental forces of nature versus those of our modern, urbanised world. Alarming population predictions. Footage of machines changing the planet to our convenience. 'Nature and man,' went the portentous narration, 'there is a balance if we can find it, every day less of nature, every day more of man, this is the shadow of progress.' Scum floats on rivers. Smoke is belched. Photochemical smog hangs over cities. 'The push of people, every day unrolling the concrete carpet further.' Shots of English suburban sprawl. 'Every year less solitude, less green spaces, less wildlife.' Unless you're an insect of course, at which point the documentary goes full-on John Wyndham and accompanies the arrival of aphids, caterpillars and beetles with discordant sci-fi horror music. These are creatures 'with a capacity for reproduction only a computer can comprehend'. DDT is dropped by plane and sprayed by terrifying-looking farm machines. And then we reach BP's darkest fears, second only in their mind to a loss of shareholder value: oil spills at sea, bubbling slicks and dead birds. As this frenzy of catastrophe reaches a climax the film neatly throws the problem back at the audience. All of this progress, it says, is not our fault: it's yours. You wanted it, we were only your handmaiden. The real monsters are you.

In the unseemly scramble of corporations to position themselves as compassionate, the Tory government formed the Department for the Environment in 1971. Here they were also attempting to shake off the shadow of progress, to reflect the nation's new-found spirit of environmental responsibility. The name was, of course, as shallow as the nation's own lip service to environmentalism. The benefits of car ownership and the products of factory farming and petrochemical industries proved too alluring for modern consumers and the companies feeding their habit. With their new conservation-friendly-sounding department, the government attempted to say we understand this frightening world, and the tide of chemically made death sweeping across it. We are the good guys. We know what you need. We will protect you.

My last happy memory of Marjorie is of sitting in our front room as we listened to *Pet Sounds* by the Beach Boys. For most of the autumn of 1997 she'd been quieter than normal. Her part-time job, hiring out buses to community groups in Croydon, was getting too much, and more worryingly, she was rapidly losing weight. At those first few ghost notes of *Wouldn't It Be Nice*, the chimes of a distant ice cream van trying to find its way back from the past, she was suddenly animated, flooded with joy. It's a song of hope, of being young, of imagining a happy future, of escaping to somewhere you might fit in. The album took her back to those days before she and John had moved to the edge of the country, when a new life for themselves seemed a distant dream rather than a soon-to-be-achieved reality. The harmonies filled the dusty living room with a swirling sense of nostalgia and she lay back in her chair smiling, eyes closed, basking in it. 'I love this one,' she said, when *Sloop John B* started, a song she remembered Paul singing at a school concert. It was a memory from their early days on the estate, when life had been so different. A time of polyester clothes, lurid wallpaper and delight at the countryside across the road.

Marj made it through that Christmas but something was very wrong. She was emaciated and in constant pain. As she lost weight, large pressure sores began to form and fluid was constantly draining through them. A bed was delivered, a monstrous thing with air compressors beneath it that meant she could lie down with the minimum of discomfort. It filled the entire living room and made a noise like a passing dustcart. She was taken into hospital at the start of the new year, a defeat she felt keenly. It was only her willpower that had stopped it happening sooner.

'I remember the last time I saw Mum,' remembered Ian. 'She was waiting for the ambulance to take her. And she was on the doorstep with Dad, and her hair was unkempt, which was unusual. Mum said, *Look after Dad*, and that was the last time.' She hadn't wanted to go in but things weren't so easy. John was weak, recovering from a series of operations for bowel and liver cancer. Looking after the pair of them at home was beyond us.

And so she was taken to hospital and put in a side room all by herself, a place with no windows, in which she lay in an even bigger pressure bed, like a baby lost in an old-fashioned pram. With her unable to move and isolated in this hot, dark, noisy room, it reminded me of the thing she most feared: an iron lung. Here she was struggling on alone, disconnected from her friends, the life she had created, from the outdoors. I kept a journal. *Just visited Mum in hospital*, went the entry from 28 January. *V weak and so thin. "Like someone from Belsen," Dad said. Trying to drink so she doesn't get put back on a drip. Had op to remove some dead tissue from her pressure sores. Refused anaesthetic and is still refusing painkillers.* I'd forgotten this particular outrage, the paranoia and control freakery that led her to reject anaesthetic. Any lapse of concentration on her part would be fatal, she decided. Every cut of the scalpel would be proof that she was still in control. She wanted to be alive to it all.

Hospital visiting is always a strangely alienating process. John, long since invalided out of work, spent most of his days there, running errands and nodding obediently to the doctors and nurses. Paul would drop by after work, between his regular office hours and the demands of his newborn twins. My visits were at the mercy of the bookshop's byzantine rota system and fuelled by chocolate and panic attacks. We were none of us big talkers and the room wasn't exactly conducive to companionable silence either, underscored by the din the bed made, like a tethered hovercraft in a shed. She wasn't grabbed by the P.D. James I'd lent her or the heap of magazines we'd brought in. Her pale blue eyes were bloodshot, her cheeks sunken, skin hanging off her bones. How I wish everything had been different. That she'd made it home. That we'd at least filled that room with something better than weak smiles and desperation. That we had made her feel safe. But Marj was the strong one. Without her lead we were hopeless.

For the indestructible superwoman, held together with Disprin, tea and irony, surely there had to be an escape plan? One last miraculous trick, the atoms of the universe bent to her will one last time. But even if *she* hadn't given up, it appeared that the medics had, with little effort being made beyond trying to keep her comfortable, which was the one thing she was not. The night staff terrorised her, she said, but the longer she was in there the more prone to strange hallucinations she became. *Dad arrived on Sunday to find her hidden beneath the sheet, emerging frighteningly, eyes dazed and immobile,* I'd written in my diary at the start of February. *"Tell them," was all she said.* And then later: *She says they have a month to get her better and then that's it, she's never going back into hospital again.* It was at this point that John's cancer nurses took him off to a hospice for a week of respite care. The commute between bookshop in Covent Garden, hospice in Sydenham and hospital in Croydon was a particular low point. It seems curious that I didn't take time off work, but I suppose I assumed there would be many more weeks like that and this was a new normal. It all seemed endless, that time which now feels so fleeting.

By the middle of March, after ten weeks in hospital, she took a turn for the worse. On the 19th, when I arrived, she was in the grip of a fever, screaming for John. Seeing little improvement, I decided to stay with her the following night, and slept in the upright vinyl chair next to her bed. It was like trying to sleep in a boiler room on a ship. The hours passed slowly but I was used to long nights awake, thanks to a mixture of anxiety and clubbing. Time would bend in strange ways on those bus rides home from the city centre to the edge of the estate. Those extra hours to watch and think. One time, making my way along Fairchildes Avenue at 4 a.m. on a Sunday morning, I'd seen a badger swaggering about across the road. It was a beautiful sight, made all the more extraordinary because just a couple of hours earlier I'd been dancing in a packed club in Vauxhall. In the small hours, time seemed elastic, and the boundary between these different worlds porous and flexible. But in Marj's room there was no window to watch the sunrise or hear the birds singing before dawn. Instead nurses trudged in and out through the night, working around me as I curled up in the chair, holding Mum's hand, talking if she wanted to. At some point, if your parents live long enough, you realise that the roles reverse. You become the adults and they the children. If I'd twigged this sooner maybe things would have been different. At the time I felt that night had been a futile interlude. Now it feels as if it was the only time I behaved like an adult.

On the 27th we were told Marj could be home by the weekend. She died in that room three days later. *Just hours before she died*, I wrote in my diary, *she leant forward and put her hand on my cheek and looked long and hard into my eyes, suddenly still and strong again*. A moment filled with love, an unspoken word in our family, even between the two of us in that room. It was to be her last moment of lucidity. Time passed and

John and I sat there, waiting for something to happen, even though the thing most likely was the one we wanted least in the world. When it came, there was no ambiguity about her death. I'd never seen a dead body before, but there it was, in its full unknowable absurdity. Without her incredible self-sustaining will, her body was suddenly as empty as the wheelchair left gathering dust in the hallway at home.

We didn't want to leave, and couldn't wait to get away. Just exiting the building seemed to break the oppressive spell of the place, and when Dad climbed up into the driver's seat in his Transit van he began to weep. We sat there for a long time, and eventually when he turned the key in the ignition the van was filled with the sound of Radio 2. In those moments we might have hoped for something deep and meaningful. They were playing *High* by the Lighthouse Family. Soothing words of being close to tears, remembering that it would all soon be over, and that somewhere in the sky we would be reunited. It seemed terribly profound. The mildly soaring music continued in its open, modestly meaningless way. We listened to it all the way through in silence. The banality of that moment all neatly wrapped up in a song about nothing by a band neither of us liked. Even at that instant I was painfully aware that Marj, a fan of Blondie and Ian Dury, would not have approved. I recorded in my diary how lucid and love-struck John remained in those moments after her death. How much he appreciated the life they had lived together. And then he started up the van, and drove us home.

When sickness comes it can be devastating. Dutch elm disease, a fungus spread by bark beetles, arrived in Britain in the 1920s. A more virulent strain arrived in the 1960s, to which Britain has so far lost 25 million elms. A more recent threat is ash dieback, another fungus, this time affecting the second most common tree in Britain. It was first spotted in 2012, and is expected to wipe out almost all of the country's 80 million ash trees. Well, unless the tenacious boring beetle *Agrilus planipennis* gets there first. The rain was falling in Selsdon Wood when I asked Croydon's forestry team, Richard Edwards and Simon Levy, whether there had been much sign yet of ash dieback in the borough. Simon told me it had been spotted in Warlingham, near Fairchildes Farm.

'It probably is here to be honest,' he said, 'but we haven't picked it up yet.' Most of the borough's woodland wasn't ash, but where it was, in neighbouring Kent, it was causing devastation. Richard was hopeful that the ash would survive.

'It could be that it's got such genetic diversity, ash, that we'll lose some but others will be resistant,' said Richard. 'It's a case of wait and see what happens to them.' Invasive species, such as Japanese knotweed and giant hogweed, weren't a big problem here either. Knotweed had colonised the old electricity substation in Rowdown Wood and there were patches elsewhere, but the team were on it. It was far from the screaming disaster movie-style headlines of house price crashes and even demolitions caused by the weed, with an infestation in one in every ten square kilometres estimated in the UK. The main invasive problems in Croydon and in much of the Metropolitan Green Belt took other forms: the glossy-leaved shrubs beloved of nineteenth-century landscape gardeners: cherry laurel and rhododendron.

The most invasive species of all is, of course, us. In an interview with *The Times* in 2014 the then Environment Secretary Owen Paterson talked up the advantages of offsetting the human destruction of ancient forest by planting new ones. He cited the positive example of the M6 toll road around Birmingham, constructed in the West Midlands green belt, which passes through six ancient woodlands. It was estimated that 10,000 mature trees were lost in the project, and a million young ones were planted. 'Now people will say that's no good for our generation,' said Paterson, 'but, over the long term, that is an enormous increase in the number of trees.' Can it really be that easy to lose ancient woodlands but gain new ones?

'It doesn't work like that,' said Simon Levy with a heavy sigh. 'The reason ancient woodlands are so important is that they're species diverse. You get many, many more species in an ancient woodland than you do in a secondary woodland. And you can't just reproduce it, because it's not only the trees and plants, it's the soil. Everything. All these relationships that have built up over millennia. The definition of ancient woodland is that it is understood to have existed in the same spot since the Ice Age, i.e., when Britain first became afforested again.'

We wandered into another area of the wood, and Simon pointed out some tall, scruffy larch in the distance, like a pack of Afghan hounds in need of a comb. They were the remains of a plantation, of the sort popular in the mid-twentieth century, where existing woodland was chopped down and coniferous trees brought in to replace it. The Forestry Commission's bombardment of Scottish hillsides and valleys with these trees is perhaps their most infamous use in Britain, but I was surprised to find some in the middle of a nature reserve in Surrey.

'In here was a monoculture of larch, which had been neglected,' said Simon, 'so it was all falling over. This area's known as East Gorse. So we felled the larch, scarified the soil and all the seed was still in the seed bank. And up it came.' And what grew in East Gorse was, unsurprisingly, gorse. Tons and tons of gorse, rising higher than our heads. A thick, dark green mass of tightly packed branches and stems, spiky needles unfriendly to the passing traveller, but great for the diversity of the wood, creating the perfect habitat for ground-nesting birds away from large predators and curious dogs. 'We never expected it to be this good,' said Simon. Out of the death of one introduced species comes back the life of another much older one. The woodland has shown incredible resilience.

I don't recall how John and I came to be discussing the apocalypse, in a Vauxhall Astra just outside Biggin Hill. Maybe we'd gone there to take photos of the aircraft or shamble about in the scrubby green belt valley at the end of the runway. Regardless, it wasn't long before things took a darker turn, and he was describing to me how he thought the world would end.

'First,' he said, with untypical gravitas, 'the sun will go out. And then there will be the darkest *inkiest* blackness you could ever imagine. And then it will get cold, the *iciest* cold there ever was, and everything will die.' Now, I was an infrequent reader of the *New Scientist*, but I was pretty sure that this wasn't how stars died, like a standard lamp in a power cut. Instead, dying stars were supposed to expand and reach outwards, burning everything in their slowly dispersing fire. But John's vision was far more frightening, like the premise of a 50s B-movie. *The Day the Earth Caught Fire*, only not. And despite physics, this vision of the apocalypse came to pass for him when Marj died. John wasn't consumed in some hungry cosmic fire. Instead Marj's light was extinguished abruptly, and he was left there, in the cold, waiting his turn.

I had written something for Marj's funeral, and read it out like it was a school assembly. Afterwards

Ian's ex-girlfriend came up to me and said, 'John, you are a man of many words.' She hadn't meant it as an insult, of course, but it was true. Those words hadn't represented Marj at all. Memorialising her seemed beyond all of us. John returned home and put a picture he'd taken of Marj on her makeup mirror in the living room, as though she was staring back out of the looking glass, while we could only see her reflection. The mirror sat on top of a trolley, the place she'd kept the detritus of her life. A plastic lacquered box of what she called 'tat': home-made earrings, bracelets and brooches; Dial-a-Ride meeting minutes; Olbas Oil; a pot filled with leaky biros; bottles and boxes of prescription tablets; afro combs and hair-spray; cheap necklaces she never wore; black-and-white snaps of her family; two old pocket diaries belonging to her father; a bottle of her favourite perfume, Opium; a bag of makeup hanging from one side; a couple of broken watches; membership cards to the video shop and garden centre; disability allow-ance books and cheque books; plastic lanyards; a souvenir Roman coin; a floppy felt hat; nail clippers; and, in profusion, notebooks full of doodles, as well as old shopping lists, phone messages and Scrabble scores in her familiar italicised script. The photo sat there for the next two years, turning the once-practi-cal trolley into a holy relic. Like my eulogy, it was a hopeless and poorly considered attempt at preserving her image.

It was just over two years after Marjorie died that John went too. The progress of his bowel cancer had been recorded, curiously, in the 9 June 1998 issue of *Woman's Realm*. That week the magazine carried a large feature on John and his revolutionary new treatment. I remember the interviewer and photographer arriving, a couple of months after Marj's death. The photographer had coaxed John and his two-year-old twin grandkids, Lily and Daisy, over the road and onto the municipal green belt in front of the school. The resulting photo shows John smiling nervously, with Daisy sat in his lap and Lily on his shoulders, both children glaring unnervingly at the cameraman. Flicking through the magazine, there he is, on the health page, opposite features on cholesterol and thrush. His beard is bushy and full of white, his hair wild and uncombed. Marj would have been rolling her eyes. The headline, a jaunty cerise, says 'Freezing away cancer'. It starts as all good articles should, with an intriguing proposition. 'In the summer of 1996, John Grindrod, then fifty-seven, went to his GP complaining of constipation.' The article details how he was diagnosed with bowel cancer, and had an operation that summer to remove a tumour. 'Funnily enough,' he is quoted as saying, 'once I knew exactly what the problem was I felt better.' But on Christmas Eve of that year a scan revealed that the cancer had spread. 'I was very disappointed,' said John. 'What a Christmas present!'

It goes on to record the two sophisticated new types of treatment he received. A pump inserted next to his large bowel, delivering the chemotherapy chemicals directly to the area rather than flooding his whole body, and an even newer treatment: cryotherapy. Here, using keyhole surgery techniques, the surgeon could go in and freeze away tumours with liquid nitrogen as soon as they were spotted. The operation was so cutting edge it was even filmed by the BBC. This was in November 1997, just as Marj had begun to get seriously ill. 'This isn't a cure,' explained the surgeon, Professor Tim Allen-Mersh of Chelsea and Westminster Hospital, 'but another potentially valuable treatment for bowel cancer.' In one way John's replies to the journalist don't sound like him at all, because they catch nothing of his fumbling, chaotic, jokey voice. But his recorded responses do capture one thing: his no-fuss positivity. 'I feel well, I'm in my own home with my family around me, and I'm happy. You can't say fairer than that, can you?'

Everything he did used to revolve around Marj, often to her extreme annoyance. *Get out from under my feet*, she'd say, trapped in some corner by her flapping husband who was *only trying to help*. Now he had to find a reason to carry on for himself, and he was ill suited to that. He spent the next couple of years in and out of hospital and St Christopher's Hospice in Sydenham. By the end he was yellow with jaundice and as gaunt as a ghost. Polaroids of him with Paul, Ian and I in the garden in the spring of 2000 emphasise how quickly he was slipping away. With so many kindly helpers it felt curiously managed, unlike the neglectful chaos of Marj's exit. Perhaps that is the difference between dying of a known illness and proving a puzzle to the doctors. When it became clear he had only days to live the hospice discharged him, because he wanted to spend them at home. And so, in that final week we became his carers. A bed arrived, and we set it up in the living room, where Marj's had been two years before. He was feeble and confused, distressed at losing control of his bodily functions, but still attempting the odd comforting smile for our benefit should we catch his eye. For three brothers who never really accepted the mantle of responsible adults this might have been a disaster, but it wasn't. It was easy to look after him because we loved him, and easier too because our reticence to express that had been broken by the loss of our mother.

After John died I went and stood outside, looking over at the bare trees all coming into bud, the crows dancing from branch to branch, daffodils and crocuses pushing up through the wet leaves in our neglected garden. That was it, I thought. The circle of green. Inside it was all over, while out here it was beginning once again.

One day in the mid-1990s John and Marj had driven their Astra through the end of a rainbow. Or so they said. It happened on a quiet stretch of dual carriageway near Maidstone in Kent. They'd seen the rainbow across the sky, and as the road curved round, there it was before them, the base of this arc of light springing out of the wet tarmac. Moments later they had driven right through it, like a couple of gamers collecting some form of bonus. I was never altogether sure I believed them. I'm not even sure that is possible. But why would they make up something like that, the sort of treacly image straight out of the Steven Spielberg playbook? In their final few years we had got used to them heading off on one unlikely jaunt or another, testing out the new trams the council were thinking of introducing, or being invited to various parties in recognition of Marj's charity work. In the summer before Marjorie had died, she and John went on their last adventure together.

It had been Paul's idea, that we buy them a sightseeing trip by helicopter for their wedding anniversary. And so that summer they redeemed their voucher, and I went along to wave them on their way. It was a jolly affair, the airfield at Biggin Hill one of many in green belts around Britain, including Prestwick, Manchester and Bournemouth. Marj was carefully lifted into the small copter, and John clambered in after her with his camera. They looked so excited as the rotors started to spin, and the little craft began to ascend. There they were, smiling down, waving, and then looking around them in delight as the fields and houses below began to reveal themselves. The helicopter pulled away and continued to climb, and I watched it fly over the green valley of Fairchildes Farm towards our house.

They were only gone for half an hour but in that time they saw a lot. They flew over New Addington in its sea of green fields, and onwards to the metropolis of Croydon. From there the urban mass stretched all the way to the Thames. They reached the river, circling above the abandoned hulk of Battersea Power Station, over the crowded streets where they'd grown up. A few minutes in the air and they had travelled the short distance their lives had taken, and the gulf between those worlds. Before they could process what they'd seen, the pilot turned the craft around and took them back to the outskirts. Was that little dot I could see the helicopter, returning so soon? Was that them, over-head, coming in to land? They were descending now with a roar and blasts of air from the rotors, the craft settling on the ground before me, those few moments of touchdown as tentative as first steps. I wheeled Marj's chair out to meet them. She was giggling and beaming and clapping her hands. John looked dazed, camera in hand, awkwardly hopping down onto the tarmac like he'd just been rescued rather than venturing up voluntarily. *It's so green*, they kept saying. *All over the city, it's so green!*

8

Secrets and Lies: It's Not as Green as it Looks

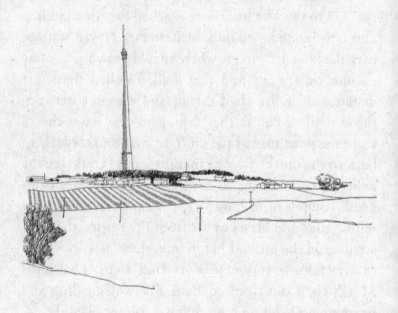

It is amazing the things the green belt can conceal. In December 1972 the Angry Brigade were standing trial. The left-wing revolutionary group had been behind the planting of twenty-five small explosives around England in the previous two years. They targeted banks, embassies, the homes of Tory MPs – including Keith Joseph – and a BBC Outside Broadcast van filming the 1970 Miss World contest. The Angry Brigade had grown out of the anti-Vietnam protests of 1968, and the radicalised students and their friends were keen on disrupting the cosy security of Edward Heath's Britain. Four of the main protagonists went to prison for ten-year stretches. One was Hilary Creek, a Watford Grammar School girl who abandoned her course at the University of Essex to live in a squat in London and imagine a better world. Rather than reflecting the supranational concerns of a terrorist death cult, Creek's protests derived from surprisingly tame-sounding issues: adventure playgrounds in inner cities; winter fuel payments for the elderly; refuges for domestic violence victims. At the trial Hilary described her background as 'conservative and green belt, where I never had to question anything'. Even then, by the early 1970s, the green belt had become synonymous with conformity and the status quo. Yet it was both incubator and perfect camouflage for unexpected secrets.

Green belts and bypasses are part of a system that shuns the centre and clings to the outskirts. Often road and belt are the same thing, because our green girdles are formed from unpromising components. I faced one at Frognal Corner, where a scratty forest of signposts and poles led me down through a vast concrete interchange over a thundering urban motorway. This walkway was suspended high above the junction on the

Sidcup Bypass in south-east London. Signs riveted to the railings announced that the subway lights had been vandalised, an oddly pessimistic permanent fixture contradicted by the reality that all were in working order. *Expect the worst and you'll be pleasantly surprised* might well be Sidcup's motto. In the suspended concrete drum I could hear the roar of traffic all around. Tenacious shoots of pyracantha offered unreal clusters of red, orange and yellow berries to any passing pedestrian. It could have been a dehumanising place, but the changes in planting, texture and scale made it feel oddly human. But then again, I do love a bit of concrete.

Infrastructure was a word barely known before the 1950s. Its use has grown up with the creation of the rationalised connecting tissue of modern life: sewers, electricity and telephone wires, gas and fresh-water plumbing, the network of roads, railways and airports. *Infra*, from the Latin 'below', and *structura*, 'to build'. These days it summons up images of politicians in hi-vis jackets and hard hats, nodding earnestly on TV news clips as construction processes are explained. It also hints at something hidden – below – like infrared, undetectable to the naked eye. Just as green belts aren't necessarily green, so infrastructure isn't always hidden. The pylons running between power station and town. Water treatment works whose smell announces them long before you catch a glimpse. And, most of all, roads. Narrow country lanes skirting field boundaries and hedgerows. Mighty motorways cut deep into hillsides or crossing high on concrete flyovers. B roads snaking away from the bustle and hurry of the long haul. Or those long, busy A roads, the congested trunk routes of a pre-motorway age lined by clapped-out semis.

If most construction is forbidden on the green belt, infrastructure doesn't require anything like the same lengthy process of planning permission. 'Roads and traffic can be exhilarating like airports and railway stations,' wrote Nan Fairbrother in 1970, 'and the number of people who park by choice beside busy main roads proves that silence and solitude are by no means what everyone wants from their day in the open.'[1] Those were the days when people still went to motorway service stations for the thrill of it all, when the thought of parking up in a layby by a pile of loose chippings with a flask of tea and some sweaty cheese sandwiches was a perfectly acceptable day out in itself. I used to be obsessed with stopping at Happy Eaters or Little Chefs, magical places where everything was wipe-clean, even the food. Motorways were boring, interspersed with these incredible oases of Formica and fish fingers.

No road-building project was bigger or more inti-mately part of the green belt than the M25. Almost every inch of it is not just constructed within the green belt, it *is* green belt. The few small exceptions are those places, like Waltham Cross in Hertfordshire, where it dashes through a short stretch of urban land. London's orbital motorway opened in 1986 and Chris Rea was minded to write his hit 'The Road to Hell' just three years later, after a trip on this new thoroughfare. Given its endless circular form, 'The Road to Purgatory' might have made more sense as a metaphor. Ideas for an orbital road around London went back almost as far as the green belt itself, the broad tree-lined boulevard being central to early twentieth-century proposals. Abercrombie made them more explicit still in his plans for London, imagining alongside the various belts a series of ring roads, from the inner to the outer. The inner ring road, known as the *motorway box*, was seriously considered in the 1960s, and land was quietly bought up for it, but when the residents of Chelsea, Brixton and Islington got wind of the idea of mass demolition they weren't so keen. This was also the very moment that protest movements and people power were beginning to make themselves felt. Pretty soon the motorway box idea became political poison and was put back in its motorway cupboard. The outer one, the orbital motorway, was less contentious, but only just. Forty inquiries, the same number as for the green belts, were launched in the early seventies as the northern parts of the ring road began construction. In September 1975 the first section was completed in the midst of the Hertfordshire green belt, between South Mimms and Potters Bar – that's junction 23 to junction 24 if you wish to take a sentimental journey.

Not every section was finished so smoothly. Secretary

Lesley Lovelock took the government to court in 1972 over proposals to plant the road 300 yards from her garden in Cranham, Essex, and was defeated eight years later. Thousands of losers all over the Metropolitan Green Belt couldn't believe that the sacred designation might not save them from this gigantic new road. One satisfying casualty was Sir Horace Cutler, head of the Greater London Council, who discovered his large house in Gerrards Cross in Buckinghamshire was also a victim of the ringway, even more immediately than Lesley Lovelock's had been. The M25 would actually pass through the grounds of his home. 'The irony is that I have been pushing for years for this to be built,' he told reporters, 'but I didn't realise it would go through my garden.'[2]

In January 1986 John Ezard from the *Guardian* met up with villagers from the Harlow to Waltham Abbey stretch of the M25. Richard Padfield, a sixty-five-year-old farmer, described the scene of what used to be there before the road came: 'a little stream running alongside the quiet village road; over there Oxleys Wood, which in a couple of months would have been showing promise of bluebell time'. His account was romantic and heartbreaking. 'We used to be able to see the stars,' he said. 'Now at night we have a great amber glow which diffuses over the whole sky. But perhaps greater than these is the wall of noise.'[3]

The motorway also passed by Croxley Green in north-west London, and Peter Wiles pointed it out as we drove to the edge of the suburb. Suddenly, as we sped along the country road, there it was. From overlooking fields and overhanging trees we were ourselves suspended over eight lanes of traffic cruising along beneath us, hidden away down a steep cutting. The M25 was part of a late-eighties obsession with everything being out of town. Offices in business parks. Supermarkets. Entire shopping centres, like Bluewater in Dartford, or Merry Hill outside Birmingham, built on the edge of green belts, flung ever outwards from town centres by the centrifugal force of modern suburban living.

Back at Frognal Corner in Sidcup I was negotiating another of those unpromising urban highways. On the far side Scadbury Park Nature Reserve ran beside the road, offering a bit of unlikely country to this otherwise urban scene. I'd come to visit the nearby River Cray, and so took a walk there along the edge of the busy A20, a road as much part of the Metropolitan Green Belt as country parks and cornfields. At the next junction I thought I'd found a short cut. Cornwall Drive housed a handful of 1930s semis, shielded from the mammoth raised junction nearby by a narrow stretch of scrubby embankment. The surface of the road was churned up, as if on a building site. This shortcut was a cul-de-sac. I reached Tintagel, the final house, whose name was emblazoned on a large iron gate.

Beyond that something was up, but I didn't quite

spot the enormity of it at first. A colossal industrial gate stood at the end of the road, plastered with warning signs of all sorts. Further on lay the grim industrial mess of a recycling yard. This belonged to a company called Waste4Fuel, which create what is known as refuse-derived fuel from tyres, plastics, cardboard, metals and paper. It was only when I stopped at the gate and looked around that I began to see a bigger picture. Beyond the rusty huts and tipper-truck tracks I could see the beginnings of a grey hill of waste. I looked to my right, and there was an outcrop of tall, slim leylandii trees, twice the height of the houses, forming a barrier. And then I saw something that made me retch. Behind the tall trees, and rising higher than them, rose an enormous mountain of rubbish. It was Godzilla-sized, a frightening peak of ash-grey refuse, making the houses feel tiny and insignificant. What must it be like to live here, I thought? Flyover, embankment, lorries rumbling by and that sinister tower of debris at the end of the road growing ever higher. It was like *Mad Max* rebooted in Brookside Close.

The heap was estimated to be 50 feet high, 60 feet wide and to weigh 18,000 tons. Alan Cowburn, a retired printer and one of the poor unfortunates living in this cul-de-sac, told the *Daily Mail* in 2014: 'The smell can be overpowering outside, like burnt plastic. I've been violently sick on occasions. I'm sure we get more flies round here than we used to, and I've seen a few rats.' His neighbour, Nasrin Sultana, told them: 'About every eight weeks the children feel sick for a couple of weeks. They weren't like that before we moved here.' A battle had been going on between Waste4Fuel and the Environment Agency, which had first told them to remove all the rubbish from the site by June 2013. They were in and out of court, the company got into financial trouble and then collapsed, and now this unmanaged tower of trash is prone to catch fire. Three years since they went to court the mountain remains, and the locals fear for their health. The Environment Agency has been monitoring pollution levels and insists that they are below the mean concentrations expected for London. The residents, however, just want the mountain moved.

As darkness began to creep up on one of the shortest days of the year, I had to face it that I wasn't going to make it past this extraordinary landmark to the River Cray after all. And so I turned my back on the mountain and began a long return walk to the train station in Sidcup, where I hoped I would be able to warm up and regain some sense of perspective away from the darker extremes of green belt life.

By the 1970s a green belt had been planned around many of our urban areas. In England there was the Metropolitan (London), the North West (Merseyside and Greater Manchester), Dorset (Bournemouth and Poole), Avon (Bristol and Bath), the North East (Tyne and Wear, Durham and Hexham), South and West Yorkshire (Leeds and Sheffield), the West Midlands (Birmingham), Nottingham and Derby, Stoke-on-Trent, Oxford, Cambridge, York, Gloucester and Cheltenham, and the least famous of all, at Burton upon Trent and Swadlincote. Scotland had eleven in the pipeline, at Aberdeen, Ayr, Clackmannanshire, Dundee, East Lothian, Edinburgh, Falkirk, Grangemouth, Glasgow, Midlothian and Stirling. Wales had just the one, between Cardiff and Newport. Meanwhile in Northern Ireland where the threat of speculative building was a problem spiralling out of control by the sixties, planner Robert Matthew proposed a simple 'stopline' around Belfast rather than a green belt. Inevitably, perhaps, the stopline was co-opted for sectarian ends. It wasn't until the end of the 1980s that the stopline became a green belt proper. A vast amount of land across the UK came under new green belt rules, these days amounting to 16 per cent of Northern Ireland, 13 per cent of England, 2 per cent of Scotland and a negligible figure in the tiny sliver of green belt in Wales. Cities, towns and villages would not encroach, and greenness would remain green. Although, what exactly had been protected by the green belt? If on the one hand we were protecting urban areas from themselves, like inmates in Broadmoor, what was happening in all of this safe space beyond the walls? After all, just having a green belt doesn't actively promote anything, not even landscape conservation.

Frederic Osborn, the garden city mastermind, was keen that green belts shouldn't be cut up into small chunks round urban areas, because that would create problems for farmers. 'Under these conditions,' he wrote in 1969, 'land can be properly farmed right up to the very edge of a town, and untidiness and waste can be avoided.'[4] But a year later that sharp observer of the modern landscape, Nan Fairbrother, remained unconvinced. 'Here we need to create a new type of scenery,' she wrote, 'the man-made wild – a landscape which seems natural but is deliberately designed and managed for recreation. At present we have almost no idea at all how to do this.'[5] And so she suggested in her influential 1970 book *New Lives, New Landscapes* that green belts should be 'divided into green-urban and rural landscape'.[6] She believed that the straggling line drawn up at the edge of housing made it impossible to integrate town and country successfully. But could it be done better? Should we move industry there, she wondered? Well, we've had a go at that, and now business parks and out-of-town shopping centres are a familiar sight thanks to Nicholas Ridley and Keith Joseph in the 1980s. Or we could create tree belts, she thought, mini-woods with urban stuff in them, dividing city and country. What she struggled with was the unhelpful administrative name *green belt*. It doesn't describe what's in it and often gives quite the wrong idea. Couldn't we hope for a more subtle, nuanced description?

Describing what is in the green belt is far more complicated than you might think. In fact, if you ever fancy playing detective, one of the strangest cases you can take on is trying to uncover just what is actually in it. Much of it isn't green at all, of course. Gravel pits. Landfill sites. Factories. Refineries. Motorways. Service stations. Caravan sites. Victorian mental hospitals. Sewage treatment works. Government research establishments. Prisons. Airfields. Glasshouses. Solar farms. In 1963 there were protests about proposals to put up a power station at Ratcliffe-on-Soar in the Nottinghamshire green belt. Regardless, it was built in 1968. In 1973 four 235-foot radio masts designed to transmit London's two new commercial radio stations were erected in the Metropolitan Green Belt beside the Barnet bypass in North London. Many TV, radio and mobile phone masts have been erected in the green belt, but none so conspicuously as Europe's tallest man-made structure: Arqiva Tower, more commonly known as the Emley Moor mast in Yorkshire. I asked local resident Karen Keenan how the concrete structure fits into the landscape.

'You can see it from our front window,' she said. 'If we have visitors who come to our house from any distance, especially if they've got children, we always take them up to see the mast. There's a car park, a little pull-in off the road, where you can stop.' Arqiva, the telecoms company, ensure through high fences that visitors can't get too close, but they have provided an information-and-interpretation board to appease any tourists who do turn up. 'We laugh that there's always an ice-cream van in the car park. So it is a little local attraction. I thought it was quite funny that it's in the green belt but we go to see a concrete structure! It's spectacular.' But the mast wasn't always the brutal concrete it is today. In 1969 the original metal mast became encrusted with ice and collapsed. 'We didn't have ITV for five days,' recalled Karen. Quite a to-do. 'The funny thing was, when we moved to our house we had terrible TV reception! We're too close to it, so the waves go over the top of us.'

The transmitter isn't the only odd interloper in the green belt near Skelmanthorpe where Karen lives. Old pit and spoil heaps have been removed, the slag heaps re-landscaped and adorned with grass and trees. This kind of reclamation of old industrial sites has been a slow process. Back in 1955, the year that the government green belt circular was sent out, townscape expert Kenneth Browne was talking about how this could be done in the 400 acres of wasteland outside Leigh in Lancashire. Most of the area he described as 'sunken, boggy and rubbish-strewn'.[7] A colliery tip overlooked a lake. 'Deciduous trees should be introduced,' wrote Kenneth, 'not to cover the conical tip, but to act as a foil to it, and to screen the distant housing.'[8] Having been a war artist, Browne supplied his own illustrations for this feature in *Architectural Review* magazine: pictures of the slag heaps as they were, and then as they might become, the dereliction now a boating lake with a jetty and trees planted around the perimeter.

Working out what to do with derelict land on the edge of towns wasn't easy. Staffordshire had a go in 1967 to salvage eight acres in the Black Country with the help of the National Coal Board. They hoped to create a landscape fit for housing, industry or woodland. In 1971 the West Riding of Yorkshire gave 'environmental exchange' a try – swapping bits of land currently in the green belt, which were needed for new coalfields, for derelict land elsewhere which could be reclaimed as green space. Leslie Fraser, the county planning officer, said this brand new concept would be applied in Sheffield, Doncaster and Maltby. 'On a cost-benefit approach,' he told the *Guardian*, 'it is better to get rid of ugliness even if it means using some green fields for industry.'[9] At the time a thousand acres had been made over, while another thousand waited patiently for their turn.

Policing that boundary between town and country was a job for Richard Edwards and Simon Levy in Croydon. They have spent a lot of time restoring the woods around New Addington, which had been slowly spoiled by human habitation.

'Simon did a huge project of fencing off the woodland to stop people getting into it,' said Richard, 'and pulled out something like fifty burned-out cars.' I thought back to the many incinerated hulks I'd seen in the woods back in the day, new ones blooming rust-red on blackened steel branches, older remains grown through with nettles and blackberries. They were as much a part of New Addington's woods as mud and midges. They were the estate's sacrificial gift to the country. You can almost hear the country saying *no, you shouldn't have*. The amount of dumped cars has dwindled in recent years, due to their increasing scrap value. Proof that positive incentives work where negative warnings have failed. But not all of the vehicles here were burned out. A cinder track in the woods used to encourage scramble biking there, but has long since vanished. I asked Malcolm Mott what happens now with the bikers. Turns out they liked having a go in his fields.

'I've tended to crack down on that something wicked,' he told me. 'Because it's not so much the one kid from Addington on his scramble bike. They've got like a jungle telephone, and the minute you get one they're coming from bloody Swanley, Brixton ...' These days he fells trees to block entry to fields where they break in and ride. 'Whereas before you had a couple of lads who did it and it wasn't so bad, it just goes completely haywire now. With technology and mobile phones and Facebooks. The minute they find it the place is swamped.'

All this talk of subversive activities reminded me that one of the first places I'd gone to begin research of the green belt was the London office of the Campaign to Protect Rural England. A serious meeting ensued, and I diligently made notes. As I got up to leave, one man remained lurking by the doorway, looking suspicious. 'You should investigate dogging,' he said, and hurried off. *I don't even know you*, I thought. But it confirmed something that I might have guessed. The green belt is stuffed with sex.

There are more innocent forms of liberation for the human body in the green belt than dogging of course. Nudism began to become popularised in the health- and efficiency-obsessed 1920s, where getting close to nature didn't just mean rambling. Green belts have played a significant role in the emergence of naturism in the UK, with early camps near Wickford in Essex and St Albans in Hertfordshire. By the 1960s The North Kent Sun Club in Orpington was one of the biggest examples. The cause of saucy jokes and liberated spirits, this site was referred to as '50 acres of paradise' by founder Jack Watkins. In August 1970 it played host to the 12th International Naturists Conference. There were delegates from twenty-one countries, including Brazil, Denmark, Guadeloupe and Rhodesia. The Queen sent her best wishes, and the press followed with endless bawdy cartoons at the expense of an Anglican clergyman who held a service on site. Quite mind-blowing for the conservative green belt and for a country whose idea of liberation at the time (and possibly still) was Pan's People, *The Benny Hill Show* and *No Sex Please, We're British*.

Also long before the era of dogging in the green belt was the arrival of swinging in the suburbs. The 1960s had heralded the beginnings of sexual freedom for a few, with the invention of the pill. But it was the 1970s that saw the mass suburban domestication of it. Soft porn films such as the *Confessions* series saw unlikely figures such as Robin Askwith, Lynda Bellingham and Jill Gascoine romping through the flares and flock wallpaper of mid-seventies suburbia. Wife swapping is one of the phenomena that we most associate with the age. No matter that there was little evidence of swingers parties, it made great salacious copy in the national press. All of this activity was symbolised by a plant: swingers supposedly grew pampas grass in their front gardens, as a signal to fellow travellers.

But really it was the arrival of the internet in the 1990s and social media in the noughties that helped create a boom in group sex in Britain. The media cottoned on to it in 2003 and a new phrase entered the Oxford English Dictionary four years later. *Dogging* was coined by the police after the behaviour of exponents, who, if stopped, claimed to be merely out walking their dogs. *The Times* called it a 'public sex epidemic' and interviewed Richard Byrne, a senior lecturer in countryside management at Harper Adams College in Shropshire, who had sent out questionnaires to wardens of country parks to discover the extent of the incidence. Doggers appeared to be mostly men, out to watch – and perhaps take part in – public heterosexual sex. 'They seem generally respectable with decent cars,' he said. While dogging and public sex in general is not illegal, other offences such as causing alarm or distress to others, public indecency or exposure could land you with a prosecution.

Because of its proximity to towns, the green belt has more than its share of dogging hotspots. There was one near where I lived, the Addington Hills, a thickly wooded area with a handy car park, ideal for doggers. The far end of the wood had long been a gay cruising ground, another green belt speciality, before the dawning of an age of decriminalisation, equal marriage and swiping right made such activities as archaic as rationing or dancing the polka. Cannock Chase, an Area of Outstanding Natural Beauty in the West Midlands green belt, was another popular spot for doggers. It was here that footballer Stan Collymore was caught dogging by a tabloid journalist. By 2013 police estimated that there were 222 dogging sites across the UK, an astonishing 93 of which were in a single county: Surrey. And the most notorious spot there was the Hog's Back, part of the North Downs in Guildford. Long before that, it had been a favourite haunt of Jane Austen, who is probably not the patron saint of public sex, despite the subsequent slash fiction written about Elizabeth, Darcy and that wet shirt. These days, with 3,250 homes set to be built on Blackwell on the Hog's Back, it looks like nature in its many colourful hues may be permanently disrupted by Guildford's local council.

It wasn't just sex that was making the earth move in the green belt. The threat of death on an unthinkable scale was offered in similarly unlikely sites too. In 1982 at Naphill, outside the Anglo-Saxon village of Bradenham, Buckinghamshire, protesters met to fight the arrival of a nuclear bunker which would house the new headquarters for RAF Strike Command. The Wycombe Peace Council was a local offshoot of the Campaign for Nuclear Disarmament, and they were trying to protect lives and the wood. You'd have thought it was pretty protected already: as well as being green belt it was National Trust land and an Area of Outstanding Natural Beauty.

John Nott, the Defence Secretary, had said reassuringly that what was being built wasn't a nuclear bunker 'as such'. Rather, he said, 'we are simply replacing our current Operations Centre with more up-to-date facilities and equipment'.[10] That's all right then. In one sense this was true: the original shelter at Naphill, known as Southdown, dated back to 1938, and had been built for RAF Bomber Command. It accompanied a nearby US airbase at Daws Hill. To keep the building secret, each tree dug up from the site was labelled and then replanted in its original position once the underground structure was finished. By 1978 the Ministry of Defence was looking to create a more high-tech Strike Command headquarters and the site of the old bunker was chosen. But this time it would be more than just their control centre. It was also nuclear bomb-proof, just in case. Because of the old shelter and airfield, the small Buckinghamshire town had long since been listed as a likely nuclear target. In the event of the Cold War turning hot, an MoD report estimated that High Wycombe and the surrounding area would have been devastated by two 500-kiloton missiles and two one-megaton bombs. No amount of green belt legislation was going to stop that.

The Wycombe Peace Council had been alerted to the proposals for Naphill by Trevor Hussey, a local philosophy lecturer and CND member. 'No one would listen to me for 18 months, not even the CND', he told the *Observer*. 'I got very depressed. Although I'm a member of CND, long before that I was just someone who lived here.' The work was taking place at Hollybush Farm, whose land had been leased to the MoD by the National Trust for ninety-nine years. In their defence the National Trust told reporters that the land was not beautiful. And it certainly wasn't when the cranes, lorries and earth-moving machines moved in, dumping a great pile of chalk where the crab apples, hawthorn and birch had stood. Three-and-a-half thousand tons of concrete and 4,000 kilometres of steel were used in the construction of the command centre. And, as in 1938, extra care was taken when restoring the landscape after construction. That is, apart from the two new seven-foot-high security fences and a suspicious mound estimated to stand thirty-three feet high. These days the bunker is painted

a scrubby green to blend in with the Chilterns countryside, with trees and bushes growing on the roof.
Work goes on 180 feet below the surface to direct RAF
operations in a facility designed to survive for months
if disconnected from the outside world. 'It is so sad,'
said Trevor Hussey. 'If you had lived here all your life
you'd feel it like I feel it.'[11]

It's amazing what you can hide if you want to. No one
had taken Marj seriously in 1962 when she'd told them
she was pregnant. Marj with her mystery illness, Marj
with the stoop, Marj who found it hard to get about.
Fragile, hospital-fodder Marj, and her doting, silly
new husband John. There was no way she could be
pregnant. Her family knew that. The doctors told
them so. And, faced with a wall of refuseniks, as well
as still bitter at the treatment she'd received back in her
teenage years, Marj stopped mentioning it to anyone.
She dealt with it all by herself. No midwife visits, no
check-ups, no advice. She was quietly sick and made
no mention of it. She grew a small bump, but her stoop
hid that. She made her own clothes, hid the evidence,
furiously kept it all in. On the third floor of Gresley
House, surrounded by her brothers, her parents, her
gran, the comings and goings of a busy block of flats,
she hid it from everyone. One day John, at work,
covered in motor grease in a filthy pit beneath a lorry,
got a message. He was to come at once. Marj was in
hospital. Marj had given birth.

A baby boy, months premature, so small they called him dormouse. A miracle baby, seemingly from nowhere. Marj and John got some funny looks after that, she for shutting them all out, he for being given the run-around. They called the baby Ian. Ian Albert. Albert was the name of her beloved, mercurial father, who bestowed on Ian his silver tongue and a kind of roguish glamour. John went from doting, clueless husband to proud, clueless father. Marj didn't even bother reminding people that they had told her she was a liar or delusional. The proof was there. She'd been right all along, she knew her own body. And all of those attempts to pigeonhole her, to tell her that this wasn't her place, was impossible, couldn't come to pass, were dismissed in one furious bout of effort. Childbirth.

Afterwards you might have expected them to have dined out on this extraordinary story. Instead they barely ever mentioned it, and if they did it was with a shrug and a mysterious smile. It was just something that happened. Once or twice they laughed darkly about it, John with a smile hovering between shame, bafflement and pride, Marjorie taking delight in her confounding strength. She'd proved she didn't need any of them, not her family, her friends, her husband even. They'd humiliated her through their lack of belief. And so she'd got them back with the indisputable proof that she was right. Marj's miracle. The woman who couldn't get pregnant now nursing her newborn baby in St Thomas' Hospital. It's fair to say that John would have wanted to believe. He'd have been her only ally, if she'd let him. But in the face of his fear, concern, wide-eyed wonder, she must have decided he wasn't going to be any help. Instead it was easier to control it, to keep the world and its stupid opinions out. A pregnancy hidden, not by disability, but by the low expectations of others. She kept it all in, until of course, she could no longer.

In my family, keeping it all in was the very least that could be expected of you. Forget public displays of affection, we could barely manage private displays of acquaintanceship. It wasn't that we didn't like each other; we did. It would just be soft to express it. Ian recalled the nose-tapping and *none of your business* that shut down conversations as effectively as a super-injunction. And one of the biggest issues was money. The secret Christmas clubs and Provident loans traded off against crazy overtime and going without.

'How *broke* they were. *Every* year, year on year,' recalled Paul. 'And they still gave you the presents you wanted.' He shook his head, exasperated. 'Would it have made a difference if I'd known? I don't know. They never said *no*. They never said, *sorry, we can't afford that*. They always put us before anything. They would rather give us something, make sure we got some food, and they wouldn't eat themselves. It was ridiculous.' He was sounding emotional now, not something either of us was particularly comfortable with. And it was so frustrating to recall these moments, secret acts of love and kindness that almost killed them, none of which they ever let on about. We were struggling with the logic, the pig-headedness, the sheer hidden *love* of it all. 'Why didn't they just say no?' wondered Paul. There was something simultaneously heroic and appalling about all of this secrecy. What did they think was going to happen if they opened up about things? *Don't tell them, we don't want to affect them.* He sighed. 'The pressure that they must have been under, every day, *constantly*, beggars belief.' He looked up and shook his head. 'We were probably horrible shits as kids.'

I told Paul something I'd heard from our dad after Marj died. The year before I was born, the year they moved to New Addington, she had a miscarriage. It was a girl, they were going to call her Amy after John's mother, who died a year later. So powerfully depressed was Marj that she took to destroying every photo of herself she could find. So John took to hiding them. A part of their past up in flames, a part of their past hidden away in wardrobes and dusty boxes, a part of their past they never talked about. Paul knew nothing of this miscarriage. He looked pretty shocked, but it made a horrible sort of sense. That distance we'd faced from Marj as small kids hadn't come from nowhere. Living in a new and unfamiliar place, depressed and refusing help, it was as if she had taken a step back from the world. A decade of cold misery would settle over her like a harsh frost. As with everything, this was something she could control, she didn't need us, or anyone. She needed to prove that to herself again and again, like an addiction. Perhaps it was no coincidence that she and John moved from Battersea at the same time as the miscarriage. It might well be that we owe our lives on the edge of the green belt to this tragedy. There is no one I can ask to find out.

Of course, you could always just put up something in the green belt without permission and see what happens. Recent history is littered with hundreds of examples of it. There was George Woolhead, who, back in 1962, had to smash up his Hertfordshire house with a hammer. He, his wife and their two sons had lived for four years in the home he'd built without permission. Afterwards they moved out to a caravan, from the place he'd built with £500 of savings.

A bigger problem cropped up in Buckinghamshire in 1967. Fulmer Grange was a charming brutalist college built by the Cement and Concrete Association in the grounds of an old house in the countryside near Slough. The state-of-the-art centre contained eighty study bedrooms, four lecture theatres, three labs, a workshop, a teaching drawing office, a dining room and a coffee lounge. *Concrete Quarterly* ran an article in June 1967 with glamorous pictures of the luxurious coffee lounge with its lofty columns of exposed concrete. There was the dining room too, with its board-marked concrete ceiling, and the exposed concrete walls of the study bedrooms. The centre offered courses, including ones for architects on the supervision of concrete construction and one on surface finishes. It was a modernist's paradise. It was also built without permission.

The council said the scheme was 'fantastic' – but not in a good way. 'The county planning committee was horrified that a firm this size should do this', they told *The Times*. But the college was equally cross. 'It is three-and-a-half years since we applied for permission, and two years since the council wrote to say it was their intention to grant it' was their response.[12] With so much public squabbling, both sides found the moral high ground eluded them. What soon became clear was that what had at first seemed to be a simple green belt dispute was in fact a grudge match between the council and college. 'They are really sticking their necks out,'[13] said a county spokesman. In the end the college was allowed to keep their swanky new building, and they even added ones alongside, just in time for the economic slump of the seventies and the backlash against concrete of the eighties. The complex closed in 1987.

Yet one story dominates all others, more dramatic, epic and implausible than an episode of *Game of Thrones*. This is the tale of Honeycrock Castle. Television is full of people encouraged to build their dream. And so in 2000 farmers Robert and Linda Fidler decided to give it a go. Their dream was a mock-Tudor fort, canons and ramparts and all, in the grounds of their farm in Salfords, Surrey. Because they guessed they might not get permission to erect it in the green belt, Robert and Linda did what any reasonable people would do, and secretly constructed it anyway behind bales of hay stacked forty feet high. The resulting fortress was a noble edifice of half-timbering and stone, all wood-panelled galleries and chandeliers on the inside. It was the ultimate green belt Tudorbethan house, a monument to a world of faux nostalgia, and the kind of folly that John Betjeman would have loved: phoney as the Croxley Revels and just as charming. Robert, Linda and their son Harry soon moved into their castle, which was still hidden from view by a giant wall of haystacks. 'We thought it would be a boring view,' said Linda, 'but birds nested there and feasted on the worms. We had several families of robins and even a duck made a nest and hatched thirteen duck-lings on top of the bales.' Then in 2006 they removed the hay, and Honeycrock Castle was suddenly out in the open. An instant landmark. Robert had been hoping to take advantage of a law which stated that because no one had objected within four years it would be allowed to stay. But it didn't go quite as planned. The council pointed out that no one had been able to object, because up until that point it had been completely hidden. Short of being kitted out with heat-sensitive goggles their neighbours would have struggled to see it. The local authority demanded it was demolished. 'The council are no different from vandals,' said Robert. 'I'm not worried as I don't believe I've done anything wrong. I can't believe they want to demolish this beautiful house.' The threshold between naivety and cynicism here was precariously thin. 'Our position is that the land is green belt land,' said council leader Lynne Hack, 'and, unless there are very special circumstances to do so, you can't build on green belt land as it is very precious. We didn't think that building a castle qualified as special circumstances.' Not that she was without respect for the Fidlers' achievement. 'It's a shame,' she said, 'because he obviously put a huge amount of time and effort into building this thing and it is a beautiful house.'[14]

The epic High Court battle ended on 9 November 2015. Mr Justice Dove informed Robert that he had to demolish Honeycrock Castle by 6 June 2016 or go to prison. 'It will break my heart to demolish it', he told the *Independent*. 'It's like asking Rembrandt to rip up his best oil painting.'[15] The castle has been hidden once more by the Fidlers and by all accounts has been reduced to a shell. Their fortress has been returned to that nether world of those things that almost don't exist in the green belt, from nuclear bunkers to dogging sites. A place where secrets and surprises lurk, ready to confound our every expectation.

9
Wide-open Space: The Green Belt Must Be Stopped

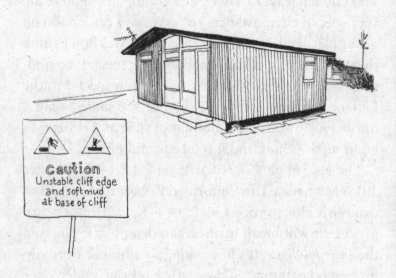

Caution
Unstable cliff edge
and soft mud
at base of cliff

In August 1972 a massive 170-square-mile extension to the Surrey green belt was announced. This one act increased the already sizeable Metropolitan Green Belt by a fifth. 'This is the start and there is much more to come in other counties,' said Graham Page, Minister for Local Government. Within a year they had either added, or were in discussions to add 127 square miles of Buckinghamshire, 130 square miles of Kent, 150 square miles of Oxford and Berkshire, and 550 square miles of the West Midlands. And by 1974 there were reports that the amount of green belt in England and Wales would double, to cover 3,000 square miles. By the end of the 1970s some planners began to think that perhaps enough space had been protected.

In Scotland, nothing illustrated this like the case of Dundee. They'd had a belt since 1962, and had given themselves plenty of room for the city to grow too. But the problem here was that the population of the city began shrinking instead, while that of the surrounding villages started to grow. And so, by 1980, an element of realism was needed. A report for Tayside Regional Council recorded that the success of the green belt was a moot point. 'Some housing developments have leap-frogged the green belt and have used good quality agricultural land on the edges of surrounding towns and villages.'[1] And so the city's entirely ineffective 37,000 acres of green belt were abolished in 1982. The Scottish Government website lists the new Dundee and Angus strategy, which includes 'supporting development in rural areas which sustains viable communities, protects and improves the country-side and maintains the quality of valued landscapes and the natural and built heritage'. There we have it. The only city to have abandoned its green belt. You can't imagine that happening in paranoid, hysterical England, although the ever-expanding areas around Cheltenham and Gloucester are having a good try.

What if central government cooled on the green belt like Dundee had? On 18 April 1979 the Labour Environment Secretary Peter Shore confirmed that although he was keen on protecting the existing Metropolitan Green Belt he wasn't interested in any further additions, such as the proposals for Tunbridge Wells, Gravesend and Chelmsford, which would have stretched a further thirty-five miles from London. He'd already put a stop to the new towns programme, and the final one, Milton Keynes, was well on its way to being built. But his thoughts were in vain. Just sixteen days later this ailing government was swept aside by a revolution, a new tough-minded form of Conservativism, led by Margaret Thatcher. What would this mean for the green belt? Well, the Conservatives had long been the protectors of it, in no small measure because that's where many of their voters lived. Those prosperous outer suburbs and counties around London, Manchester and Birmingham were famously Tory. It was in their interest to protect it, you'd think.

Michael Heseltine, Thatcher's first Environment Secretary, wasn't so sure. By January 1980 he was insisting that not only would he not be extending the green belt any further, but he would be releasing some of it for private building too. A thousand acres in Berkshire, for example, the area designed to stop Reading, Bracknell and Wokingham coalescing. Surrey and Hertfordshire had dreams of becoming almost entirely green belt. Now Heseltine was suggesting that Surrey should find space for 13,000 new homes. It was all a bit of a shock to counties used to being cosied up to. While in opposition, Heseltine had made no secret of his frustration at the lack of private construction going on – he called it *jobs locked in filing cabinets.* Now in power, he was blowing the locks off those filing cabinets, and presumably spraying big-haired women and red-spectacled men with reams of paperwork in urgent need of rubber-stamping. Not that he was pro-construction in every case. In November 1980 he placed a moratorium on council house building. The programme, part of the postwar system that had created green belts, new towns and slum clearance, had built up to 250,000 new homes a year at its peak in the 1950s, but following Heseltine's ruling it dwindled to almost nothing by the 1990s, never to recover. At the same time he announced the Right to Buy scheme for council residents, a souped-up version of a programme offered by Heath's government in the 1970s. And then there were the league tables, to show which local councils hadn't handled their planning applications in the required number of weeks, to shame bureaucrats who might be obstructing construction. Planning, after all, was at odds with the free market, the presiding god of the Thatcher era and beyond.

Heseltine's Housing Act would change forever the composition of Britain. The housing problems we face today, particularly of a decline in new house building and a lack of social housing, are a direct consequence of the enduring failure of these policies. The Thatcherite fetishisation of Victorianism ironically attempted to undo all of the progressive work championed by those eminent Victorians the first time round: Octavia Hill, Ebenezer Howard, John Ruskin and the rest. The new regime saw virtue only in private enterprise and philanthropy, rather than in collectivism and public ownership. And for getting in the way of those ideals, the green belt has been drafted in as a convenient scapegoat ever since.

Heseltine had been a whirlwind. His successor, Patrick Jenkin, sought to be even more radical. Following the 1983 election he decided to take on the planning system, and this time that would mean the green belt. He published a draft circular, a kind of anti-Sandys, which would have seen the withdrawal of green belt status for any land surrounded by existing building: parks, open spaces and playing fields, for example. The Greater London Council were just one of the many parties outraged. 'Even with the present strict controls,' said GLC planning chairman George Nicholson, 'the average loss of green belt is running at nearly 30 acres a year for Greater London. It will accelerate dramatically if rules are relaxed.'[2] At this point the green belt around London accounted for four times the urban area controlled by the GLC. The acceleration of this loss was exactly what Jenkin wanted. His accomplices would be a new gang of private mega-builders – Consortium Developments – who swiftly announced proposals for fifteen new villages to be put up in the South East.

Headed up by Lord Northfield, who had been head of the Telford new town development corporation in the seventies, the consortium was like Marvel's *Avenger's Assemble*, with considerably less spandex. Here the superheroes were Barratt, Beazer, Bovis, Ideal Homes, Laing, YJ Lovell, McCarthy and Stone, Tarmac, Wilcon and Wimpey. But at the Tory Party Conference in October, Jenkin's remarks on green belts caused a panic. He'd been full of optimism about his fashionable free market ideas, and poured scorn on those who wished to protect the status quo. Retired planner Ian Tant remembered Jenkin's description of 'the *I'm-alright-Jack-pull-the-ladder-up-behind-me* mentality of those who lived on the edges of green belt'. It might have thrilled the consortium, but back-bench MPs and party members from the Home Counties were less impressed with their minister. Within a month they had created a consortium of their own: an alliance of farmers, conservationists and local authorities to fight these new incursions on their beloved countryside.

Two months later and suffering a sustained monstering in the press, an under-pressure Jenkin backed down. 'There is no question of rolling back the green belt,' he said, presumably through gritted teeth, 'or of allowing building to take place wherever developers choose to build.'[3] He dropped intentions to overrule local objections to Consortium Developments too, who were understandably furious with Jenkin for caving in to backbenchers. 'The Environment Secretary has been blackmailed by a minority of Shire Counties MPs,' said Tom Baron, the consortium's Chairman and Heseltine's former housing policy expert. 'He's just accepted the easy way out.'[4] Even so, they pushed ahead with their first project. This was for Tillingham Hall in the Essex green belt. There would be 5,100 homes, as well as industrial units and schools. Like a postwar new town, but without the public service ethic driving it. It was submitted for planning permission in 1985, at which point all hell broke loose at a public inquiry. It was turned down in 1987. Killing off the construction of council housing and new towns before their replacement private schemes were assured meant that the government's – and the nation's – housing policy was suddenly in jeopardy.

Vocal public objections to anyone wishing to build in the green belt characterised the era. In January 1984 it was the turn of the Ministry of Defence, when they bought 630 acres of land at Luddesdown in Kent to practise the laying of mines. They couldn't have chosen a more protected area. Not only was it in the green belt, it was also an Area of Outstanding Natural Beauty, a Site of Special Scientific Interest and an Area of High Nature Conservation Value – one of those many smaller designations I had never heard of. Forty groups sought to challenge the decision, ranging from the Ramblers Association to the CPRE, fighting alongside eleven parish councils, two district councils and Kent County Council. More embarrassingly for the MoD many of the protesters turned out to be retired service personnel. 'I take my hat off to them', said Colonel Drake of the Ministry. 'It is a clever and well-orchestrated objection . . . but it makes it hard for us to teach their sons to protect the nation.'[5]

Ian Tant was working for Hertsmere council in the eighties, his job to revise the local plan. In the prevailing political climate he was told to think short term.

'Just identify exactly the amount of green belt required to meet the housing requirements of the structure plan and let the future look after itself.' What a job for a young planner, to get caught up in this unsatisfactory bodge. He was part of a small team whose job it was to identify potential areas for expansion. 'We drove out,' he said, bringing back memories of Abercrombie and his team doing the same forty years before. 'We started with the map, and what looked like reasonable enclaves, and then we went to have a look at the site.' It was confidential work, the local authority only too aware that any leak at that stage could be catastrophic. This was strange cloak-and-dagger stuff. Eventually they took a draft of their report to local councillors, who initially seemed very keen. But then, the next step would have been sounding out representatives from the public utilities, such as water and electricity, to see if their blueprints were possible. This caused the local politicians to take flight, scared that their proposals would become public knowledge. And so what happened was precisely nothing, and in the end Ian Tant decided to move on.

By 1986 the green belt covered 10.5 per cent of England and Wales, an astonishing 110 per cent increase in fully approved green belt in a decade. This was mainly because, since the 1950s, councils had been operating with a vast amount of unapproved green belt, which was only now finally being given the thumbs up. If, during my research, I'd found the boundaries almost impossible to pin down on the ground, unapproved ones would prove doubly tricky, ghosts barely appearing on any map. London's population reached a high point of 8.7 million in 1939, when war broke out. By 1951 half a million people had left the city. With planners aiming to thin out the population of big cities still further through the creation of new towns, London's population continued to fall until it reached a low point of 6.8 million in 1983. Yet at this time the Metropolitan Green Belt held a population of 1.75 million people – an increase of 1.3 million since 1939 – either living in expanded towns and estates, or in increasingly densely populated villages packed with commuters. It is curious to see that it was the protected green belts and not the rapidly changing city that saw a population increase in the postwar period.

Since then immigration has been one of the largest factors affecting the rise in London's population, just as migration from across Britain had been at the heart of the city's population rise in the nineteenth century. At the turn of the millennium there were almost eight million people living in London. And in 2015 it had finally reached that 1939 figure again. This massive fluctuation in population over time has not been reflected in housebuilding, or in adjusting policies like the green belt, designed to contain the city. It is for this reason that London's green belt has come under the most pressure in recent years, and has stolen all the headlines.

It seems hard to believe that a yet more abrasive figure could be employed as Secretary of State for the Environment than the recent incumbents, but on 21 May 1986 controversialist Nicholas Ridley was installed. He had a message for Tory MPs who represented green belt constituencies, which he delivered in a cruel imitation of their whiny lobbying voices: 'Look, we know you are right, but it doesn't make a ha'penny worth of difference – we must not have any more development on our patch,' he said. Well, he couldn't agree with that. 'I cannot and will not say because I have a nice house and a good life that I do not care about anyone else. Those *anyone elses* are my children, your children, your neighbour's children.' Which was, it had to be said, a good point. But it was a speech that left those backbenchers 'absolutely hopping mad'.[6] Even

Michael Heseltine went on the offensive about proposals to build on the green belt, the architect of radical reforms suddenly sounding like a thirties moderate. 'If you argue that a demand only has to exist for it to have a right to be met,' he said, 'then in the end, from the Weald of Kent to the Berkshire Downs, from the Chilterns to the Channel, you will go on building till you reach the sea.'[7]

He was reacting to a series of proposals that were being considered for villages around Reading in Berkshire. There was a scheme by planning company Barton Willmore, which was representing a fashionable consortium of five developers, to build to the east of the village of Three Mile Cross. Meanwhile another speculator, Speyhawk, was angling to have a go to the north-west of the village at Great Lea. Combined, the two proposals took a thousand acres of land for 6,750 new homes. These were just two of eleven private projects to put up 23,000 houses in the area between Reading and Aldershot in Hampshire. The sticking point was the motorway, which formed the edge of Reading's built-up area to the south, and which these estates would breach.

Even champions of private housebuilding had their limits, and Ridley's hypocrisy was revealed on ITN, when an interview on *News at One* on 14 June 1988 went spectacularly wrong. After all of his public humiliation of fellow MPs pleading special cases, it turned out that he'd been objecting to a neighbour who intended to build on a field next to his house, a Queen Anne rectory in the Cotswolds. After being asked about it three times live on air he stormed out of the interview. Meanwhile the Adam Smith Institute, the praetorian guard of the market, were busy peddling their own monetarist outline for the green belt, catchily titled the Green Quadratic. Estimating that a further million homes were needed in the South East, they recommended building on a whopping tenth of the Metropolitan Green Belt. 'The casual traveller through the green belt will scarcely be conscious of the increase in population,' they purred reassuringly, 'though the resident of long standing will no doubt harbour wistful memories of the time when "all the hillsides were covered in green fields"'.[8] Bless those wistful locals and their charmingly irrelevant opinions. After all, the institute claimed 40 per cent of the green belt was derelict or damaged 'brown' land as they called it. For a think-tank so bound up in the practice of number crunching, that absurd percentage and their awkwardly applied geometric shape showed some creative accountancy, if not a total maths fail.

It was left to a more emollient incoming Secretary of State, Chris Patten, to dismiss many of the green belt building projects his predecessors had encouraged. Rather than the central diktats of Heseltine, Jenkin and Ridley, his watchword would be local choice, a liberating phrase which meant in reality shoving all the hot potatoes back at local authorities for them to deal with. And those fifteen new villages proposed by Consortium Developments at the start of the decade? Not one of them made it through. Patten's decisions might have been kinder to the green belt authorities and their Tory MPs, but they created a huge hole in the government's planning policies. Where would all of these new houses go, if not in the places the various consortiums had wanted? Would they get built elsewhere, or at all? If not, how would the government be able to reverse the fall in construction caused by the end of council house building? What were their new ideas to stave off a future housing crisis?

'I went from sanity to insanity crossing that road,' said Ian. He was recalling the day our family moved to New Addington in 1969. And for once he wasn't exaggerating. 'It was like everything a child could want! There were trees, fields of wheat, I'd never seen anything like this. Didn't know what to say, didn't know what to think. It just blew me away. And I walked into the farmer's field and I looked at all the wheat, and it was just like . . . wow!' He paused. 'That's when I became agoraphobic. That *very* moment. I remember it, having to walk backwards under the tree because it was too big. Too much sky. So much sky! That's what I noticed. I could see for *miles*!'

To a seven-year-old who had only known the city, Ian couldn't quite process what he was seeing. It was so different from the view from their old flat in

Battersea, where within a few metres tall buildings were interrupting his gaze, and the sky appeared small on the elevated horizon. In the high fields around New Addington he took to hiding beneath trees, keeping his eyes down, averting his gaze from the all-too-much. The advantages of green belt living – space to play, country air, wildlife – were bypassed by this sudden, unexpected affliction.

'It was the best thing in my life and a curse, that field in Fairchildes,' he said. Tracey, his wife, had walked in while he was talking, and heard him eulogising about this field. She gave him a funny look.

'Weirdo.' And then she pottered off again.

He remained on in the house in Fairchildes Avenue for a few months after John died, until the council wanted it back. Following John's death there didn't seem to be much holding the three of us together: unemployed Ian with his unpredictable ways; Paul with his twins and responsibilities; me about to turn thirty and emotionally not yet even a teenager. Ian had to clear the house before he moved out, and wheeled the entire contents on endless barrow trips to the rubbish dump at Fishers Farm, a mile away.

'That was horrible,' he recalled. 'I remember moving the last lot, using a stack barrow.' When he closed that front door for the last time he told me he'd felt Marj and John's spirits rushing at him from the house, angry and vengeful. He'd slammed the front door and never looked back.

Back in the 1970s Ian found that having all that space as a playground, with all the woods, hills and fields, was fantastic.

'But I couldn't cross the field,' he said. He learned instead to run all the way round the edges, to catch up with his mates. And that's how he got into an early hobby, fossil hunting. 'My very *first* fossil was a tooth from an ancient type of cow,' he told me. 'I took it to school, gave it to my science teacher and he sent it off to the British Museum. The teacher received a letter confirming what it was. 'I said, "Can I have it back?" He said, "Oh, they've kept it!"' Fossil hunting worked because Ian found he could cope with the great outdoors if he had something else to focus his mind on. 'Because otherwise I start thinking how small we are and how open everything is,' he said. 'How big it is. And it just gets bigger and bigger and bigger. But that's a challenge. I try to go out there and take photographs of it – what it means to me. Some of those photos, that sunset, I *love* that one.' The sunset he was referring to was a photo he'd taken in the field opposite our old house, getting on for fourteen years ago. It was of the valley, the tall trees in the middle of the field, those relics of the landscaped garden of Fairchildes Lodge. This was the place our dad returned to throughout the seventies, eighties and nineties, taking photos of the sun setting behind the big trees in winter, the silhouettes giving further definition to the dying rays of the day as they lit up the clouds. His persistence was like that of an impressionist painter, returning to quickly capture the light on hay bales or the lily pond when the light was just right. 'You can look at all the different patterns in the sky, you can see the tree,' said Ian of his version of the sunset. Dad's sunset, but not. 'What I know, and what I see, is an agoraphobic in a field overcoming it to take that photo.'

After John died Ian moved to an eighth-floor flat in the centre of New Addington. He couldn't enjoy the view. He kept the curtains closed at all times, and never once looked out his windows let alone ventured onto the balcony. It was also difficult being in the centre of the estate. He missed the trees and the fields. A childhood in the town had spoiled him for the green belt, and now the green belt had spoiled him for the town. Nowadays, all these years later, here he was back in a council maisonette, exactly like the one we grew up in, and only two streets away from the woods. He still tried to make the occasional effort to go over there, but he found it hard.

'It's exhausting,' he said. 'I really want to go out and do something but by the time I've got myself ready I've argued with myself so I'm absolutely cream-crackered.' I remembered all of those years after John died when he barely went out at all. 'Oh, I'm still like that,' he said briskly. 'I haven't been out, *properly* out over the woods for a while. I doubt if I've left the house this week. I didn't leave the house last week, I know that.'

Here he was, trapped by panic attacks and night terrors, still unable to function.

One occasion he did go out, he took a friend's dog for a walk and stuck to the field boundary.

'I needed a jimmy,' he recalled. 'There was an oak log, great big, cut down. I thought that'll do, there's no one around, I'll have a jimmy there. I had shorts on and I just felt something go – ' and he mimed jabbing – 'on the back of me leg.' He couldn't see what had caused it and so carried on with his walk. Towards the end he felt his leg swelling up, so much so he found it hard to walk. 'I was wondering how I was going to get the dog home!' He managed to make it to the local GP, and they had a look. He'd been bitten by an adder. Perhaps he'd been right all along. Maybe it was dangerous out there.

After ten minutes trudging through the rain, Lorna, my old flatmate, her two kids and I emerged from between the chalets to a clearing at the top of the Dorset cliffs. Two wooden benches stood stoically overlooking the English Channel. On the grey, drizzly horizon I could just make out the faint shape of the Needles, the rocks and lighthouse that trailed like ellipses to put a soft end to the Isle of Wight. Along the clifftops and down the escarpment, buttercups and gorse were in bright yellow flower. As I peered further over the bank I could see a forest of horsetails growing up from crumbling soil on the steep cliff face,

Carboniferous survivors on the Jurassic coast. The four of us tried to convince ourselves that some parts of the drenched benches were drier than others and perched there for a moment. Chalet curtains twitched as we did so, but surely these holidaymakers staring at us were used to idiots coming here to admire the view in the rain? After all, it is one of the great pleasures of a British seaside holiday.

Being here in 2016 reminded me of the first train I ever went on, almost forty years earlier. It was a pink stuccoed chalet made from old railway carriages, part of this holiday park in the 1970s. Only later did I discover that trains didn't usually have net curtains hiding large, splayed spiders, oddments of Utility furniture dotted about the place, or space for a wheelchair, unless you wanted to be loaded into the mail coach next to the bikes and parcels. So it was with a curious sense of irony that these vehicles had been turned into wheelchair accessible chalets. While my brothers spent all week playing World Cup football outside, I roamed all the tucked-away bits round and about, the bushes, ditches and streams, lost in a fantasy world of adventure, mysteries and secrets. None of the holiday homes we stayed in after that were anywhere near as exciting as that magically transformed train. It had been part of Naish, a holiday village built on the green belt by the sea at New Milton in Dorset, the place I had come back to explore with Lorna decades later.

When it comes to wide-open space, some green belts have more than any other. These are the coastal ones: on the banks of the Mersey; around the quayside at Bristol; along the oil-rush coast of Aberdeen; and abutting much of the Northern Irish coastline. One of the longest stretches ran along the seafront and around towns and villages in Hampshire and Dorset. Here the green belt meets the blue belt. Hampshire had been both repelled and attracted by the idea since the 1950s. The dangers of not having one were obvious: the entire shoreline between Portsmouth and Bournemouth would soon be taken up with houses and flats, and all the famous views and their tourist potential would be lost. It wasn't just bungalows: industry had long been attracted to the Solent estuary too. The arrival of the Fawley refinery at Southampton, for example, prompted the expansion of housing and amenities for the new workforce.

When the green belt proposals for Hampshire had been revealed in 1958 they had been unexpectedly controversial. Both Portsmouth's and Southampton's ambitious district councils were desperate to grow and objected to being hemmed in. Hampshire's chief planning officer said with some understatement that 'the creation of the green belt will not always suit the ambition of local authorities with thoughts of expansion, nor in all cases will it suit landowners and speculative developers'.[9] Twenty-two towns and large villages would be affected, where only essential construction would be permitted. For fifty-four smaller villages, their rural character would be protected. The fighting paid off: Southampton and Portsmouth evaded belts completely, and could comfort-eat the countryside round and about to their hearts' delight. But from the western end of Hampshire through the New Forest fringes of Dorset and around Bournemouth and Poole, a green belt was declared. Of course, here the danger of encroachment didn't just come from builders, but from the sea itself, which carried away great lumps of the green belt with complete disregard for the rigours of planning permission.

The steep cliffs, the open sea, the green falling away, each of these things proved a nightmare for Ian. He kept his head down and away from the edges, much as it pained him not to be at the centre of things if we went for an evening stroll to see the sea. The car journey was bad enough. I'd sit next to him, and he'd be jammed into the back seat of the Mini, one hand wedged against the roof, the other holding tight to the side, feet twitching in maximum anxiety. Every year we returned to Naish holiday village and each time it was a little more eroded. Coming back to spot the changes was as much fun as seeing the tourist sights that remained just so. Yes, we loved seeing the seaside charm of our old favourites, almost as much as we did seeing them being tragically wrecked by landslips and avalanches. Here geology worked as effectively as Godzilla on a high-rise cityscape.

Nearby, the sturdier houses and bungalows of residents met their fate as surely as the lightweight chalets of the holiday park. We'd spend ages looking at the ruins of homes built too close to the edge. How awful for the owners, we'd say gleefully. It might have been my first intimation of the passing of time and of mortality. Morbidity for sure, for our fascinations were ghoulish, like the Addams Family on a day out. Every year the landscape was remade, remodelled, some of it even intentionally. The old railway carriages eventually went too, lost to the sea or replaced by modish wooden cabins or static caravans, we couldn't quite recall.

Nowadays Naish is called the Hoburne Holiday Park, and it was strange to revisit it with local resident Lorna, and her two boys, Dylan and Rufus. A stream, Chewton Bunney, runs through a nature reserve next to the park, and as Lorna's car sped over the little humpback bridge that crosses the watercourse we all went *oooh!* For a second I was taken back to being a kid, when John's reckless driving used to bounce us in the air over that bump, our stomachs in our mouths. The green belt skirts the houses nearby, but the holiday park is very much in it. Presumably the work here had been allowed because the caravans and chalets were temporary structures. Of course, as the locals had long since discovered, all the houses here were temporary, no matter the quality of their foundations or the sturdiness of their construction. The insatiable white horses galloped happily over the rocks twice daily to drag away more victims.

The first thing I noticed was how crowded it had become. Back in the 1970s there had been far more green space, but then the cliff had robbed the owners of that luxury. I remembered these wooden cabins being built. It was comforting somehow to see that they still dominated the park, a houndstooth check layout of chalets on repetitive diagonals. It was easy to feel lost among them, each still wearing their once-fashionable dark wood stain. Marj used to turn her nose up at them. Poky, she said, though we never went inside to find out. Expensive was more like it. Seeing the cabins again unlocked a yearning I'd not felt for almost forty years. They had looked mysterious and exciting at the time, and now they looked unbearably alluring. The modernist dream of clean lines, glass fronts, flat roofs and treated wood. Some even had the original white plastic italicised numbers screwed to the exterior, and the little wooden bin stores beside them, like a small friend taken under their wing. Released by the open space at the top of the cliffs, the boys raced off, and made catapults from the tough sedge grasses. They were near the age I was when I first came here and I was reminded of how everything could be an adventure, every landscape an opportunity for dreaming.

I bent down to examine some of the clifftop ruins, where tiny wildflowers and grasses flourished. Lorna told me about a botany project on Hengistbury Head, another green belt area a couple of miles up the coast, which revealed that much of the flora there had been the result of smugglers centuries before. Bringing in illegal goods from the Indies, they had left a trail of spore and seeds from the sacks of grain they were lugging ashore, and now some of the resulting grasses and wild flowers could be traced back directly to Jamaica. We'd scattered Marj and John's ashes at Mudeford, a nearby harbour where we'd once come to fish for crabs and hide out of the wind around the corner behind mariners' cottages. We'd released them near a bench that overlooked a mudflat, where gulls and oystercatchers roamed, and the rigging clanked quietly on the masts of a hundred small boats, like a slightly apologetic samba band warming up. Behind them loomed the crest of Hengistbury Head, the long spit of land that curved round to form the bay. I suppose we thought Marj and John were at one with their favourite view, the green belt with the sea beyond. A final escape.

On the way back to the car I picked up a brochure from the holiday park shop. How to buy a chalet here or in their other desirable locations. I stuffed it into my bag. Research, I told myself, though for weeks afterwards I would keep going back to look again at the brochure, imagining myself sat on one of those little wooden verandas living the 1970s modernist dream. Until down it came, bin store and all.

~

Back in 1973 respected town planner Peter Hall said the system under which he worked had 'a pronounced preservationist bias'. For him it was a 'civilised version of apartheid', keeping classes and income groups comfortably separate, the wealthy sharing the green belt between them as if it were some great private estate encircling the rest of us.[10] In some ways it was hard to square with estates like mine, where the urban poor had been shoved to the edges of the town, accidentally getting the best view in the borough. But by the nineties there was another equally controversial land classification coming into common usage. Brownfield sites were in many ways as mysterious as both green belt and white land. The idea was that they were land that had already been used for building or industry at some point. Quarries. Factories. Prefab estates. Landfills. Schools. Hospitals. Airfields. They might even have had houses on them. Yours, perhaps. All of us live on potentially brownfield land. And some of that was available to be built on. But it came with problems of its own. Ownership was often a complicated affair, especially if you wanted to aggregate different bits to create a chunk sizeable enough to redevelop. And then there was the hangover from what had been there before. It might be polluted from industrial chemicals; it might be unstable from mine workings; it might just be an awkward site to build anything meaningful on. In the early seventies there were lots of these wastelands to be found in the midst of towns and cities, places captured in gritty TV shows like *The Sweeney*, where the rough, ruined scraps could be exploited for scenes of handbrake turns and dramatic violence. They might have been bombsites from the war that had never been reclaimed, or the ghosts of failed schemes gone unbuilt. Perhaps they were blighted by redevelopments that never happened or urban motorways that did. Back in an age of plenty they were often just too small for the bigger construction firms to care about. They were the stray ends of the epic rebuilding programmes of the sixties. But by the 1990s a lot of these sites had finally gone.

Like 'nimby', 'brownfield' was another US coinage, this time from a 1986 Congressional Field Hearing of eighteen 'rustbelt' states trying to work out what to do with their derelict and vacant industrial sites. The term became a favourite of John Prescott, New Labour's colourful Secretary of State for the Environment, Transport and the Regions. It's hard to tell if the fabulous comment attributed to him, that the green belt was 'a Labour achievement, and we mean to build on it', is actually true, but it's become one of the enduring quotes of the era. 'Experts estimate that as much as a quarter of the metropolitan green belt is derelict wasteland', wrote Richard Morrison in *The Times* in March 2003, 'largely devoid of landscape beauty or amenity value. Exactly the sort of *brownfield sites*, in other words, that the Government is so keen to get builders to use.'[11] But, of course, it wasn't as simple as that. Prescott's position was as confusing as his language, as he defended the green belts on one side, while insisting on phenomenal housing targets on the other – targets that just couldn't be met on brownfield sites alone.

The New Labour era, from 1997 to 2010, saw renewed battles over the green belt. In the heady days of 1997 they set a target of 50 per cent of new builds to be constructed on brownfield sites, but that looked a lot in the cold light of day. Kent faced a housing boom, with 116,000 new houses to be built by 2011, and Essex expected a further 106,000. Plans were most advanced in Hertfordshire, at Stevenage, the first postwar new town, where the local council had approved the construction of up to 10,000 new homes on 2,000 acres west of the town. The proposal attracted one of the largest protests of the era. And it was one with history. Many demonstrators were the descendants of protesters who'd fought against the construction of the new town in the 1940s. Alongside Friends of the Earth and CASE – the Campaign Against Stevenage Expansion – the protesters were joined by Conservative MPs, former environment minister John Gummer and new leader William Hague, keen to make the Conservatives out to be the party of the green belt once again after a period in government which suggested quite the opposite.

Protesters from CASE certainly knew what they thought of it. 'The county council believes that by planting a few cherry trees and calling it a garden city, that automatically makes it environmentally sustainable,' said one, 'and anyone who doesn't agree is labelled a nimby.'[12] Prescott's love of all things brownfield just wasn't going to be enough, and county councils like Hertfordshire were realistic about having to lose some countryside if they were to accommodate this growth. The county had done well to reach 68 per cent of development on brownfield sites. But the rest, well, farmland – such as the two square miles outside Stevenage – would have to suck it up. The man with the unenviable decision to make was Peter Jackson, the county council's director of environment. He told the *Guardian* that 'we had a real dilemma. We had been given guidance in terms of how many houses we had to provide; we have the green belt which surrounds most of the settlements in Hertfordshire; and we were trying to plan sustainably. It was impossible to tie all of them up together. One of them had to give. The one which gave way was the green belt.'[13]

The village of Sandy Lane in the Pennines was in a similar bind. Bryant Homes came to build ninety-two houses here in the green belt valley in January 1998. There they met the Residents' Action Group for the Environment (RAGE), whose protesters occupied two caravans on the site, blockading the entrance. Carol Simpson, whose house overlooked the field, told journalist Andy Beckett, 'at first, we were naïve. We thought the council would listen to us. But at the last planning meeting they were just chatting away among themselves. That was when we got really, really angry.' And then the fight got considerably more active than the odd placard and letter to the paper. Occupying the caravans and denying the developers access created a huge headache for the local council and the builders. Bryant Homes sought injunctions through the court, but Oliver Robinson, a local experienced anti-roads protester who lived in a tree house, helped fire up local residents with his new direct action methods to achieve their goals. 'We want to hurt Bryant as much as possible,'[14] he told a local community meeting. The pain would come in the form of negative publicity, phoning TV and radio stations, picketing other Bryant ventures and painting the walls with slogans. It was a form of direct action that builders like Bryant were unused to dealing with. And it wasn't just the residents of Sandy Lane taking action against Bryant Homes. On 2 November protesters occupied their head office in Oxfordshire while their annual general meeting was going on, campaigning for *Homes for Need not Greed*. Fighting in the green belt had become a very dirty business.

The landscape of Britain was broken down into its constituent parts in a 2011 report by the Centre for Ecology and Hydrology. Its findings might seem surprising:

Arable and horticulture – 25 per cent
Grassland for pasture, silage or recreation – 25 per cent
Mountains, heaths and bogs – 16 per cent
Semi-natural grasslands – 13 per cent
Coniferous woodland – 6 per cent
Broadleaf woodland – 6 per cent
Urban areas – 6 per cent

That's right, you read correctly, built-up areas account for just 6 per cent of Britain. Maybe those green belts have been doing their jobs after all, containing that urban sprawl? These figures, as I'm sure you'll have spotted, add up to 97 per cent. I'm not sure what the other 3 per cent are. I'm imagining it's a combination of decking, roundabouts and old mattresses. The Office for National Statistics environmental accounts for 2012 analysed exactly what 'urban land' in England was made up from too. They estimated that over half of the area could be described as green (gardens, parks, verges, etc.), reckoning that only 2.27 per cent of England is actually built on. Which goes to back up the thoughts of those planners from the 1930s, that it's not the building that's necessarily the issue, it's the sprawl it creates if not tightly managed.

Protests to protect green belts have largely been confined to England. But with devolved administrations in Scotland, Northern Ireland and Wales keen to attract as much business and investment as possible, everything is being re-examined. For example, Edinburgh's proposals to expand into its green belt has awakened a network of campaigners. I spoke to one of them, Duncan Campbell, a retired landscape architect who now volunteers for the Edinburgh Civic Trust.

'The government is so fixated on new build, and build and build and build,' he told me when we spoke in April 2016. 'There's just been a press release this week that the government is going to call in all planning applications of more than 100 houses which have been appealed, in order to facilitate building 50,000 affordable houses in the current planning period. That means enormous pressure on green space. You cannot accommodate all of that on your brownfield sites by any stretch of the imagination. But my hero is William Wilberforce! It took thirty years to abolish slavery. It'll take about that time to get a better balance in the planning system, I think.' Or to abolish the green belt, if Campbell's opponents have their way. Currently Edinburgh's population is just under half a million. With a booming local economy it's expected to rise to over 600,000 in the next twenty years, a dramatic change in the rate of growth. Can they continue with existing policies when facing that kind of transformation?

A veteran of many voluntary bodies, Duncan has also been recently press-ganged into the Green Belt Alliance, which is part of the Association for the Protection of Rural Scotland. Such groups are behind sister organisations like the Campaign for the

Protection of Rural England, which carries out detailed surveys about everything from our attitudes to the green belt to detailed studies of changes to the boundaries.

'The developers around Edinburgh and elsewhere around Scotland, they make their money from suburban houses with gardens,' said Duncan. 'They don't make their money necessarily on affordable housing on brownfield sites. So there is a bit of a conflict between the Scottish Government's motive for affordable houses, which I support, and those of the developer, with a profit incentive, who don't see that as a way to protect their profit margin.'

While governments across Britain have become increasingly scared of green belts and the power of protest, they haven't quite yet managed to hive off all of the decisions to local authorities. As district councils drag their feet to implement local plans, time and again government finds itself pulled back in as final arbiter.

'Although there are protestations about the local decision being taken out of their hands,' said planner Ian Tant of the government's attitude, 'they're very happy because they can wash their hands of it. *It's not our fault!*' He laughed at the pettiness of it all. As authorities hold the line, new building is pushed ever further out beyond green belt boundaries. Take Oxford, for example, where new homes are built not in the city but in the surrounding towns of Bicester,

Didcot, Witney and Banbury. The added commute for these workers and shoppers makes the growth of these towns quite unsustainable while Oxford remains the draw. 'What's been recognised in debate after debate is the most sensible place to put new development is on the edge of Oxford,' said Ian. 'And then you're into the green belt and the whole emotive issue about green belt review.' It's as if we have learned nothing from the whole experiment. One of the biggest mistakes in the history of our green belts is the story of white land, that area along the edge which can allow building. With all of that land long gone, and few strategic planners brave enough to redraw boundaries to create more, the fears of Duncan Sandys' civil servants have finally become manifest. We have run out of flexibility. The situation seems to be a bit of a joke. Ian had faced these issues in Berkshire in the 1980s and nothing much had changed since then. 'The spaces that were left between the edges of the town and the green belt to allow for expansion have long been taken up,' he explained. 'And that's why we're facing the challenge now: of having so fiercely protected the green belt, and by and large done relatively little to change it since then.' And so, afraid at what we might encounter, with fingers in ears and eyes closed, we march onwards, denying both environmental and social disaster.

'I haven't been over there for about a year,' said my brother Ian. 'I really want to do it but I just haven't felt up to it. But I love it. It takes so much hard work just to get there.' I'd hoped to coax him out into the woods, but since I'd suggested it his anxiety levels had been increasing all the time. A wildly tapping foot, an arm restlessly moving, a look of discomfort and shallow breathing. I'd asked him to describe how he felt when he went to the fields. 'Small,' he said. 'Small. Agoraphobics can visualise infinity. You feel so small.' He thought back to that very first experience. 'Those tiny bits of grain, all those in that head of corn. And look at that, all those heads of corn. Thousands and thousands. And that field over there. And,' he gasped, 'you look up and take a step back, and that's what I done. Went under the tree.' The feeling was intense, overwhelming. 'I get it in waves and there's no think-ing, there's nothing. You just want to hide. They tell you try and control your breathing, but when you don't know when it's going to happen and it starts . . . *try not to clench your teeth, keep your shoulders down* . . . I explained this to a psychiatrist. You're walking in the field, you're having a lovely day. I'm in an aircraft with no wings that's just about to crash. That's what it feels like to me, every single second. It can't get any worse. It's fear. Fight or flight. It goes so mad that there's not any conscious thought in the end.' But Ian is all contra-dictions, feeling the pull of the country all the while knowing what it might do to him. 'They questioned me on that, "How can you be agoraphobic and you like to do that?" I said, "No, I *love* to do it, but I *can't* do it." Every time I seem to beat something – it's like a balloon, you squash it that way, it just changes shape. The problem's still there.'

It just wasn't fair on him to push it. I waved goodbye and took a slow walk out to the edge. It was a hot August day and the trees were in their magnificent pomp, a few early flecks of brown and yellow creeping into the high canopy. Here was the valley, through a barrier of saplings grown up to protect Malcolm Mott's farmland. A large field with a fold in the centre. The ploughed surface was rough with clods of clay and large chunks of flint churned up by years of working. Remnants of old crops grew here, the stalks dry in the sun. All manner of weeds and wildflowers had occupied the valley too: a small red poppy still in flower, great patches of thistle, scraps of leggy ragwort and tall stems of greater celandine in yellow bloom, chickweed, goose grass and bindweed hobbling along the rough ground in search of something to support them.

There were more trees in the field than I remembered. Eight of them dotted about. A hornbeam covered in hanging fruit waiting to fall on their spiralling leaves. A sickly-looking maple. A moth-eaten chestnut. A number of beech trees, one giant and several smaller varieties, their trunks sturdy and ancient looking. But the largest by far was the star of all of those photos, a prosperous-looking lime tree. It was higher up the valley than the rest and dominated the ploughed landscape like a lighthouse above rocks. At the moment it was in full leaf, but soon those leaves would fall, and in the low winter sun the bare branches would stand in stark silhouette. This survivor of the landscaped grounds of Fairchildes Lodge was the most beautiful of all the trees here. It drew us back with our cameras and our most romantic instincts.

I'd never walked through the centre of this field before, didn't remember it being left fallow. Ian had never made it out this far into the open. This was the landscape that both repelled and attracted him. Eventually I reached the lowest part of the valley and looked up at the lime tree, something Ian could never do, something I'd never done either, in all the games I'd played round the edges. I felt spooked out here, in the baking sun, vulnerable at the lowest point of the ploughed field. For a second I could glimpse what it might be like for Ian, the crushing, overwhelming size of it all. Climbing carefully back up the rough ploughed ground I made my way to the familiar edges once more. Ian was right. It felt better under the cover of the trees.

10
Pale Green Ghosts: Town and Country Divided

One of the chief virtues of the green belt is that it's a bit boring. It can't match the spectacular landscape of the National Parks or the urgent thrill of the city. Rather it occupies a similar place in the British psyche as *Reader's Digest*, Rich Tea biscuits and *Blue Peter*. Rather prim and middle class, and dependably unexciting. That was what I thought when I started these travels, and now I had reached the end, well, I wasn't entirely convinced I'd been proved wrong. Yes, there were bizarre elements – landfills, bunkers, airports – and beautiful ones too – views across the Chiltern Hills, say, or the Mole Valley. But generally speaking most of the green belt was a bit quiet. Large fields farmed or left fallow, some turned to meadows due to EU environmental schemes. Patches of derelict land on the edges of towns. Country parks and trunk roads. And golf courses, *so many* golf courses. They exert the most peculiar stranglehold on the countryside, a status symbol as flash and selfish as any shiny BMW that might attempt to force you off the road. Housing expert Colin Wiles estimates that 2 per cent of British land is given over to golf courses, almost double the amount used for homes across the country. Golf is the corporatisation of over thousands of square miles of British land.

Back in 1963, Michael Frayn described the difference between the two philosophies attempting to control Britain after the war: the herbivores – guilt-bound liberal intelligentsia behind the BBC and the Festival of Britain – and the carnivores – 'if God had not wished them to prey upon all smaller and weaker creatures without scruple he would not have made them as they are'. The green belt was certainly created by herbivores, those Fabians and ramblers, town planners and grandees chomping on the green grass, protecting it and, in the process, the leafy places where they lived too. The policy was a way of neutralising the carnivores, preventing them from buying and selling the scenery round towns for swift profits, as had happened in the interwar years. These days it's all rather more confusing. Both carnivores and herbivores form coalitions on either side of the argument: the housing campaigners and town planners alongside the big developers; the environmentalists alongside the nimbys and vested interests. It's hard to tell if those are sheep grazing in the paddock or wolves creeping around in expensive woollen jackets.

An image keeps recurring as I wander the edges of New Addington: diggers in the field opposite our old maisonette. The beginnings of a road through the hedgerows, the foundations of houses laid out into the valley, across the muddy expanse like stepping stones for a giant. I've seen it time and again in farmland outside Milton Keynes, say, or Aylesbury, growing towns where the green belt doesn't reach, places saddled with huge housing targets because of it. The image isn't unprecedented in my old street. A small cul-de-sac had been built at the end of Fairchildes Avenue in the 1980s, above the tangled hawthorn and briars of Hutchinson's Bank, the steep slope that haunted generations of kids on cross-country runs. Now, as you walk down that track you can look up and see the fences and gables of the little red brick houses through the branches and leaves. The chalk grassland of the bank itself has become a nature reserve, home to twenty-eight species of butterfly, including such splendours as the Glanville fritillary, the green hairsteak and the dingy skipper. London Wildlife Trust, who manage the area, encourage local people to get involved in cleaning it up. A generation of New Addingtoners connecting with the nature on their doorstep. But what if the rest of the valley was swallowed up by the estate? I can't pretend I wouldn't be upset, the landscape I have known all my life chewed over by mechanical mouths and laid out for houses, the very land itself receding into history like the creatures, plants and people who had once known it. People have to live somewhere. Finding those somewheres is not easy.

Recurring as that image is, it's not those fields that are most likely to be built on next. These lie at the other end of the estate, on the way to Croydon. They are the pick-your-own fields of Gravel Hill, where strawberries ended up in your mouth as often as they did in the punnet, and the old horses' fields beside the tram interchange at Addington village, which remain as scrubby and unkempt as ever. In the eighties a gaggle of stroppy geese had lived here, and enjoyed bursting through the fence and onto the dual carriageway. There they would stand about, rudely interrupting the modern world that had surrounded their field, making their presence felt like a bunch of protesters reminding everyone that they were still here. They couldn't do that now: the fields are all surrounded by tall temporary steel barriers, the land literally going to waste.

Persimmon, one of the biggest housebuilders in the UK, has been trying to gain a foothold on these sites for several years now, and the local council have said that they are willing to look at every option to find suitable places to reach their housing targets. There have been protests against it, most tellingly by the local MP, Gavin Barwell, who was appointed Minister of Housing by Theresa May in 2016. 'I do feel very strongly', he told the *Croydon Guardian* in January 2016, 'that unless there is literally no alternative we shouldn't be building houses on green belt.'

It was estimated by London Councils that the city would need an extra 800,000 new homes by 2021, when the population was expected to reach nine million. Obviously many of the problems facing London are not due to the green belt, but as Dame Evelyn Sharp predicted in the 1960s, for councils hemmed in by rigid barriers it is a contributory factor. So what should we expect of housebuilding in this new era? Precisely what we have seen for the last thirty-five years, I suspect. The feeble stop-start of private enterprise winning small battles and failing to make a dent on the housing shortage, the green belts as sacrosanct, the brownfields slowly exhausted, existing social housing sold off and none built, and everyone dissatisfied with the entirely predictable outcome. I am willing to be pleasantly surprised.

With all of these fields surrounded by a network of busy roads and tramlines, and after decades of containment, it seems only a matter of time before New Addington starts to grow once more. The council recently began looking again at their local plan. The CPRE noted that there were twenty open-space sites around the borough that were being earmarked for building, including three encampments for Irish traveller families. The outrage in the paper, the fractious meetings, the push and the pull of it between these contested boundaries, and little to show for it all. The carnivores and herbivores at war, each side looking suspiciously like the other.

It's always strange to go back there, the place I lived for thirty years, somewhere which has changed so little. Fairchildes Avenue, the outskirts of the outskirts, is a brisk ten-minute walk from the final tram stop. The houses a little scrappier than I remembered, with satellite dishes, leaded UPVC windows and elaborate white plastic front doors fussing up the exteriors. When I reached our old maisonette there was little evidence of our having lived there. No circle of flowers on the front lawn, no blousy roses growing up creosoted poles, no hastily-bolted-together dexion fence, the functional ramp John had built for Marj now a fairytale path snaking its way across the garden. Trying not to look too suspicious, I dodged across the road where long grass grew beneath tall trees. Beyond that were the fields, tricky to access through the dense tangle of shrubs bursting into leaf. But there were desire paths etched into the ground and they took me to a gap in the undergrowth, and from there I could see the valley. Scattered around for a metre or so were those classic pieces of evidence of the creep of civilisation: empty fag packets, choc ice wrappers, plastic bags, flattened cans and clear plastic bottles half-full of murky liquid. A couple of metres beyond and it was as I ever remembered, the steep valley, the mud ploughed up in regular divots, a thin bristle of green beginning to show. Worried that the curtains might be twitching, I left the narrow borderland and crossed back to the pavement.

I'd seen our maisonette, and now here was our old house too. As I approached, a familiar deep rumbling noise filled the air. I looked up and sure enough, a Spitfire was banking over the trees above the school. A salute of some kind. Not looking where I was going I almost bumped into one of our old neighbours, Tracey, a woman not much older than me, who was walking along with the aid of a stick. Despite the fact we hadn't seen each other for fifteen years she recognised me instantly, and we fell into companionable neighbourly chat. She told me the story of the street since I'd moved away: newcomers, babies, the infirm, the dead. While we stood there a man emerged from old Mr Stratford's house, the man we all used to know as Steptoe because of his fascination with collecting junk from over the woods. 'Look at this!' he'd say to me, standing there in his string vest, braces and flat cap, waving a rusty piece of metal at me. 'Camshaft. *Messerschmitt*. Found it over the fields.' And he'd laugh a great braying chuckle, never at anything remotely amusing. But this man wasn't Mr Stratford. For one thing, he looked pretty natty. 'I've been waiting to see who lives there!' said Tracey, excitedly. We talked each other through family illnesses. With a major back problem she was finding it difficult to move about. But, she said, whenever she felt low about it she thought of Marj, and of how she never complained and just got on with it. 'Your mum was an inspiration,' she said. Of course Marj sometimes did complain, and on occasion didn't get on with it, but I knew what she meant. She had been the Olympic champion of hope springing eternal, scooping the World Cup of making the best of it.

We waved our goodbyes and I headed off to the end of the street, where the estate stopped and the roads led out into the countryside. On one side was Keston Showmans' Park, a temporary encampment for fairground travellers like a relic from the Middle Ages. Past my old school and into the country, of sorts. A field punctuated by telegraph wires strung between tall poles on a dogged diagonal, the soil stony and unforgiving for any sort of organised growing. This field was surrounded, not by hedgerows, but by a bank of trees at least ten metres deep. On this early March day hazel catkins hung down like a thousand hungry caterpillars and hawthorn was bursting into flower over a month early. At the far end there was a small patch of wood. The ground was thick with oak leaves, through which I could catch the odd bloom of blue polythene or yellow canvas, builders' debris thrown out of sight. Sacks of rubble sat among the dead ferns and sprouting blue-bells. In the bare branches of shrubs were the tangled remains of plastic bags. It was a sorry sight, worse than it used to be. Accumulated decades of trash mingling with the wildlife, laying partial claim to the woods. They were evidence that life had gone on, I supposed.

'Though Addington was a dump,' Paul told me, 'still is, I don't think I could have had more fun growing up.' It was a reminder that for many people from the estate, the surrounding country wasn't a dumping ground, it was a constant mystery and inspiration. 'I never would have done half the things I did. Whether it's made me a better person than I would have been, who knows? Who cares, really? I had fun as a kid, and that was that. It's what growing up's all about, having fun and learning.'

In 2012 Grant Shapps, that shape-shifting entity from the Department for Communities and Local Government, announced a rather ponderous-sounding new initiative, the National Planning Policy Framework. In it lay the current definitions of the purposes of green belt land in England and Wales. They are to:

1. Check the unrestricted sprawl of large built-up areas.
2. Prevent neighbouring towns merging into one another.

3. Assist in safeguarding the countryside from encroachment.
4. Preserve the setting and special character of historic towns.
5. Assist in urban regeneration, by encouraging the recycling of derelict and other urban land.

The third is really just the first turned on its head, and watered down at that. But the fifth is a curious nimby-friendly notion, making a virtue of the bind that politicians now find themselves in. If you can't build on the green belts then you're forced to look again at the land where you can. Back to the cities it is, wearing out one pair of shoes to spare another. In an era of missed opportunities this new definition was just a feeble retread of the old, a fig leaf to disguise a lack of action.

Also published in 2012 was the Landscape Institute's guide to modern landscape architecture. The language was fascinating, the kind of buzzwords usually surrounded by circles on whiteboards: 'strategic planning, delivery and management'; 'vision'; 'engage stakeholders'; 'interaction with the environment'; 'public realm'; 'creating value'; 'infrastructure'; 'optimisation'; 'partnerships'; 'underpins visioning work'. In my research I'd become more used to their twentieth-century equivalents: 'amenity'; 'landscape value'; 'overspill'; 'development plans'; 'preservationism'; 'townsman'; 'countryman'. It made me wonder what the green belt would be called if it were created today. Stakeholder Green Space? The Urban Lungway? The Customer-Optimised Landscape InfraRealm? Not that it *would* be created today, of course. That's its unique value and chief annoyance. To housebuilders in our post-privatisation world it has all the appeal of the Lord Chamberlain censoring representations of sex or finding yourself chaperoned on a date.

Still, the Landscape Institute is trying to address some of the problems facing our green belts and the towns they contain. It is aware that within this zone of country we have acres of intensively farmed land, industrial waste or dereliction that has all the wild natural abandon of the HR department on the Death Star. The Landscape Institute's head, Merrick Denton-Thompson, has suggested the creation of management bodies, equivalent of those of National Parks, to oversee them. These managers could foster not just good planning but an increase in biodiversity, as well as helping to improve the health and wellbeing of city dwellers by encouraging them to use this open space. After all, with the green belt being such a passive policy, these kind of positive uses aren't officially encouraged or promoted.

The Landscape Institute is not the only organisation thinking again about the green belt. A new generation of academics, architects, economists, planners and students have been looking at it afresh. There's Urbed, for example, a design consultancy that won the 2014

Wolfson Prize for its modern garden city project. It proposed doubling the population of towns of 200,000 people through minor incursions into the green belt and the creation of managed green space. Such was the public relations panic about this abstract proposal that the government, which had nothing whatsoever to do with either the prize or the plan, immediately condemned it. Housing Minister Brandon Lewis said the government was 'committed to protecting the green belt from development as an important protection against urban sprawl'. Like a spooked entrepreneur from *Dragons' Den*, Lewis was quick to declare *I'm out*: the 'proposal from Lord Wolfson's competition is not government policy and will not be taken up,' he said.

Then there were the students of the Royal College of Art School of Architecture, who in 2013 produced *The Green Belt Atlas*, a series of maps revealing just what was in the Metropolitan Green Belt. They showed the AONBs, the SSSIs, the grasslands and woodland, but also the built-up areas, the voting patterns over time (increasingly Tory) and the current and historic locations of landfill sites. This kind of research and data visualisation helps counter some of the more outlandish claims made about the green belt from either side of the debate. The *Atlas* was then used as part of a report by planner Jonathan Manns for a resurgent London Society, an organisation that had been instrumental in the creation of our green belts a hundred years ago. 'Central to success', he wrote, 'will be the way in which new housing is integrated with the green belt; whether through the release of parcels on the city fringe, expansion of existing satellite towns or development of new settlements elsewhere.'[1] In the ongoing green belt war Manns' work was attacked in the *Sunday Times* as lobbying for large house builders, while he defended it as his 'professional judgement.'[2]

Ailing, fragile and exploited, our green belt policy presides over much of our country like King Lear. Its reign has been long and surprisingly stable but as the heirs – politicians, builders, nimbys, planners – have begun to circle for position and power, the whole situation has begun to descend into madness. This is a version of *King Lear* stuffed with Gonerils and Regans, with the odd Gloucester thrown in (or plucked out), and a conspicuous lack of Cordelias. In 2015 it was reported that the number of houses given planning permission on green belt land in England had more than doubled since 2014, five times more than it had been just five years earlier. This increase isn't being achieved in a carefully planned way; instead it's a careless nibbling away to little effect on either housebuilding or conservation. Then there's London's predicted population increase, two million more people by 2030. Given the chance, it's difficult to believe that huge rural landowners like the Crown Estate wouldn't sell off their green belt acres in a heartbeat if they could. And then we might see the full storm of a Shakespearean tragedy begin to unfold.

Well, this was embarrassing. It turned out Marjorie hadn't died after all. I'd returned to my childhood home on New Year's Eve 2015. I could have sworn we'd left the house years before, and yet here it was, just the same. That fancy Georgian-style wallpaper in the living room, the faded cheap blue flowery carpet, the same threadbare old furniture in the same places, just as I'd last seen it. A lovely, friendly, homely mess. And there, facing the window, in the place she'd parked her wheelchair forever, was Marjorie, smiling serenely. Here she was, back from California, she told me. And I was supposed to have known this. Why couldn't I remember? Why had I persisted in this fantasy for seventeen years that she was dead? These were extraordinary times, I reminded myself. Why, just the other day Kathy Beale had returned from the dead on *EastEnders*. Don't get me wrong, I was delighted to see my mum, but a sense of mortification was overwhelming me too. *Just like you, John*, I could imagine the rest of my family saying, when they found out. *Head in the clouds*. The very same head you'd forget if it wasn't screwed on. But this, this was worse than the time I'd left that suitcase on the train, or my front door keys on the chest freezer. Forgetting a beloved parent was alive and well, or as well as any of us sickly runts could claim to be. It had to be said, Marj didn't seem particularly emotional about it. Seventeen years, get over it. Instead it was like two acquaintances bumping into each other in the street. We traded formalities, made noises of polite surprise, nodded with more vigour than was strictly necessary. All those years stood between us. Even so, some of the differences were unexpected. Despite her time in California she had taken on an Australian accent. And she was full of ideas on how I could improve myself. Perhaps plastic surgery, she suggested.

What had I been up to, she wanted to know. I mentioned I'd been writing and she was chuffed to bits, and sat there, expectantly. I was reluctant to hand over the manuscript. How to break it to her that in the book I was writing I thought she had died. That, indeed, for years I had told everyone she was dead. That somehow I'd forgotten that my own mother was actually alive. *Hello Mum!* No zombie apocalypse, this, or soap opera fireworks. Instead there was stifled confusion, guilt tied up with embarrassment. Was this all that coming back to life amounted to? In the event I stalled on the whole death thing for as long as I could, and instead we chatted about the house, the garden, the weather. I squatted down next to her chair, and suddenly I was looking up and around as I had as a child, holding on to her armrest and eye-level with the stickers on the side – one of the Red Arrows, another that said *I'm With the Royal Air Force*. I looked round the room as she spoke, and it was all there as it ever had been: the music centre, John's tatty wing-backed chair, Marj's trolley, stacked with papers, cheap jewellery, boxes of medicine and pots of pens. Light came dazzling in through the front window, from the garden, the avenue, the acres of school fields and valley beyond. The sensation of being a child again, holding on to the arm of her wheelchair, looking out on the world from the edge of it all, was overwhelming. In the corner of the room there was a figure I couldn't get a fix on, couldn't quite see. A patterned acrylic jumper. Tracksuit bottoms. Wild hair. Short and stout. A man on the periphery, out of reach.

When I awoke it was, indeed, New Year's Eve 2015. I was in my flat, my partner Adam asleep next to me. I lay there in the dark, trying to unscramble this visitation. I felt shaken. The physical sensation of being next to Marj. Of returning to the old house. An aftershock of mortification flowed through me. In the dream I had forgotten she was alive. And now, in reality, I had to remember that she was dead. I reached over and switched on my bedside lamp, with its ceramic painted trunk and canopy of faded green embroidery silk, made by Marj some thirty years before.

I never dream about my family or my past, and so this one stayed with me all through the day and into the new year. When I should have been thinking ahead I remained jangled by the past. It wasn't the soap opera outrageousness but the details I'd not thought of for years that haunted me: net curtains, acrylic carpet, patterned wallpaper, enamel chipped from the wheel-chair. Cheap man-made fabrics, objects fallen from long-halted production lines, colours seldom seen today, patterns only revisited in irony and contempt. Time masked how much I missed it all: Marj, John, the house, the avenue, the trees and country beyond, the life we had lived for many years. All that day it felt so close again. And then it faded, lost to the edges.

Paul Shepheard was fascinated by the unlikely people, like his father Peter, who had founded the green belts.

'It all came from the top, didn't it?' he said. 'It's all the ruling class. They are the landowners, these people, which is interesting.' He paused. 'I'm just wondering where the impulse to stop this hyperinflation of land is going to come from. As far as I can figure out no one can see how to stop that, and it's wrecking the place. Maybe extreme localism would be one way to do it. Like you can't buy a property in Switzerland unless you have lived there for so many years.'

We talked about how people look at architecture and appreciate it was 'modern', but they don't look at the green belt and see the same. My interest in it partly comes from the fact it's as much part of the postwar city as tower blocks, flyovers and streets in the sky. The green belts we ended up with are part of the same story, created by the same people as part of that same solution, not separate from it. The kind of lazy bar-room criticism you hear of postwar planning never extends to the green belt. Nimbys should be blowing kisses to tower blocks, hugging the concrete bollards of council estates, scattering rose petals on high walkways. They are as much the heroes of this story as the green belts, because without them and the planners who attempted to fit together the many conflicting and complex things that make our modern lives possible, we would have deregulated sprawl everywhere we look. Although, sure, that free-for-all is increasingly the world we now inhabit, thanks to the negligent short-termism of modern politics. The feeding frenzy over those pre-Thatcher assets, from council housing to the green belt, has now gnawed through to the bone.

I needed to cheer myself up. Do people at least still enjoy the green belt country near our towns? Figures for urban folk visiting green belts were sketchy, the CPRE claiming that there were 1.3 billion visits to England's green belts in 2013–14, which sounds like a lot, but also hard to visualise. The survey suggested there were no barriers depending on class or income, but I can sense the ghost of Octavia Hill raising an eyebrow at that. Access to the countryside for urban people is limited as much by a lack of confidence and knowledge as it is by money or transport. Would my family have ever ventured into those fields and woods if we'd remained living in Battersea? I doubt it. It was a different world, a culture shock from which it took years to adjust: for Ian, an ongoing process. And certainly there is a significant lack of black or ethnic minority people living and working in the countryside. All of my walks presented a rather monocultural picture: middle-aged white people, mostly affluent, usually with a prop such as a bike, dog or child to make the visit permissible. I asked Karen Keenan whether she ever explored the green belt outside her home of Skelmanthorpe in Yorkshire.

'Yes, I suppose we do,' she said. 'We walk. The local parish council is pretty good. They've got a country-side officer, and they've done a set of a dozen village walks. Each village has a walk, usually a circular one, that you can do. But if you drive ten to fifteen minutes you can be closer to Holmfirth, you can be up on the tops. There's reservoirs to walk round.' The country-side officer had produced a series of leaflets promoting various walks. 'The Denby Dale one's good because that tells you all about the history of the pies.' It appears that, along with the Emley Moor mast and Yorkshire Sculpture Park, her local area has another eccentric trick tucked into its green belt. The village of Denby Dale has a history of baking huge commemorative pies, going back to 1788 to celebrate, of all things, George III's recovery from porphyria. 'One pie they made, it went off straight away,' explained Karen, referring to the one commemorating Victoria's Golden Jubilee in 1887. 'And they had to bury it somewhere in quicklime to get rid of it. So there's somewhere you can go where the pie was buried. Quirky things like that!' Even the local dairy has become a tourist attraction. 'Half past three every day they bring the cows in for milking,' she explained, 'and they've got a viewing platform. So you go up from the café, out on the platform, look down, see the cows coming in, see them milked, see the milk filling the containers.' It is an image straight from one of those progressive Ladybird books from the sixties and seventies, where rural images were often interrupted with combine harvesters or cooling towers. Proof that even the mechanised processes of modern farming and the industrialised landscape can be viewed as entertainment.

I'd been haunted by one of the things that Croydon's Tree Officer Richard Edwards had said as we were walking around Selsdon Wood. Part of their job, he'd said, was to manipulate time. He meant that by progressively cutting down trees in different areas they could help reproduce the same effects of nature on a larger forest over time, creating diversity where there was none. Ideas about how to make our green belt land more biologically diverse should be welcomed, especially with the threats to our landscape posed by ash dieback, neonicotinoids and the rest. But the cutting of local authority funds means that countryside stewardship projects are at the bottom of a long list of urgent priorities. In many ways this acts as the start of a massive programme of privatisation, one prefigured by recent suggestions that the government hand over some planning functions to private companies, taking decisions out of the hands of local authorities and putting into those of businesses like Barton Willmore. Running down an amenity due to underfunding and then breaking it up and selling it off is the only form of management modern politicians and policy makers seem to understand. It's impossible to imagine the green belt will be any different. In twenty years' time no amount of careful woodland management tricks will be able to turn back the clock on large areas of our green belt.

As much as we might want to engage in a debate with the ideas of Octavia Hill or Patrick Abercrombie, their voices speak to a culture that is dying. In many places we cannot protect a green belt that is worth saving or build the homes we desperately need because we have abandoned both the systems and the morality that brought them into existence in the first place. Instead, all we hear are rousing soundbites that appear to link us to a fantasy of the past.

For something so abstract, the green belts have changed an enormous amount of the physical landscape of Britain. By keeping 13 per cent of our landmass in stasis, change is kept at bay, while a significant percentage of urban land is controlled too. Of course, many of our large towns don't have green belts to protect them. Swansea. Brighton. Southampton. Portsmouth. Plymouth. Middlesbrough. Ipswich. Taunton. Norwich. Leicester. Carlisle. Lincoln. Swindon. Hull. There's Dundee too, of course, though that was their own perverse, or enlightened, choice.

Even though these cities and towns don't have green belts, many are beside other protected landscapes, such as AONBs or National Parks. Little of the land round our urban areas would allow for unrestricted growth.

In martial arts, the belts, or obi, denote the skill level of the wearer. In judo there are nine levels, and green is fourth from bottom; in karate it's the middle of nine. Appropriately enough, the green belt is all about fighting. Fighting to save it. Fighting for decent housing for all. Fighting for shareholder value. To some it's a joke, like wrestling a rubber snake in a B-movie. To others it's life or death, like the belts the murderer uses in Alfred Hitchcock's 1972 shocker *Frenzy* to strangle his helpless naked victims. To city dwellers the green belt is tightening around our throats. To country folk we are ignorant barbarians, intent on its destruction. Once the green belt was a mechanism for trying to help us get along. Now it is the chief cause of antagonism.

Back in 1969 Dame Evelyn Sharp, that sharp-elbowed senior civil servant rolling her eyes at the incompetencies of her ministers, was one of the many eminent planners who forecast the problem we now find ourselves in. 'The failures, or the supposed failures are all too evident', she wrote. 'The inability of some of the great cities, hemmed in by green belts, to open up their crowded areas or meet their housing needs.'[3] In the same year the greatest living planner of the age, Peter Hall, wrote something that chimed perfectly with Sharp's view of events:

In the fast-growing London region of the post-1945 period, there is in fact a serious danger that the green belt may become a device of anti-planning, used by the counties around the conurbation – which are understandably reluctant to take more overspill than they can help – to make sure that the London émigrés go anywhere rather than their sacred plot.[4]

These predictions have come to pass. Where Abercrombie and his ilk saw flexibility, the next generation saw only rules that had to be obeyed or rebelled against. And so rather than being engaged with and positively developed, the ideas behind it have atrophied or been debased. David Eversley, a former GLC chief strategic planner, wrote a forceful piece in 1974 called 'Conservation for the Minority', remarking that 'a tiny minority of self-appointed arbiters of taste dictates what the living standard of the rest of us shall be'. And who might they be? 'The ever present ancient establishment . . . They are continually mourning for a past where they, and they alone, had a right to tranquility, the open countryside, distant coasts, spacious surroundings.'[5]

Is the green belt primarily an environmental issue? Of course it is. But then so is every element of our lives. The environment will always remain the biggest issue we face, whether it's protecting the countryside or using our resources to make food that we throw away, the energy to power our workplaces and leisure, or our cars and home comforts. Just supplying the energy to keep us alive, to feed and clothe and heat us, helps destroy the world a little bit more. Environmentalism is seeing our lives and existence as part of the whole ecology of our planet. Just as they did with garden cities and new towns, planners have to look to sustainable solutions, which limit car use and journey times as well as making a minimal impact on the landscape and resources.

'Green belt is the one part of planning policy that people think they understand,' said planner Ian Tant. But for him, the myth of the circular town surrounded by green was killing any chance of doing right by the cities and the country. A 1930s model for solving a 1930s problem. 'If you want to develop sustainably and limit the distances people have to travel for work, shops, schools, the best place to put development is on the edges of those towns.' He talked me through the Copenhagen model, where fingers of development are allowed along transport corridors and around major transport hubs. Transport was one of the big issues for the green belt. If we can't build enough homes within a city then we're pushing commuters out to the other side of the girdle. Is commuting long distances a viable option? Roughly a fifth of all London's employees are commuters. In the decade to 2014, rising house prices and the financial crash of 2008 contributed to a 72 per cent increase in people travelling to work over two hours a day across Britain, according to the TUC. In

2015 the Royal Town Planning Institute examined data about people's journeys to work in the Metropolitan Green Belt. They looked at five medium-sized towns, such as Bracknell and Watford, with railway lines directly connected to central London. Only 7.4 per cent of commuters used these routes, while 72 per cent went to work by car, often to jobs not in London but based locally or elsewhere. The misery of commuting, the time wasted and the pollution caused is one of the green belt's less attractive legacies. So could the Copenhagen model help? Ian Tant couldn't imagine a politician brave enough to suggest it in the UK. 'It's getting the political traction for that, because the first politician to stand up and say, "I think the green girdle idea is the wrong thing to do, what we ought to be doing is . . ." – you can just imagine the lambasting they're going to get for that.'

'It may be that we're fifteen to twenty years away from where we get a mass reconsideration of green belt policy,' said Ian. 'But that debate has to happen now. Because people have to start changing their conception of green belt. It's not the sacrosanct, written-in-stone, long-term thing that tends to be the conception. It's a policy. And if it isn't serving the problem correctly, change the policy. Let's look at a different way to see these things.'

Mick Wills, the retired Worcestershire planner, came at the problem from the local authority perspective rather than that of a private planning consultancy. He could see where the ideas of Ebenezer Howard and Patrick Abercrombie had gone wrong.

'Up until the Thatcher era we had a fairly large planning department,' he recalled. 'We were able to get ahead of the race and do forward planning, and actually work out where new development ought to go. That's been lost now because planning departments have been cut and cut and cut. There aren't enough to do planning in the way it ought to be done. And a corollary of the green belt is that you can protect this bit, but you have to be able to say where these developments should go. And I don't think it's adequate to rely on the market, because they'll go where they can sell them, not where it's best for the county.'

The green belt is one of the many victims of a modern malaise. A lack of people adult enough to debate complex subjects in a reasonable manner with a sense of mutual respect. Forget Brexit, Corbynmania or Kanye West, the green belt has been bringing out the very worst in people since the 1950s. Neither side is listening; instead we face increasingly extreme and unreasonable behaviour, a white noise of yes/no. Housing and conservation, both precarious, both essential. The adults have left the room. The adults were, in this case, the regional and county planners, abolished by successive neoliberal governments. In 2004 New Labour ditched the strategic County Structure Plans invented in the sixties. Less than a decade later, the coalition disposed of their replacements, Regional Spacial Strategies, which had been costly and didn't deliver their promised housing targets. So we no longer have county or regional planners, just local ones, relative minnows with little power to affect the big picture.

A recent report by homelessness charity Shelter and planning company Quod suggested that to solve the housing crisis no elements should be discounted as possible solutions. In fact, they proposed that we needed a bit of everything – brownfield, building high, new garden cities, estate and town centre renewal, building along transport corridors, and losing 0.8 per cent of the London green belt – to reach the 50,000 new houses we need a year. It was calmly reported in the London *Evening Standard* as 'Build on Green Belt NOW'. No grown-ups, it seemed, were available for comment.

Our housing crisis has been on the cards ever since Michael Heseltine put a moratorium on council house building in 1980. Private builders need to keep the price of houses high, so it's in their interest not to flood the market with new homes. Instead they have been 'land-banking' – buying land and not building on it. Because the market doesn't provide what we need, which is new housing, and instead warps the existing resources we have to its own ends, we cannot trust speculators with the green belt. Council house building programmes, although not perfect, would at least inject some fairness back into the British housing scene. They would also allow for the inclusion of green space in new building, something that developers are seldom keen on. Thinking in a more joined-up way might just save our green belts from complete unsustainable collapse.

In January 2017 the government unveiled the sites for 200,000 homes to be built in 14 new 'garden villages' and three 'garden towns' in England, with little but the name to link them to Ebenezer Howard's vision. Some, like the one on the border between Essex and Hertfordshire, would be in the green belt. The government's Housing White Paper was spoken of in radical terms, until it was unveiled. One suggestion that failed to materialise was environmental exchange, allowing councils to move the position of their green belts to suit house building. Instead, the finished item assured everyone that all of the old green belt protections would remain. 'There is no need to take huge tracts of land out of the green belt to solve the housing crisis,' was minister Gavin Barwell's ambiguous soundbite.[6] The bullets dodged, the decisions unmade.

Am I pessimistic about the green belts? I think I am, yes. Because we are living in an era when many of the things from which they sprang – a desire to make things better for everyone, not just an elite; a determination to understand and address fundamentally important issues such as conservation, bad housing or homelessness – are now more debased than at any point in my lifetime. When public life is dominated by the shabby and the shallow, how can fundamental decencies be argued for with any hope of success? I do not think that every square metre of our green belts is worth retaining, or indeed can be retained. But without the requisite grown-ups in the room how can we hope to make the best of what we have and work out what we need? In a bear pit of lies and instant gratification something as abstract as a green belt ultimately stands no chance.

'We sold a field here,' said Malcolm Mott of Fairchildes Farm. 'If you go that way back to Addington, a ten-acre field backs up to the school playing field.' This triangle of land was split down the centre between Kent and Surrey. 'We sold it when I bought the farm, because they thought it was a good prospect for building on, so we got a good price.' The firm who bought it haven't been able to touch it since 1989. 'And now they have a wood,' said Malcolm. 'It's turned into a wood! The trees are now eight, ten or twelve foot high. That is what happens if you leave it. I think they thought they had a result when there was talk of pulling the school down and building houses. But that never happened.'

And so, after we'd spoken I made my way back to New Addington the way he suggested, the long fields full of new crops growing in the spring sunshine. I cut through into a patch of aged woodland and then to my left was a familiar sight – a glimpse of rusted railings, the end of the immense school field. Here I looked back from the green belt onto the estate. Beyond the distant school buildings was the street of semi-detached council houses where I'd grown up. It had once been Fairchildes High School. Now it's Meridian, an academy, facing all the same problems of poverty and apathy, and failing as much as it ever did in the face of all their hard work.

The fence continued for an age, and curved around so I was back walking straight towards the estate. Then I began to see it. On my left, the tall, thick barrier of the old growth beside the school fence, mighty trees and dense shrubs cut back to help form a path. And on my right, the young trees, a great clearing of them, light and fragile beside their elderly relatives. Once Malcolm's farmers field, now a developer's thicket. Dense grass ran into the abandoned lea. The oaks were late into bud. It was impossible to walk in the thicket; young ash, hawthorn and silver birch had sent spindly stems high into the air in a desperate competition for light. They formed an impenetrable barrier. Dandelions were in flower at the base of slender saplings. Hazel and hawthorn had come into leaf and were spreading outwards, trying to crowd out their taller neighbours. Brambles arched up and around these slender stems, their barbs ready to catch you should you stray from the well-worn path. The remains of last year, the brown leaves and tall bleached grass stalks, lay at the foot of the trees, as new growth of geranium, wood anemone and ash pushed through.

Sycamore saplings had grown most lustily here, the big hand-sized leaves spreading out to catch the spring sunshine and shade the floor of this new woodland. Their century-old parents stood beside the school fence and towered above me, trunks splitting off into complicated swooping patterns. Alder and may tree created a dense wall of green. In some places the green belts have preserved the old landscape to the extent that it's like discovering ancient civilisations lost in the rainforest. But not here. This new young woodland was a school, inspired by the one the council had built beside it in the fifties. A nursery for trees and shrubs springing up on the edge of this estate. A green belt accident, one of those of which there are countless. A plot which has thickened with trees and shrubs rather than houses and flats. A new wood on old farmland, enabled by a company jumping the gun and a strange old policy standing firm.

Like so much of the green belt, this wasn't what anyone had imagined would happen. A speculator's misstep creating a new wood, seeded and managed all by itself. It was yet another reminder that the generalisations I'd heard about the dereliction beside housing estates were so often misplaced. This land might be nature reserves or chalk pits. Landfill sites or ancient meadows. Converted barns or motorway embankments. Electricity substations or nuclear bunkers. Astroturf, managed forests, busted fridges and litter. A walk in the green belt is a reminder of what we have done to the landscape. Created the picturesque and practical over centuries, farmland and forest, land since despoiled, built on, protected or improved. It's a reminder too of the artificiality of our countryside: the houses beyond the trees, the motorway cutting through, the airport in its midst. There is the rubberised or concrete mesh laid out in car parks, to stop weeds growing and the soil from eroding. These 'geosynthetic grass protection systems' all have brilliant names. GridForce. EcoGrid. BodPave 40. They allow the green belt here to be turned into car parking, while still letting grass grow. All the appearance of green with none of the troublesome consequences of growth. They remain the most green belt thing I have seen. Maybe one day this is what the countryside will be, rolling fields of BodPave 40, and meadows underlaid by GridForce. The green belt holds within it a myriad of twentieth-century dreams, from the garden city enthusiasts and ramblers to the planners and technocrats, the technologically advanced farmers and the earthy environmentalists, the politicians and builders, the nimbys and protesters.

As I continued walking I emerged, suddenly, by the side of a road and the school gates. On the green belt, looking outwards to the estate. From the old lanes: Featherbed; Sheepbarn; North Pole; Skid Hill. I took a slow stroll back along my street; a place that was no longer my street, no matter what my dreams might suggest. What hope for families like mine now, finding a flat in the centre of London or a house on the outskirts? All those years I'd lingered here and taken it all for granted – the space, the light, the constant spectacular parade of the changing seasons.

Growing up where I did it was easy to feel that the town didn't want me, and the country wasn't too bothered either. Now I'm older it feels that this classic green belt scenario, of being trapped between conflicting things, is what living in the twenty-first century is all about. Maybe we can't have it all – town *and* country – but we can't afford to lose either. It's a false choice, of course, to decide between them. Both are essential for our continued existence, and the green belt, for all its flaws, is just a way of policing that. And undoubtedly better than nothing. Without compromise there is no love story or progress. It's all part of being a responsible adult. In these polarised days it's something we need to be reminded of.

A curiosity I noticed on my way to the tram was that the holly tree we'd planted in the front garden of our house was now the only remaining relic of our time there. Once a tiny, insignificant aside beside the delphiniums, dog roses and lupins, now it was an ugly brute, up to the windows of the top floor. One of Marj's cuttings gone wild, something none of us had particularly cared for. And so the rules which govern our landscape, the laws and policies, plans and whims, become like this garden too. All the things we might have nurtured, discarded by successive generations.

What remains is meaningless totems, the asides they thought nothing of, the weasel words nobody intended. Patrick Abercrombie and Octavia Hill might look over the green belts we have now with the same sense of bewilderment as I did our old garden. Why did they keep *that*, they might think, and lose all those good things? That wasn't what we meant at all. But then we are not beholden to people and ideas from another time. We are the grown-ups now, and the world we live in not anyone else's fault or design. Once, before all of the infighting and blame, the green belt was an inspiring idea, an attempt to make order out of chaos. Much as we might want to rise above it and make decisions afresh, like all things green belt we are taken round in circles over and over. Just looking out onto it is to bring back echoes of history that quickly overwhelm us. And so, filled with all those age-old contradictions, anxieties and suppressed feelings of hope I walked away from the edge, and kept on going.

APPENDIX
Government Circular, 3 August 1955:

I am directed by the Minister of Housing and Local Government to draw your attention to the importance of checking the unrestricted growth of built-up areas, and of safeguarding the surrounding countryside against further encroachment.

He is satisfied that the only really effective way to achieve this object is by the formal designation of clearly defined green belts around the areas concerned.

The minister accordingly recommends planning authorities to consider establishing a green belt wherever this is desirable in order:

a) to check the further growth of a large built-up area;

b) to prevent the neighbouring towns from merging into one-another; or

c) to preserve the special character of a town.

Wherever practicable the green belt should be several miles wide, so as to ensure an appreciable rural zone all round the built-up area concerned.

Inside a green belt, approval should not be given, except in very special circumstances, for the construction of new buildings or for the change of use of existing buildings for purposes other than agriculture, sport, cemeteries, institutions standing in extensive grounds, or other uses appropriate to a rural area.

Apart from a strictly limited amount of 'infilling' or 'rounding off' (within boundaries to be defined in Town Maps) existing towns and villages within a green belt should not be allowed to expand further. Even within the urban areas thus defined, every effort should be made to prevent any further building for industrial or commercial purposes; since this, if allowed, would lead to a demand for more labour, which in turn would create a need for the development of additional land for housing.

A Planning Authority which wishes to establish a green belt in its area should, after consulting any neighbouring Planning Authority affected, submit to the Minister, as soon as possible, a Sketch Plan, indicating the approximate boundaries of the proposed belt. Before officially submitting their plans, authorities may find it helpful to discuss them informally with this Ministry either through its regional representative or in Whitehall.

In due course, a detailed survey will be needed to define precisely the inner and outer boundaries of the green belt, as well as the boundaries of towns and villages within it. Thereafter, those particulars will have to be incorporated as amendments in the Development Plan.

The procedure may take some time to complete. Meanwhile it is desirable to prevent any further deterioration in the position. The Minister, therefore, asks that, where a Planning Authority has submitted a Sketch Plan for a green belt, it should forthwith apply provisionally in the area proposed.

I am Sir, Your obedient servant,
B. Valentine, Under Secretary

Acknowledgements

Thank you to the many people who have helped me write this book and have assisted in its publication. Particular credit is due to the brilliant advice of my agent Nicola Barr and editor Drummond Moir. Thanks too to Eleanor Crow for her wonderful illustrations, and to the publishing team, Nikki Barrow, Jenny Campbell, Fleur Clarke, Lucy Hale, Richard Peters, Caitriona Horne, Nick Fawcett and Joe Hall.

As well as the people I interviewed for the book, my research was greatly assisted by Gillian Darley, @DiamondGeezer, Rachel Cooke, Will Wiles, Les Back, Charles Holland, Paul Lincoln, Katie Lock, Julia Thrift, Shane Brownie, Joseph Watson, Euan Leitch, Kate Ashbrook, Bartley Shaw, Kevin Trickett, Ewan Tant, Neil Sinden, Paul Miner, Mura Quigley, Camilla Smallwood and Julie Gough.

Thanks are also due to the support of Eddy Rhead, Jack Hale, Ben Yarde Buller, Justine Crow, Jonathan Main, Joseph Watson, Neil Denny, Mike Althorpe, Catherine Croft, James Ward, Helen Day, Kesewa Hennessy, Tim Dunn, Jason Hazeley, Karen McLeod, Helen Day, Salomon Frausto, Mark Pimlott, Susanna

Round, Richard King, Andrea Butcher and many writers, booksellers, librarians, archivists and enthusiasts who have made the process of producing this book so enjoyable.

I'd especially like to thank my brothers, Ian and Paul, for giving up their time and for being so supportive and enthusiastic for such a curious project. I'd also like to thank Fern, Lily, Daisy and Tracey Grindrod for all of their love, time and kindness, as well as Susan and Dennis Le Baigue, Donna Payne, Matt Haslum, Mary Newbrook, Katie Hall, Richard de Pesando, Lorna Rees Coshan, Chris Gough, Colin Harvey, Sally Lee, Christian Manley, Andy Miller, Noel Murphy, Anna Pallai, Sarah Wickens, Dawn Burnett, Bunmi Western, Helen Zaltzman, Bob Stanley, Karen Duffy, Sid Fletcher, Catherine Daly, Julian Loose and Steve Archer.

This book could not have been written without the miraculous support of my partner, Adam Nightingale, his family, Ann and Jane, and his ever-curious and inspiring father Ray, who passed away in January 2017.

Further Reading

I read many hundreds of books and articles in my research, but these publications in particular proved invaluable sources:

Patrick Abercrombie, *The Greater London Plan*, HMSO, 1945.

Clough Williams-Ellis (ed.), *Britain and the Beast*, J.M. Dent, 1938.

Martin J. Elson, *Green Belts: Conflict Mediation in the Urban Fringe*, Heinemann, 1986.

Nan Fairbrother, *New Lives, New Landscapes*, Penguin, 1972.

Jonathan Manns, *Green Sprawl: Our Current Affection for a Preservation Myth?*, London Society, 2014.

The Ministry of Housing and Local Government, *The Green Belts*, HMSO, 1962.

Dr Michael Murray, *The Politics and Pragmatism of Urban Containment: Belfast Since 1940*, Avebury, 1991.

Royal College of Art School of Architecture, ADS2: Amelia Hunter, Andy Matthews, Rowan Prady,

Benjamin Turner and William Young, *The Green Belt Atlas*, 2013.

David Thomas, *London's Green Belt*, Faber, 1970.

The West Midlands Group, *Conurbation*, The Architectural Press, 1948.

Notes

Introduction

1 Patrick Abercrombie, *The Greater London Plan*, HMSO, 1945, pp. 154–5.
2 Ibid.

Chapter 1

1 Thomas More, *Utopia*, 1515.
2 W.G. Hoskins, *The Making of the English Landscape*, Pelican, 1955, p. 91.
3 Sir William Petty, *Essay on the Growth of London*, 1682.
4 John Ward, *Information Relative to New Zealand*, 1841.

Chapter 2

1 Frederic Osborn, *Green Belt Cities*, 2nd edition, Evelyn, Adams and Mackay, 1969, p. 66.
2 Ebenezer Howard, *Garden Cities of Tomorrow*, 1898.
3 Extract from Prospectus of First Garden City, Ltd, 1903, in Osborn, *Green Belt Cities*, p. 183.
4 Osborn, *Green Belt Cities*, p. 56.
5 *Garden Cities and Town Planning*, April 1921, p. 92.

6 Osborn, *Green Belt Cities*, p. 68.

7 C.E.M. Joad, in Clough Williams-Ellis (ed.), *Britain and the Beast*, J.M. Dent, 1938, p. 80.

8 A.G. Street, in Williams-Ellis (ed.), *Britain and the Beast*, p. 126.

9 Howard Marshall, in Williams-Ellis (ed.), *Britain and the Beast*, p. 171.

10 Dame Evelyn Sharp, *The Ministry of Housing and Local Government*, George Allen & Unwin, 1969, p. 163.

11 S.D. Adshead, *Journal of the London Society*, 21, July 1919.

12 Juliet Gardiner, *The Thirties*, Harper Press, 2010, p. 249.

13 Sylvia Crowe, *Tomorrow's Landscapes*, Architectural Press, 1956, p. 137.

Chapter 3

1 Neville Chamberlain, in *Ministry of Housing and Local Government: The Green Belts*, HMSO, 1962, p. 2.

2 Raymond Unwin, *Architects' Journal*, 58, 1923, p. 608.

3 Raymond Unwin, in Andrew Saint, *Politics and the People of London*, Hambledon Press, 1989, p. 227.

4 *Manchester Guardian*, 2 May 1935, p. xiv.

5 Ibid., p. 13.

6 CPRE, 'Sheffield's Green Belt', 1945 (leaflet).

7 *Scotsman*, 21 August 1935, p. 8.

8 *Croydon Advertiser*, 20 July 1935, p. 10.

9 Ibid., p. 11.

10 *Croydon Advertiser*, 1 April 1938, p. 15.

11 R.G. Bolton (letter), *Croydon Advertiser*, 28 September 1935, p. 16.

12 Sheila Kaye-Smith, in Williams-Ellis (ed.), *Britain and the Beast*, p. 43.

13 R.C. Sherriff, *Greengates*, Persephone Books, 1936, p. 198.

14 Ibid., p. 241.

15 *The Times*, 26 August 1936, p. 13.

16 *Observer*, 7 March 1937, p 11.

17 Patrick Abercrombie, *Greater London Plan 1944*, HMSO, 1945, pp. 154–5.

18 Bruce Watkin, *Surrey: A Shell Guide*, Faber & Faber, 1977, p. 38.

Chapter 4

1 Lord Howarth of Penrith quoting Nazi law of 1935 in Williams-Ellis (ed.), *Britain and the Beast*, p. 284.

2 C.E.M. Joad, *The Untutored Townsman's Invasion of the Country*, Faber, 1944, p. 37.

3 Peter Hall, *The Containment of Urban England*, Allen & Unwin, 1973.

4 Ministry of Works and Planning, 'Report of the Committee on Land Utilisation of Land Use in Rural Areas', HMSO, 1943, p. 71.

5 *Scotsman*, 1 March 1941, p. 5.

6 Grieve quoted in Glendinning and Muthesius, *Tower Block*, Yale University Press, 1994, p. 159.

7 Rowland Nicholas, *The Manchester City Plan*, Jarrold and Sons, 1945.

8 The West Midlands Group, *Conurbation*, The Architectural Press, 1948, p. 100.

9 *The Greater London Plan*.

10 Crowe, *Tomorrow's Landscapes*, p. 157.

Chapter 5

1 See Appendix.

2 Sharp, *The Ministry of Housing and Local Government*, p. 150.

3 J.R. James, in David Thomas, *London's Green Belt*, Faber, 1970, p. 89.

4 Martin Elson, *Green Belts*, Heinemann, 1986, p. 22.

5 *Manchester Guardian*, 30 June 1955, p. 2.

6 *Manchester Guardian*, 25 October 1952, p. 9.

7 Richard Crossman, 'December 5 1964', *The Diaries of a Cabinet Minister Volume One*, Hamish Hamilton and Jonathan Cape, 1974, p. 86.

8 Crossman, 'December 6 1964', *Diaries of a Cabinet Minister*, p. 87.

9 Crossman, 'December 9 1964', *Diaries of a Cabinet Minister*, p. 92.

10 Crossman, 'December 10 1964', *Diaries of a Cabinet Minister*, p. 93.

11 Crossman, 'December 13 1964', *Diaries of a Cabinet Minister*, p. 98.

12 *The Times*, 15 January 1965, p. 8.

13 Crossman, 'June 16 1965', *Diaries of a Cabinet Minister*, p. 252.

14 *The Times*, 26 June 1956, p. 6.

15 *Guardian*, 6 April 1960, p. 4.

16 See https://www.theguardian.com/business/2015/dec/06/cadburys-owner-paid-no-uk-tax-last-year

17 *The Times*, 31 October 1961, p. 15.

18 *The Times*, 2 March 1962, p. 4.

19 *The Times*, 3 November 1961, p. 7.

20 E.M. Forster, in Williams-Ellis (ed.), *Britain and the Beast*, p. 47.

Chapter 6

1 *The Times*, 3 January 1975, p. 2.

2 Ian Nairn, *Outrage!*, special issue of *Architectural Review*, June 1955, p. 365.

3 Ibid., p. 365.

4 *Observer*, 8 August 1965, p. 17.

5 Crowe, *Tomorrow's Landscapes*, p. 192.

6 Ibid., p. 156.

7 Lionel Brett, *Landscape in Distress*, Architectural Press, 1965, pp. 97–102.

8 Nan Fairbrother, *New Lives, New Landscapes*, Penguin, 1972 (first published 1970), p. 13.

9 *Guardian*, 17 March 1960, p. 22.

10 *The Times*, 17 February 1956, p. 3.

11 Fairbrother, *New Lives, New Landscapes*, p. 94.

12 Ibid., p. 105.

13 Ibid., pp. 189–90.

14 *The Times*, 19 November 1963, p. 9.

15 *The Times*, 15 January 1963, p. 9.

16 MHLG, *The South-east Study 1961–1981*, HMSO, 1964, pp. 88–95.

17 *The Times*, 30 November 1963, p. 6.

18 *The Times*, 30 November 1964, p. 14.

19 *Observer*, 17 September 1967, p. 26.

Chapter 7

1 *The Times*, 23 November 1944, p. 2.

2 *The Times*, 21 July 1960, p. 13.

3 Rachel Carson, *Silent Spring*, Penguin, 1965 (first published 1962), p. 22.

4 Aldous Huxley, in Carson, *Silent Spring*.

5 Conor Mark Jameson, *Silent Spring Revisited*, Bloomsbury, 2012, p. 173.

6 Max Nicholson, *The Environmental Revolution: A Guide for the New Masters of the World*, Hodder & Stoughton, 1970.

Chapter 8

1 Fairbrother, *New Lives, New Landscapes*, p. 224.
2 *Guardian*, 15 December 2005.
3 *Guardian*, 27 January 1986, p. 30.
4 Osborn, *Green Belt Cities*, p. 148.
5 Fairbrother, *New Lives, New Landscapes*, p. 248.
6 Ibid., p. 300.
7 Kenneth Browne, *Architectural Review*, November 1955, p. 310.
8 Ibid., p. 311.
9 *Guardian*, 20 October 1971, p. 20.
10 *Observer*, 10 October 1982, p. 16.
11 Ibid.
12 *The Times*, 26 October 1967, p. 3.
13 Ibid.
14 *Independent*, 10 May 2008.
15 *Independent*, 13 November 2015.

Chapter 9

1 TRC, *Tayside Structure Plan Report of Survey*, April, 1980, Dundee, para. 6.12.
2 *Guardian*, 12 August 1983, p. 2.
3 *The Times*, 11 January 1984, p. 3.
4 Elson, *Green Belts*, p. 245.
5 *The Times*, 24 January 1984, p. 8.
6 *The Times*, 11 May 1988, p. 2.
7 *The Times*, 20 May 1988, p. 15.
8 *The Times*, 9 June 1988, p. 3.
9 *The Times*, 17 November 1958, p. 12.
10 Hall in Elson, *Green Belts*, p. 48.
11 Richard Morrison, *The Times*, 11 March 2003, p. 4.

12 *Guardian*, 2 September 1998.
13 Ibid.
14 *Guardian*, 16 February 1998.

Chapter 10

1 Jonathan Manns, *Green Sprawl: Our Current Affection for a Preservation Myth?*, London Society, 2014, p. 18.
2 Andrew Gillian, *Sunday Times*, 5 February 2017.
3 Sharp, *The Ministry of Housing and Local Government*, p. 142.
4 Peter Hall, *London 2000*, Faber, 1969, p. 178.
5 David Eversley, 'Conservation for the Minority?' in *Built Environment Quarterly*, 1974.
6 Gavin Barwell on *Peston on Sunday*, ITV, 5 February 2017.

Join a literary community of
like-minded readers who seek out
the best in contemporary writing.

From the thousands of submissions Sceptre
receives each year, our editors select the books
we consider to be outstanding.

We look for distinctive voices, thought-provoking
themes, original ideas, absorbing narratives and
writing of prize-winning quality.

If you want to be the first to hear about our
new discoveries, and would like the chance to
receive advance reading copies of our books
before they are published, visit

www.sceptrebooks.co.uk

 Follow @sceptrebooks

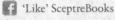 'Like' SceptreBooks

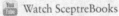 Watch SceptreBooks